D1603234

EVIDENCES AND RECONCILIATIONS

John A. Widtsoe, 1894

EVIDENCES AND RECONCILIATIONS

John A. Widtsoe
Arranged by G. Homer Durham

BOOKCRAFT
Salt Lake City, Utah

ISBN 0-88494-073-X

Collector's Edition Fourth Printing, 1995

Printed in the United States of America

FOREWORD TO THE FIRST EDITION

Books come into being in many different ways—some because writers choose to write, and some, like this one, because readers make insistent demands.

Throughout his professional life as scientist, educator, public servant, and churchman—a distinguished and almost unbelievably varied career going back nearly half a century—Dr. John A. Widtsoe has been receiving questions from confused and alert and honest and eager students—students of life, students of the gospel, and students engaged in formal academic pursuits. These questions have come by letter, in Church gatherings, from the mission field, in the classroom, and on informal occasions.

Some years ago Dr. Widtsoe began to make permanent record of such questions as they came to him and, beginning nearly five years ago, to answer in print in the pages of the *Improvement Era* those most persistently and most frequently asked. "Evidences and Reconciliations" was the general title adopted, with a subtitle "Aids to Faith in a Modern Day"; and that the series filled an urgent need is attested by the fact that requests for permanent compilation began to increase as the writings progressed through the months—thus repeating the experience of other writers who, by reason of demand, have been obliged to publish their serial efforts in book form.

Dr. Widtsoe's pen has long been active in the cause of truth—all truth. His scientific papers are numerous. His articles and books crusading for better irrigation and dry-farming practice have been translated into many languages. His Church books, courses of study, and compilations go back to his early young manhood. Books and manuals written by him and published number more than a score and a half, in addition to magazine and newspaper articles, pamphlets, tracts, and encyclopedic and other writings.

As a research scholar schooled in the finest institutions of two continents, as a former president first of a state agricultural college and then of a state university, as a consulting chemist, as director of an agricultural experiment station, as a member of government commissions and of scientific societies, as a churchman of many assignments, and as a world traveler, he has the stimulating manner of a true teacher, the open mind of a true scholar, the engaging charm of a true gentleman, and the true humility of a man of God. His pen, sparing in its use of words and direct in its approach, is nevertheless colorful in expression—and it quickly focuses attention on fact, avoiding unsupportable generalization.

With this brief glimpse of a man and his work, neither of which needs introduction, it is gratifying to bring this volume to the readers who have asked for it and to the many students, both of science and religion, who will find in it many "aids to faith in a modern day."

RICHARD L. EVANS

PUBLISHER'S PREFACE TO COLLECTOR'S EDITION

He is not dead whose glorious mind
    Lifts thine on high.
To live in hearts we leave behind
    Is not to die.

There is more than one kind of immortality, and for the kind the verse suggests Elder John A. Widtsoe the Apostle eminently qualifies. As the above Foreword indicates, his trained and talented mind addressed both scientific and religious issues in a direct and penetrating manner yet with a humility that gives his words a wide appeal.

Those characteristics mark the more than one hundred discussions of significant gospel and Church topics contained in this volume. The publisher is pleased to be able to include it in the Collector's Edition series.

CONTENTS

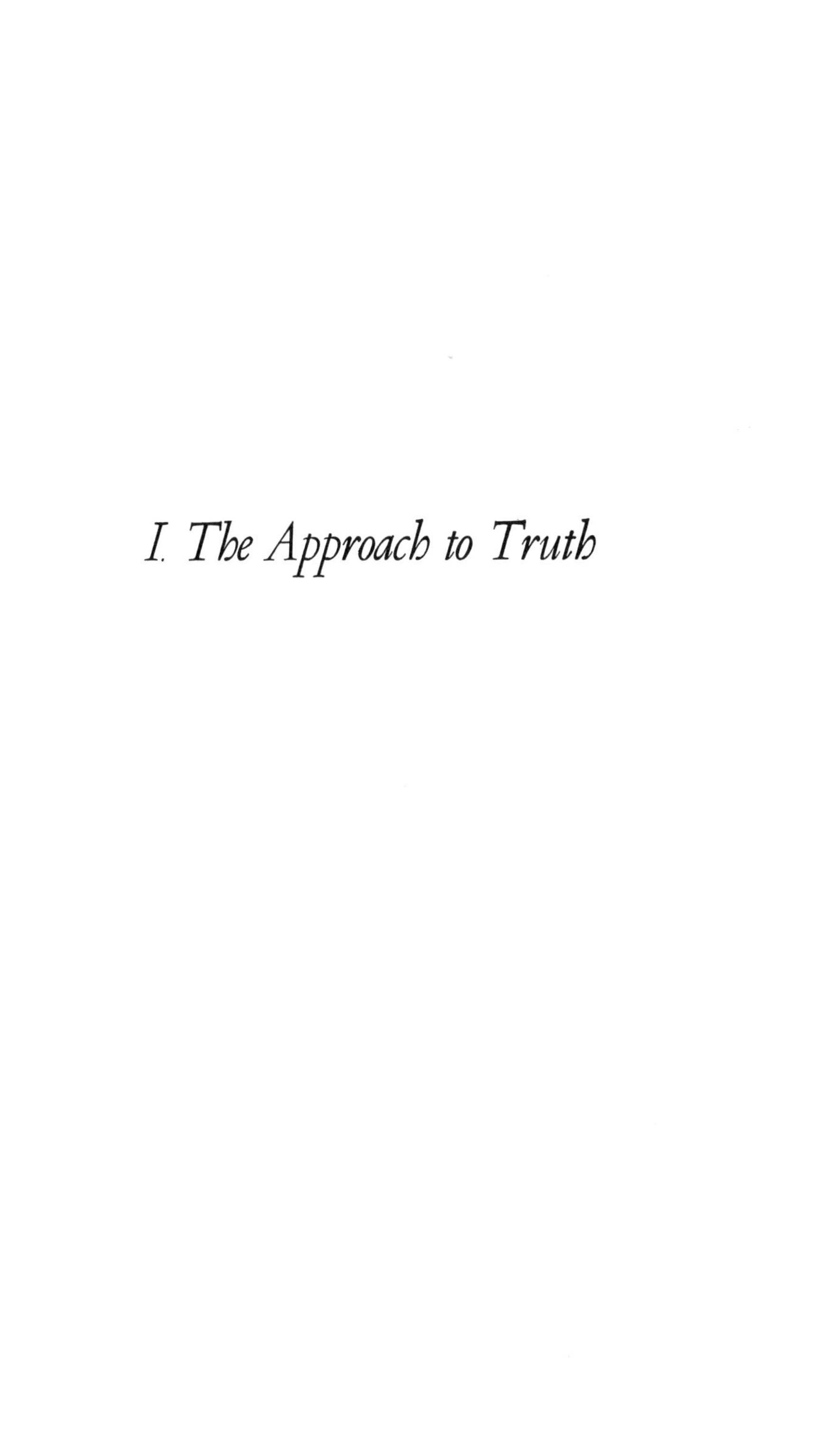

I. The Approach to Truth

1. WHAT IS TRUTH?

Truth is the desired objective of all rational human action. Science and religion alike are built on truth. Jesus, the Christ, frankly declared to Pilate that "To this end was I born, and for this cause came I into the world, that I should bear witness unto the truth." (John 18:37)

The meaning of a word so commonly used should be generally and correctly understood. Yet, subjected to philosophical speculation, truth has often been given diverse meanings, or left befogged in clouds of abstraction.

In a revelation to the Prophet Joseph Smith occurs a very simple yet comprehensive definition, "Truth is knowledge of things as they are, and as they were, and as they are to come." (D. & C. 93:24)—that is, truth is synonymous with accurate knowledge or a product of it.

This cuts away all underbrush. Without knowledge, truth may not be found. Truth is revealed by knowledge; and knowledge is gained by man through his various senses assisted by such aids as he may secure. That is, the facts of observation, in the visible or invisible world, lead to truth; and truth must conform to human experience. To the seeker after knowledge, truth is constantly being revealed.

The dictionary agrees well in one of its several definitions with the Prophet: "Truth is conformity with fact or reality; exact accordance with that which is, or has been, or will be." This also expresses the thought that truth issues from knowledge.

This throws the burden of discovering truth upon the individual. As he obtains knowledge in any field, he will gain truth. But the knowledge must be correct, factual, or it does not lead to truth.

There has been endless speaking and writing about ultimate or final truth. It may as well be admitted at once, and without reservation, that mortal man, gathering knowledge through imperfect senses—his only avenues to truth—must remain content, in many fields of endeavor, with partial truth. The eye of man, sweeping the heavens, gathers some knowledge of the universe; with the aid of telescope and spectroscope more is won; but full knowledge of the starry heavens is yet far beyond man's reach. Nevertheless, the knowledge gained by the bare eye, or by the aid of instruments, reveals truth—partial but noble truth, fit to stand by the side of all other truth. With the progress of time, knowledge-seeking, truth-loving man will ever approach the fulness of truth.

The attempt has also been made to limit man's search for truth to the material universe. This implies that there is no other universe, or that man is incapable of exploring spiritual domains. Both alternatives are unacceptable to sound thinking. Man and the eternal universe cannot be confined within the limits of materialism. Therefore, in the search for truth man may touch the source of life, as also the immobile stone; the eternal past, as the endless future; the Lord of the heavens, as the humblest of His creatures; the spiritual, as the material worlds.

In the search for truth it becomes, of course, evident that there are divisions of knowledge. One deals with facts alone; another with the use of the facts for man's good or evil; yet another, to those who believe in God, with the conformity of statements or actions to divine laws.

In a world of living things, knowledge that helps man is of greatest importance, and highest value. Indeed, knowledge of the universe is of value only as it serves man in his upward, progressive journey. Within that statement lie the truths of religion; and therein the importance of religion becomes evident. Simply to gather truth without regard to man's welfare spells an empty life. Or, to gather truth for the purpose of injuring man, makes a devil of such a seeker after knowledge. Only those who seek to find the use of truth for every man's advancement, are the acceptable seekers after truth.

In its noblest sense, truth is knowledge gathered and used for human welfare.

Truth is the most precious possession of man. Light is its fellow traveler. He who walks in the light, may travel intelligently and safely. (D. & C. 93:29, 36) There, also, is a test of truth. (D. & C. 50:23, 24)

2. HOW MAY A TESTIMONY OF THE TRUTH OF THE GOSPEL BE OBTAINED?

Members of the Church frequently "bear testimonies," one to the other. They declare that they know the restored gospel to be true, and voice the joy found in the possession of the gospel.

Such testimonies are statements of certainty of belief. They imply that the united experiences and powers of the man or woman confirm the truth of the gospel. Doubt is dismissed. Faith becomes the ruling power.

The beginning of a testimony is faith in God as the Father of the spirits of men; then in a divine plan of salvation for all men, with Jesus, the Christ, at the head; and finally in the restoration of the gospel or the plan and Priesthood authority through the instrumentality of the Prophet Joseph Smith.

The learned and the unlearned, the youth and the veteran, the high and the humble, may bear such a testimony alike. Each one learns the truth through his own powers. To each one may come the conviction that truth is the substance of the gospel and its claims. The man, rich in learning and experience, may be able to marshall more evidences for his belief than the adolescent lad; but, since both have tested the gospel with the means at their command, and found it not wanting, they may both claim respect for their separate testimonies.

A conviction of the truth of the gospel, a testimony, must be sought if it is to be found. It does not come as the dew from heaven. It is the result of man's eagerness to know truth. Often it requires battle with traditions, former opinions and appetites, and a long testing of the gospel by every available fact and standard. "Faith is a gift of God," but faith must be used to be of service to man. The Lord lets it rain upon the just and the unjust, but he whose field is well plowed is most benefited by the moisture from the sky.

Specifically, what must a person do in his quest for a testimony?

First, there must be a desire for truth. That is the beginning of all human progress, in school, in active life, in every human occupation. The desire to know the truth of the gospel must be insistent, constant, overwhelming, burning. It must be a driving force. A "devil-may-care" attitude will not do. Otherwise, the seeker will not pay the required price for the testimony.

A testimony comes only to those who desire it. Saul, as an enemy of Christ, was sincere in his persecutions. As his desire for truth developed, the Lord could bring to him the conviction of his error. Running through the Pauline epistles is the glorification of truth as the foundation of all wisdom.

Desire must precede all else in the winning of a testimony.

Second, the seeker for a testimony must recognize his own limitations. He is on a royal road, traveling towards the palace of truth, in which all human good may be found. There are truths beyond the material universe. Indeed, a testimony may be said to begin with the acceptance of God, who transcends as well as encompasses material things. The seeker for a testimony feels the need of help beyond his own powers, as the astronomer uses the telescope to enlarge his natural vision. The seeker for a testimony prays to the Lord for help. Such a prayer must be as insistent and constant as the desire. They must move together as the palm and back of the hand. Then help will come. Many a man has strayed from the road because his desire has not been coupled with prayer.

Prayer must accompany desire in the quest for a testimony.

Third, an effort must be put forth to learn the gospel, to understand it, to comprehend the relationship of its principles. The gospel must be studied, otherwise no test of its truth may sanely be applied to it. That study must be wide, for the gospel is so organized that in it is a place for every truth, of every name and nature. That study must be constantly continued, for the content of the gospel is illimitable.

It is a paradox that men will gladly devote time every day for many years to learn a science or an art; yet will expect to win a knowledge of the gospel, which comprehends all sciences and arts, through perfunctory glances at books or occasional listening to sermons. The gospel should be studied more intensively than any school or college subject. They who pass opinion on the gospel without having given it intimate and careful study are not lovers of truth, and their opinions are worthless.

To secure a testimony, then, study must accompany desire and prayer.

Fourth, the gospel must be woven into the pattern of life. It must be tested in practice. The gospel must be used in life. That is the ultimate test in the winning of a testimony.

Certainly, the experience of others who have consistently obeyed gospel requirements is of value to the seeker after a testimony. Children are wise in accepting the experiences of their parents. Beginners do well to trust those who are seasoned in gospel living. But, there comes a time when every person must find out for himself, in his own daily life, the value of the gospel. A sufficient testimony comes only to him who "stands upon his own feet."

A testimony of the truth of the gospel comes, then, from: (1) Desire, (2) Prayer, (3) Study, and (4) Practice.

This is really the formula given by Moroni, the Nephite prophet:

> And when ye shall receive these things, I would exhort you that ye would ask God, the Eternal Father, in the name of Christ, if these things are not true; and if ye shall ask with a sincere heart, with real intent, having faith in Christ, he will manifest the truth of it unto you, by the power of the Holy Ghost.
>
> And by the power of the Holy Ghost ye may know the truth of all things. (Book of Mormon, Moroni 10:4, 5)

Thousands have tried this approach to truth; and have found the testimonies they sought. So far, no one who, with flaming desire, sincere prayer, earnest study, and fearless practice, has sought the truth of "Mormonism" has failed to find it. Some, for lack of courage, though truth stared them in the face, have kept it to themselves. But, the approach never fails, so declares fearlessly the Church of Jesus Christ of Latter-day Saints.

3. HOW CAN THE EXISTENCE OF GOD BE VERIFIED?

There is really no more important question before man. And, in the words of the Apostle Peter, we should "be ready always to give an answer to every man that asketh you a reason of the hope that is in you." (I Peter 3:15)

However, it is useless to attempt to satisfy anyone who asks this question unless he really desires to know God. Desire to know always precedes knowledge.

Religious truth begins with a knowledge of God. Once the existence and nature of our Father in heaven have been established, religious doubts soon vanish, and life's proper course of action becomes clear. Too often theological misunderstandings come because the testimony of God's reality has not been obtained.

In winning a certainty of God's existence, every power and faculty possessed by man may be employed. Observation, experimentation, feeling, prayer, and every process of thought are legitimate avenues to a knowledge of God. The attempt to confine the pursuit of religious truth within a compartment away from many-sided life simply leads to confusion and mystification. In every other activity man is obliged to use his natural gifts—senses of body and spirit, and power of mind to arrange acquired knowledge in an orderly manner—so why not in the search for God? All methods by which truth is discovered may be used in finding the answer to this foremost question.

Man knows things chiefly by their effects or by reports from others.

Likewise, in the search for religious truth we often know things, conditions, persons and personages from their effects, or the testimony of others. God, who does not reveal Himself in person to all, may be known through His works, or through His revelations to others. Jesus, the Christ, declared a search for truth through its effects to be legitimate.

> If I do not the works of my Father, believe me not.
>
> But if I do, though ye believe not me, believe the works: that ye may know and believe . . . (John 10:37, 38)

By this test we, two thousand years later, may know that Jesus of Nazareth was indeed the Son of God. By this test we may know that there is a God.

So important is the question concerning the existence of God that thousands of men, from the earliest times, have sought for the answer. Out of this long search have come convincing evidences for the reality of God. These evidences have increased as men have more diligently sought God and respected truth. The existence of God, tested by all human powers, is the most firmly established fact in man's possession.

The searcher for God may turn for evidence to the external universe, to his own inner self, and to human history for his answer.

Three hundred years of advancing science have revealed many of the secrets of nature. In one respect the result of the study of nature has always been the same. Every process of nature is orderly. Chance, disorder, chaos are ruled out of the physical universe. If every condition involved in a system is precisely the same, the result, anywhere, everywhere, today or at any other time, will be the same. The sun does not rise in the east today and in the west tomorrow. That means that the phenomena of nature are products of law. The infinitely large or the infinitely small move in obedience to law. In man's earnest search for truth, no exception to this process has been found. Apparent deviations, such as the famous uncertainty principle operating in the subatomic world, are but expressions of man's incomplete knowledge, which always disappear with increasing knowledge. The universe exists under a reign of eternal law, surpassing the imperfect laws of human government.

Such orderliness, such domination by law, imply intelligent planning and purpose. Nothing happens of itself. Nowhere, in the age-old experience of man, has continued order been found except as the product of intelligent direction. Man's simplest machine, from the Indian scalping knife to the high-powered automobile, is a product of intelligent action. So convincing has the accumulated knowledge of man become that sober men of science, of foremost rank, declare that to them the universe appears as a Great Thought. The conclusion is evident. There can be no planning or purpose without a mind; there can be no thought without a thinker. The universe, itself, declares that there is intelligent purpose in nature, and that there must be, therefore, a supreme intelligence directing the universe. This is God.

Thus, every discovery in science becomes an additional evidence for God. The day of materialism is laid low. Only those who are content to gather facts without thinking about their meaning in the scheme of things are atheists in this day of enlightenment. "Faith in science is faith in God."

The evidence for God which comes from the invisible world, the world as yet only feebly explored by science, is equally convincing. Man's knowledge of the universe is not confined to the narrowly limited senses of seeing, hearing, tasting, smelling, and tactile feeling. He has other senses which enable him to gather truth from the larger part of the universe beyond the reach of eye or ear. The existence of such scenes and fields is no longer questioned by sound thinkers. It is recognized that in the invisible as in the visible world cause and effect travel together, and may be sensed by the human organism; and that when a person uses these powers, places himself "in tune," he receives knowledge pertaining to the part of the universe closed to the grosser senses.

Such, for example, is the evidence of conscience. If one seeks to do right, he is warned whenever he is tempted to stray from the proper path. Similar is the evidence of prayer. The vast majority of mankind agree that prayer helps people meet or solve the problems of life. Or, note the results of obedience to the law of the Lord. They who obey law find a joy not otherwise to be secured. From such conformity, prayer, and heed to conscience has come to millions of people the revelation, the certain conviction, that God lives and guides His children on earth. The message is as real as the words issuing from the radio tuned to the broadcaster. Certain it is that man has within himself the power to find and to know God.

The reality and validity of such knowledge or convictions, often called spiritual, is now very generally admitted. It certainly should be. That there are mountains on the moon is accepted as a fact because thousands of normal people testify that they have seen them through the telescope. That prayers are heard; that guidance is received from the unseen world; or that God lives, have been testified to, throughout the generations of time, by more thousands of honest, normal persons than have ever testified to a scientific fact. And it is notable that there is full agreement among the believers in God as to the nature of their experiences. The very tests applied to the science of the external world, may properly be used in testing spiritual experiences. And the results should be received with equal respect. Scoffing is the refuge of the uninformed.

An evidence of the highest value remains. Millions of men and women have come to be believers in God, and have sought to place themselves in harmony with him, by yielding obedience to His will. As a result they have undergone a thorough-going change. As they have accepted God fully, and in sincerity, this change has become more marked. They have become more law-abiding. They have increased in power. They have been more useful to society. They have learned to accept the vicissitudes of life with more equanimity, and to look with more tolerance upon their fellow men. Love has flowed from them. They are the ones who have moved the world forward. The study of the world's history justifies these statements. Believers in God reflect His qualities; even as the warm earth represents the warmth of the sun. Under the law of cause and effect this is a powerful evidence for the existence of God, the source of strength and love and progress.

As a supplementary evidence is the further historical fact that a number of men have declared that they have seen God, and even spoken with Him, or that they have received messages from Him for themselves and others. The historicity of their claims is in most cases well established. That which was done, for example, by Paul the Apostle and Joseph Smith the Prophet after their heavenly experiences helps confirm the truth of their claims.

The existence of God may then be verified from external nature, from the "inner nature" of man, from the effects of conformity to God's law, and from the statements of men who have seen God. The first three types of evidence rest upon the testimonies of hundreds of thousands of men and women, increasing tremendously the probability of truth.

It must be added that no knowledge of God can be won unless it is earnestly, honestly, and prayerfully sought. Those who thus seek will receive the testimony, by the Holy Ghost, that God lives.

The knowledge so received is as genuine as if God had revealed Himself in person. So, innumerable lovers of truth, who have sought Him in spirit and deed, have testified. No knowledge to them has become more certain than that God lives and directs the affairs of men. To them, "closer is he than breathing, and nearer than hands and feet." (Tennyson, "The Higher Pantheism") And they are the happy ones on earth.

4. DOES THE CHURCH HAVE A MONOPOLY ON TRUTH?

Such a question reflects a complete misapprehension of the claims of the restored Church of Christ.

A monopoly of truth would mean the possession of all available truth, and the exclusion of those not in the Church from participation in the benefits of truth.

Nothing could be farther from the teachings of the Church. It has been taught from the days of the Prophet Joseph Smith that the light of truth enlightens every man born into the earth. All who seek truth may find it, whether in or out of the Church. Those who seek earnestly in libraries, laboratories, or open nature will be rewarded from the inexhaustible fountain of truth. The Author of truth is generous. The Church urges that in every clime, by all men, at all times, the search for truth be continued; for as truth multiplies among men, human joys may increase.

However, there are many kinds of truth. Some truths concern themselves with the physical conditions of earth and the heavens, under which material things move and operate. That is valuable knowledge, which has brought humanity many of its blessings. The discovery of such truth has called into being our present civilization which speaks with the stars and gives light and comfort to the humblest home.

There are higher kinds of truth—such as pertain to human conduct, that is, to man's manner of using the knowledge that he possesses; truths concerning the God of heaven and man's relationship to his divine Father; truths that explain the mystery of the past, reveal the meaning of the present, and foretell the future destiny of humanity; truths that enable man, if he but uses them, to approach, forever, the likeness of God.

This latter kind of truth forms the framework of the plan of salvation as set forth in the gospel of the Lord Jesus Christ. The gospel is a product of the mind and will of the Lord. It teaches that a divine purpose runs through the universe, encompassing every fact, law, and principle, and enlivening all the works of nature. Thus the gospel in its fulness becomes the home of truth, into which all truth, of every kind, may be fitted. As the home of truth, the gospel includes all truth, and places every truth in its proper place and position with respect to the present and future welfare of man.

The truths of the gospel, as all other truths, are available to all mankind. Indeed, perhaps all men possess a part of this basic knowledge for their comfort. Certainly in every church professing God there is some of this higher truth. That is the doctrine of the Latter-day Saints.

The gospel is operated on earth under the authority of the Lord. He placed man on earth and gave him the gospel. He has watched over the children of men throughout the ages of time and has reestablished His Church from time to time as the apostasy of man made it necessary. To the care of the Church the gospel has been committed, together with the Lord's authority, called the Priesthood. Only the Church possessing this authority is the complete Church of Christ, and there can be but one. All others lack the necessary authority and are therefore incomplete.

The Church of Jesus Christ of Latter-day Saints possesses the full truth relative to the gospel of the Lord Jesus Christ, the one divine plan of salvation, and also the authority to officiate in God's name in the upbuilding of the Church of Christ. There is but one gospel; there can be but one Priesthood; there is but one Church which encompasses the whole truth of the gospel, and into which all truth may find its place. In that sense the Church claims to possess the full fundamental truth, call it monopoly if you choose, necessary for full salvation in the celestial kingdom of God. This the Church does humbly and gratefully, keenly sensible of its high commission and vast responsibility, to lead all mankind into a fulness of the knowledge leading to eternal progression in the presence of the Lord.

5. CAN THE EXPERIMENTAL METHOD BE EMPLOYED IN RELIGION?

Civilization and enlightenment have come when men, using the experimental method, have begun to test the correctness of their beliefs. The highway to truth is paved with such rigid tests.

On the contrary, the black cloud of superstition and confusion, twin enemies of progress, has obscured human vision when untested opinions or unverified claims or personal guesses have ruled human actions, or when assumed authority has claimed precedence over patient inquiry. The blind acceptance of unsupported statements, or placing theories upon a pedestal for human worship, has always been a source of sorrow.

Whenever men have set up devices or experiments to test the validity of their opinions, whenever men have demanded proofs of the verity of offered teachings, the world has moved forward. To test current beliefs, Galileo dropped stones of unequal weights from a height; Lavoisier weighed mercury before and after heating; Pasteur filtered air through tufts of cotton; Lister washed wounds with a solution of carbolic acid—and each destroyed a false belief and revealed a new truth: stones of all sizes fall through the air with equal velocity; mercury becomes heavier when heated in air; microscopic living things, in the air, are often capable of injury to man; in wounds are germs which if not destroyed may delay healing. Out of each of these experiments a vast volume of truth has grown. Our civilization rests upon innumerable such experiments.

The same principle appears in the field of living things, from animals to men. The complex relationships of social living must be tested for their value, if the path of safety is to be found. Though experimentation in this field is somewhat more difficult because of the human will (the power to accept or reject) yet, for example, the desirability of organization, cooperation, and democracy, and the ill effects of autocracy, tyranny, and dictatorships, have been demonstrated by actual trial.

Spiritual principles that affect human life, are likewise subject to experiment. Prayer, attendance at Church meetings, the Word of Wisdom, tithing are but remote beliefs until put into practice and thus tested for their value. Intelligent man cannot pass worth-while opinion on these and other principles until he has tried them himself or observed their effects on others.

Authority, itself, must bow before the experimental method. The reality of authority is best established by the efficacy of that which it declares and commands. Authority which is not willing to submit to such a test may well be questioned. There are today innumerable fantastic cults, leading thousands astray, which have no foundation beyond the unsupported claims of their originators.

This does not mean that the experimental method is the only approach to truth, but that it is one of the most important. Nor does it mean that every man must get drunk to learn the evils of alcohol. Human experience is filled with the sad examples of those who have toyed with evil and have been destroyed by it. We can learn from the experience of others, as from our own, as to that which is good or evil.

We can also learn from those wiser than we are. But in accepting guidance from them we must be certain of their wisdom.

The gospel of the Lord Jesus Christ advises men to test its truths in human life. It approves distinctly of the experimental method. The Savior laid down the principle in a luminous statement: "My doctrine is not mine, but his that sent me. If any man will do his will, he shall know of the doctrine, whether it be of God, or whether I speak of myself." (John 7:16, 17) On another occasion He repeated the thought: "If I do not the works of my Father, believe me not. But if I do, though ye believe not me, believe the works." (John 10:37, 38) The words of the Apostle Paul, "Prove all things; hold fast that which is good." (I Thessalonians 5:21), are of the same import. There is constant advice in the scriptures to let the effects of gospel living be evidence of its truth, as for example: "Let your light so shine before men, that they may see your good works, and glorify your Father which is in heaven" (Matthew 5:16); or "Having your conversation honest among the Gentiles: that, whereas they speak against you as evil-doers, they may by your good works, which they shall behold, glorify God in the day of visitation." (I Peter 2:12)

Joseph Smith, the Prophet, recognized this method of testing truth. He read the words of James, "If any of you lack wisdom, let him ask of God, that giveth to all men liberally, and upbraideth not; and it shall be given him" (James 1:5); and, believing in God, he went into the grove to test the reality of the promise there made. Thus came the great First Vision.

Running through the scriptures is the doctrine that truth as well as untruth may be recognized by its effects, and the counsel is given to test the claims of the gospel by rendering obedience to its principles of action. Obedience itself becomes but a call to do certain things so that certain rewards may be received. Obedience may therefore be counted as a phase of the experimental method.

All should test their religious beliefs. But all such testing must be done in the right spirit and by the right method. Every testing must be a sincere and honest search for truth. The truth or the goodness, not the untruth or the evil, of a system must be sought; then untruth or evil, if it exists, is automatically discovered. There must be no bending of means or methods to bolster up prejudice. An honest seeker after truth must accept truth unhesitatingly when found, and yield full surrender to it. The truth-seeker must be single-minded—for truth. Errors must be thrown out, however appealing they may be to man-made appetites.

The experimental method is applicable and should be used in the field of religion as in every other field of human activity. Only then can a full conviction of its truth be won. "Practicing our religion" is the most direct method of gaining a "testimony of its truth," and that should be the constant concern of every Latter-day Saint.

6. CAN FAITH BE BUILT ON THEORIES?

There is danger in confusing facts and theories. Let it not be held, however, that theories are in themselves objectionable. They play an important part in human progress. They are man's best inferential explanations of existing facts. The history of theories is largely the history of the world of thought. They have been steppingstones to the discovery of truth. Only when theories have been held aloft as unchanging facts or guides to life, have they become dangerous in the search for truth.

New facts of observation as discovered either confirm or disprove a theory. When increasing knowledge confirms a theory, that theory approaches the status of an unchanging fact of nature; if such knowledge weakens the theory, the inference must be modified or abandoned. Most theories are forever changing as new truth appears. That is the main reason why one cannot build firmly and finally on a theory, and feel assured that he is on the safe road to truth.

Claudius Ptolemy, an Egyptian astronomer, living about one hundred fifty years after Christ, inferred from the daily movement of the sun from east to west, that the earth was the center of the solar system. This theory ruled for many centuries until an accumulation of observations threw doubt on its correctness. At last, Copernicus, born 1473 A. D., from existing facts concluded that day and night result from the earth's rotation upon its axis. The theory of Ptolemy fell with a crash. The telescope was invented; more observations were recorded. All heavenly bodies were found to be in motion and rotation. Mighty men appeared: Bruno, Galileo, Kepler, and many others. Our new theories of the solar system are supported by all available knowledge. Yet we are ready to change or modify them as new knowledge appears.

The best thinkers among the Greeks believed that fire was an element, the ultimate principle of the universe. In the seventh century after Christ, a careful investigator, Stahl, set up the theory that an inflammable principle, largely immaterial, devoid of weight, escapes from a burning substance. This he called phlogiston. Every combustible body contains, therefore, more or less phlogiston. This theory was accepted by the scientific world only to be overthrown within a hundred years. Lavoisier, called the father of chemistry, showed by a simple experiment that fire is but the energy released where combustible substances combine with the element oxygen.

Modern theories of the structure and origin of the earth, of the structure of matter, of heat, light, disease, population, the mind and man, are but heirs of earlier, mistaken inferences. The history of theories forms one of the most engaging chapters of human progress. No fault is found with those who propose theories, provided they base their theories on existing facts, and treat them as theories and not as facts.

The history of the theory of evolution is an excellent answer to the question at the head of this writing. The theory of evolution, a storm center of thought for many years, has been modified until it is vastly different from its original form. Leaving aside the doctrine that all life has a common beginning (see also pages 150-158), the basic idea in Darwinism was that the many life forms on the earth could be traced back to "natural selection," the "survival of the fittest" in the struggle for existence. Students of life in every department seized avidly upon this explanation of conditions among men and lower animals. Thousands of books and pamphlets in the fields of natural, economic, and social sciences have been based on the theory of natural selection.

During the last generation, however, facts have appeared to cast serious doubt upon the validity of the doctrine of natural selection. Recently, two books, almost epoch-making, written by men of the highest scientific standing, declare natural selection to be insufficient to explain the variety in nature.[1] Moreover, these two notable investigators have proposed new explanations, inferences from their own work and that of others, to replace the doctrine of natural selection.

Dr. Richard Goldschmidt, American scientist, declares, among other things, that "species and the higher categories," originate in single steps, independent of natural selection as "completely new genetic systems." That is, they appear by sudden variation, which is mutation. He adds that he be-

-----

[1]Goldschmidt, *The Material Basis of Evolution,* Yale University Press, 1940. Willis, *The Course of Evolution,* Macmillan Company, 1940.

lieves such independent appearances to be the result of processes which are very simple. "If life phenomena were not based on very simple principles, no organism could exist." Such views would have been heretical two generations ago.

Dr. J. C. Willis, European scientist, frankly entitles his book *The Course of Evolution,* "by differentiation or divergent mutation rather than by selection." He concludes that "The process of evolution appears not to be a matter of natural selection or chance variations of adaptational value. Rather, it is working upon some definite law that we do not yet comprehend. The law probably began its operations with the commencement of life, and it is carrying this on according to some definite plan. . . . Evolution is no longer a matter of chance, but of law. It has no need of any support from natural selection. . . . The theory of natural selection is no longer getting us anywhere, except in politics (the dead hand)." He goes on to argue for the explanation of "the increasing divergencies of characters as one goes up the scale from species to family," by mutation, a law in opposition to natural selection.

In essence these two eminent experimenters and thinkers are in agreement. Future basic changes in the doctrine of evolution may well be expected.

Had the proponents as well as the opponents of evolution, as a whole or in part, kept in mind that they were discussing a theory, subject to frequent and fundamental change, the civilized world would have been spared much unseemly behavior.

Again the warning: Distinguish clearly between facts and the inferences from facts.

Certainly, it is a mistake to accept theories in building faith in anything, from religion to our everyday life pursuits.

7. IS IT WRONG TO DOUBT?

Doubt usually means uncertainty. You doubt the presence of gold in the ore, though there are yellow flakes in it; or that the man is a thief, though stolen goods are found in his possession; or that a principle of the gospel is correctly interpreted by the speaker. What you really mean is that the evidence in your possession is insufficient to convince you that there is gold in the ore, or that the man is a thief, or that the gospel principle has been explained correctly. Doubt arises from lack of evidence.

Intelligent people cannot long endure such doubt. It must be resolved. Proof must be secured of the presence of gold in the ore, or of the dishonesty of the man, or of the correctness of the doctrinal exposition. Consequently, we set about to remove doubt by gathering information and making tests concerning the subject in question. Doubt, then, becomes converted into inquiry or investigation.

After proper inquiries, using all the powers at our command, the truth concerning the subject becomes known, or it remains unknown to be unravelled perhaps at some future time. The weight of evidence is on one side or the other. Doubt is removed. Doubt, therefore, can be and should be only a temporary condition. Certainly, a question cannot forever be suspended between heaven and earth; it is either answered or unanswered. As the results of an inquiry appear, doubt must flee.

In other words, doubt, which ever is or should be a passing condition, must never itself be an end. Doubt as an objective of life is an intellectual and a spiritual offense. A lasting doubt implies an unwillingness on the part of the individual to seek the solution of his problem, or a fear to face the truth. Doubt should vanish as it appears, or as soon as proper inquiry can place it either with the known or the unknown facts of life; with the solvable or the unsolvable; with the knowable or the unknowable.

The strong man is not afraid to say, "I do not know"; the weak man simpers and answers, "I doubt." Doubt, unless transmuted into inquiry, has no value or worth in the world. Of itself it has never lifted a brick, driven a nail, or turned a furrow. To take pride in being a doubter, without earnestly seeking to remove the doubt, is to reveal shallowness of thought and purpose.

Perhaps you are questioning the correctness of a gospel principle. Call it doubt if you prefer. Proceed to take it out of the region of doubt by examination and practice. Soon it will be understood, or left with the many things not yet within the reach of man. But remember: failure to understand one principle does not vitiate other principles. When proved false, one doctrine may cast distrust upon other doctrines, but the others must be tested for their own correctness.

Doubt of the right kind—that is, honest questioning—leads to faith. Such doubt impels men to inquiry which always opens the door to truth. The scientist in his laboratory, the explorer in distant parts, the prayerful man upon his knees—these and all inquirers like them find truth. They learn that some things are known, others are not. They cease to doubt. They settle down with the knowledge they possess to make the forces of nature do their bidding, knowing well that they will be victorious; and that more knowledge will come to them, if sought, to yield new power.

On the other hand, the stagnant doubter, one content with himself, unwilling to make the effort, to pay the price of discovery, inevitably reaches unbelief and miry darkness. His doubts grow like poisonous mushrooms in the dim shadows of his mental and spiritual chambers. At last, blind like the mole in his burrow, he usually substitutes ridicule for reason, and indolence for labor. The simplest truth is worth the sum of all such doubts. He joins the unhappy army of doubters who, weakened by their doubts, have at all periods of human history allowed others, men of faith, to move the world into increasing light.

Faith is practically the opposite of doubt. Faith rests securely upon "evidences" and "assurances." Note the definition by the Apostle Paul: "Faith is the assurance of things hoped for, the evidence of things not seen."[2] Faith knows, and goes forth courageously to use knowledge in the affairs of men. It declares itself the master of things; it lays mountains low; it lifts valleys; it promotes the welfare of man.

-----

[2]Hebrews 11:1, as rendered by Joseph Smith, Jr., the Seer, *Holy Scriptures*, Inspired Revision.

Joseph Smith is an excellent example of proper doubt. The ministers of his day were contending for the membership of the boy. He went to God for help; received it; and doubt disappeared. From that day on, doubt did not reappear. His doubt was lost in the desired knowledge he gained from proper inquiry. So may every man do.

The unknown universe, material, mental, spiritual, is greater than the known. If we seek, we shall forever add knowledge to knowledge. That which seems dark today, will be crystal clear tomorrow. Eternal progress means the unending elucidation of things not known or understood today.

No! Doubt is not wrong unless it becomes an end of life. It rises to high dignity when it becomes an active search for, and practice of, truth.

Doubt which immediately leads to honest inquiry, and thereby removes itself, is wholesome. But that doubt which feeds and grows upon itself, and, with stubborn indolence, breeds more doubt, is evil.

8. HOW DO YOU ACCOUNT FOR GOSPEL RESEMBLANCES IN NON-CHRISTIAN RELIGIONS?

The great world religions have much in common. Hinduism, Taoism, Zoroastrianism, Buddhism, Confucianism, and Mohammedanism hold to some tenets fundamental in Christianity. They all believe in an overruling power, God; in man's immortality in some form; and in a divine plan for the guidance of man to happiness. All of them recognize that growth and progress come through self-effort, by self-control and self-discipline. The brotherhood of man, cooperation, and the golden rule are generally accepted as obligatory upon all men. These doctrines are impressively similar to those of Christianity. (H. M. Woodward, *Humanity's Greatest Need*)

There is a like similarity, though not so marked, in the practices or ordinances of the religions of earth. For example, baptism, the initiatory Christian ordinance, is not peculiar to the Christian Church. In some form it is practiced by many non-Christian communities; in fact, the doctrine of entering through water into a new life is very old. Among the Hebrews a practice equivalent to baptism was observed long before the days of Christ. In ancient Egypt, a corresponding rite was in operation from days immemorial. Other gospel practices likewise appear in non-Christian religions.

Even the substance of the Ten Commandments dates back into far non-Christian antiquity, and among others than the Hebrew people. The Ten Commandments were given by God to Moses among the thunderings and lightnings on Mount Sinai. Yet, in other forms their teachings were known by peoples who lived before the days of Moses. The code of Hammurabi, a contemporary of Abraham, contains injunctions for correct living resembling the Ten Commandments. (R. F. Harper, *The Code of Hammurabi*)

Such similarities might be multiplied. How may they be explained? It is a fair question.

In the abundant literature attempting to answer this question, two opposing answers or explanations appear.

The first, for the moment the fashionable one, sets up the theory of the independent development of such similarities in different lands and among different peoples. That is, religious beliefs and practices have arisen spontaneously and independently in various countries. The founders of the various great world religions developed from the foundation, and independently of other religions, their respective bodies of laws and regulations. The striking similarities that exist, despite independent origin, are explained by a "psychic unity that leads men independently . . . to arrive at the same destination." Some supporters of this theory speak of a "convergence" of human ideas towards the same conclusions. In short, the blind or chance operation of some mystic force explains the similarities appearing in the religious systems of the world.

This explanation is not confined to religious beliefs and practices, but is extended to the general cultural history of mankind. In economic and social fields, in literature, art, mechanics, and crafts, remarkable similarities exist among various peoples the world over. All these, this theory declares, had an independent origin in different lands.

Similar myths, legends, and folklore exist among all primitive peoples. The theory of "independent development" holds to the belief that from out the shadows of the forest, the presence of death, and other experiences that stir the feelings of man, primitive magic was formed alike in different lands. From this magic came religion, which in time, as people progressed, became science. (James G. Frazer, *The Golden Bough; Folk Lore of the Old Testament*)

The second theory to explain the similarities in the religions and other cultures of different peoples holds that there has been a diffusion of religious, cultural ideas from a common source or center. This theory does not deny the possibility of "independent development," but insists that such development can not be proved. It claims that observed facts are much more easily explained on the theory of diffusion.

In support of this theory are historical evidences of the diffusion of ideas, handicrafts, and arts pretty much over the whole earth. From early times the human race has traveled widely, often by sea. Intercommunication among widely separated countries has long been going on. The wisdom and the skill of man have been passed on from land to land, from individual to individual. The accumulation of facts in favor of the diffusion view is large and most interesting. Its modern founder, Sir Edward Burnett Tylor, and his followers, have produced a large and convincing literature dealing with the diffusion theory.

This theory agrees with the former that there is a gradual development of culture from primitive to more advanced peoples. It also admits that there are occasional difficulties in this as with every other theory. For example, the trilithons of Stonehenge in England, and those of Tongatabu in Oceania, though very similar, seem so far removed in distance as to have no relationship. Yet, the general intercourse of mankind, since early days, does not make it seem impossible that the idea behind these ancient monuments had a common source.

In the field of religion, it has been well established that there has been a wide diffusion of ideas. Mohammedanism is a good example. From Arabia it has spread over Asia, parts of Europe and Africa, and into many islands of the sea. What has been done in this case, within easy historical times, may have and probably has been done with earlier religious ideas. (Sir G. Elliott Smith, *The Diffusion of Culture*)

As a sidelight on this theory, it is interesting to note that the diffusionists are inclined to believe that the center from which our present culture has diffused was Egypt; and that the diffusion began about 4000 years before Christ. (Sir G. Elliott Smith, *In the Beginning*)

These two contending and opposite theories–the independent development and the diffusion theories–have followers of equal scholastic standing. As said, the independent development theory has been the fashionable one for some time. But the history of scientific theories is that they rise and fall in popularity from time to time. The diffusion theory may soon be the one in best standing.

Latter-day Saints agree with both of these theories in part, and differ with them in part.

Revelation, the communication of man with God, is fundamental in the gospel structure. Every man born into the earth may receive knowledge and guidance through the omnipresent Holy Spirit. Should it be the will of the Lord, there could be no reason why two men, widely separated, and inaccessible one to the other, should not receive through revelation the same truths. To that extent, the doctrine of "independent development" can be accepted by Latter-day Saints.

Historically, however, the doctrine of diffusion seems to Latter-day Saints the more likely in explaining the religious and cultural similarities of the varying religions and races of men. Modern revelation, through the Prophet Joseph Smith, has given the clue. Adam was taught the gospel, was baptized, received the gift of the Holy Ghost, and was ordained to the Priesthood. While details are not given, the inference seems justified that the father of the human race received a knowledge of the fulness of the gospel and all its gifts. We know that he was ordained a presiding high priest.[3]

Adam taught the gospel to his children and his children's children. Upon those who were worthy he conferred the Holy Priesthood. The gospel with its principles and practices, its Priesthood and powers, was generally known among the people of Adam's long day.

Satan succeeded in those early days to turn many from righteous lives. These people lived sinfully. Yet, as they departed from association with the people of the Lord, they carried with them the knowledge of the gospel. Such parts of it as seemed to fit their desires they retained, often warped beyond recognition. But, from the days of Adam, gospel truth was diffused among the peoples of the earth.

The same thing happened after the flood. Noah, a righteous man, ordained to the Priesthood, and knowing the gospel, taught the plan of salvation and the doctrine of the gospel to his day and generation. Some listened and obeyed, more heard the message with unwilling hearts. Self-conquest precedes full acceptance of the gospel. Nevertheless, even those who refused full obedience, took of the gospel such truths as they desired, and without authority built their religions in imitation of the full truth.

This explains to Latter-day Saints the many striking similarities among the non-Christian and Christian religions. The early knowledge of the gospel has spread over the earth,

---

[3]See Pearl of Great Price, Moses 5:6-9, 58, 59; 6:7, 53, 64-68.

as men have so spread, and as inter-communication among nations has continued. The founders of the great world religions, and of less important ones, for that matter, have used to their liking, often in their desire to serve their own people, parts of the truths of the gospel.

It may be that these founders were led by inspiration to assemble the truths of the gospel for the use of their fellowmen. Even a minor gospel truth is a blessing, and better than none. However, any such system can only be an approach to the covenant people which is the objective of the gospel.

Sacred history leaves the conviction that in the increasing purpose of the Lord with respect to the human family, such peoples as have not been prepared for the gospel have been given parts of it, as much as they could comprehend. Remember that the Higher Priesthood was taken from Israel in the wilderness because of their unfitness for the higher privilege. This view seems well confirmed by the following passage from the Book of Mormon:

> For behold, the Lord does grant unto all nations, of their own nation and tongue, to teach his word, yea, in wisdom, all that he seeth fit that they should have. (Book of Mormon, Alma 29:8)

The person who rails at Old Testament accuracy because the substance of the Ten Commandments is found in the code of Hammurabi makes little impression upon Latter-day Saints who understand the spread of the knowledge of truth from Adam and Noah. The truths embodied in the Ten Commandments are part of the gospel as taught to Adam. They were diffused among mankind. They were summarized and restated by the Lord to Moses and preserved in that form for the benefit of Israel and all the world. Much foolish Bible fault-finding disappears in the light of modern revelation.

Such then is the answer to the query at the head of this chapter.

9. HOW IS A TESTIMONY KEPT? LOST?

How may a testimony be kept?

Since a testimony is a compound of knowledge and the use of knowledge, it is much as a living thing. It is never static, like a stone. The small testimony may grow larger, the large testimony become smaller. Therefore, it must be cared for, as any other type of life. Our treatment of it is of prime importance.

First, to keep our testimony we must feed it, regularly and plentifully. The steps that lead to a testimony: desire, prayer, study, and practice, must be trodden continuously. The desire for truth should stamp our every act; help from God in all things must be invoked; the study of the gospel, which has not been plumbed to its depth by any man, should be continued; and the practice of gospel principles, in all our labors, must never be forgotten.

He who would retain his testimony is required to give constant study to the gospel. He cannot live forever on that which he learned yesterday. By a little such study every day, light will follow light, and understanding will increase. This is doubly important since we live in a changing world, which requires continuous applications of gospel truth to new conditions.

To keep his testimony, a person must increase in the use of gospel principles. There must be stricter conformity with the higher as well as the lesser laws of life—more activity in Church service; increasing charity and kindness; greater sacrifice for the common good; more readiness to help advance the plan of salvation; more truth in all we do. And as our knowledge of gospel law increases, our activity under gospel law must increase.

By such feeding, a testimony may be kept; may remain whole and sound; and may grow to become an increasingly certain guide, and a constant joy in life. There is no other way to preserve a testimony. Look about you. Have you not seen people who have fed their testimonies? Is it not good to be with them?

How may a testimony be lost?

A testimony, being a living thing, may die. Sorrowfully,

all of us may have seen such a passing. Witness the life of any apostate. Refuse to do the things that lead to a testimony, and, gradually, it will starve, wither, and perish. It does not matter how strong it may have been. It must be fed to be kept alive.

Starvation of a testimony usually begins with failure to keep properly in touch with divine forces, to pray. Then, desire to learn and to live the gospel law soon weakens. Sacred covenants are forgotten. Study of the gospel is set aside for some other study or activity. There is less and less participation in the life of the Church. Eyes are blurred so that the laws of life are forgotten.

There are many attacks by the evil one upon a weakening testimony. Commonly, a feeling of superiority, ending in ambition for office, overshadows all else and leads to testimony starvation. Personal ambition has always been a destructive force in human lives. Sometimes, and closely related to the feeling of superiority, are false interpretations of scripture. These rise to such magnitude, though at variance with accepted, revealed doctrine, that they endanger the spiritual life of the individual. The various cults that arise, like mushrooms, from time to time, are but variations of this manner of destroying a testimony. They can always be recognized, for they are in opposition to some principle or regulation of the Church.

Most frequently, however, the loss of a testimony is due to finding fault with one's fellow believers, and with the leadership of the Church. Every action of bishop, stake president, or General Authority seems wrong, to such unfortunate people. Their vision distorts the world and all in it.

The dying testimony is easily recognized. The organizations and practices of the Church are ignored; the television takes the place of the Sacrament meeting; golf or motion pictures, the Sunday worship; the cup of coffee, instead of the Word of Wisdom; the cold, selfish hand instead of helpfulness, charity for the poor, and the payment of tithing.

Soon, the testimony is gone, and the former possessor walks about, somewhat sour and discontented, and always in his heart, unhappy. He has lost his most precious possession, and has found nothing to replace it. He has lost inward freedom, the gift of obedience to law.

10. DOES HIGHER EDUCATION TEND TO DIMINISH FAITH IN THE GOSPEL?

Higher education usually means education beyond high school. Since the main purpose of education, lower or higher, is the same, the above question should probably read. "Does education tend to diminish faith in the gospel?"

Really, the constant advocacy by the Church, over a hundred years, of study and learning should be a sufficient answer to this question. Schools and universities mark the course of Mormon history. Today the largest single expenditure of the Church is for education. Mormon students are found everywhere in collegiate institutions. In proportion to its membership, no group of like size in the world has higher literacy or more graduates of colleges and universities. The Church has ever been mindful of the doctrine that "The glory of God is intelligence" (D. & C. 93:36); and its great objective is to become increasingly like God.

The Church could not do otherwise, for the revelations to the Prophet Joseph Smith are replete with instructions to gather knowledge.[4]

If education had been found to destroy faith, such support would not have been given it.

The true objectives of education—to gather knowledge, and to learn how to use it for human welfare—are fully accepted by the Church. Therefore, any decrease of faith among educated men does not depend upon their education, but upon some other coincident factor or factors. For example:

Faith in the gospel is much like a living organism. To be healthy and vigorous it must be fed. If starved, it sickens, weakens, and may die. Loss of faith may always be traced to neglect, mistreatment, or sin.

The food of faith is simple but imperative. Knowledge of the gospel must be maintained and increased by regular, continuous study; and this knowledge must be made alive by active obedience to the practices and requirements of the Church. Real intelligence or wisdom, the true purpose of

---

[4]See D. & C. 88:78-80, 118; 90:15.

education, is a compound of knowledge and the use of that knowledge for human welfare, according to the plan of salvation.

Neglect to maintain familiarity with gospel principles through regular study, coupled with neglect to practice gospel precepts in daily life, is a fruitful cause of loss of faith. It is always a pathetic picture to see a man who through long studious years has moved towards an advanced degree in some academic principle—chemistry or biology, English or economics—but who during that time has given only passing attention to his religion—sit in judgment on the gospel. It is an erroneous assumption on his part, unworthy of an educated man, that knowledge of the gospel comes as it were, with breathing, while to secure academic knowledge requires toil and more toil.

One wonders at the intelligence quotient of the man who does not comprehend that the prayerful man alone can pass upon the virtue of prayer; the Word of Wisdom keeper upon the Word of Wisdom; the tithe payer upon tithing; the regular student of the gospel upon the content and meaning of the gospel, and so on throughout the several gospel requirements. Some so-called educated men make themselves absurd by passing opinions on spiritual matters when they live only material lives. To become an adept in religion—which includes the science of human behavior—requires more study and practice than to become the master of any one of the many groups of knowledge recognized by collegiate institutions. And one cannot depend on previous knowledge. The past fades away with the progress of time. Every person whether in religion or science must keep his knowledge fresh and up-to-date, else he goes "on the shelf."

The student who, every day, will place his needs before the Lord, who will spend say ten minutes in gospel study, and conform to gospel requirements, will find his faith grows as he increases in secular knowledge. His understanding of the true meaning of all his efforts will become clearer and more comprehensive.

Excuses for neglect of Church duties are easily found by students of higher education. There may be no Church meetings in the university town; and the Sabbath is spent as any other day. Urgency of work makes prayers irregular.

A meagre purse justifies disobedience to the law of sacrifice. These are specious excuses, which, if nurtured, take on the aspects of necessity.

At least one group of three, the only Church members, in a university town, held regular Sunday meetings, partook of the Sacrament, bore testimony to one another, studied the gospel together, remembered to give of their slender means, and now after many years, rejoice in a robust faith in the gospel, and at the same time have record of distinguished service to their fellow men. Others have done likewise; and others may happily follow their examples.

Loss of faith may be suffered also by those who adopt habits of their colleagues—students or teachers—contrary to gospel teachings. They who do so have not the courage to maintain their own convictions. They are weak, timid souls, not destined for leadership. They drink, smoke, or carouse with the group with which they associate. A distinguished scholar is a nicotine victim, therefore they imitate him; another sips his cocktails; yet another scoffs at faith. They who imitate such leaders fail to understand that men are often great in some field despite their weaknesses, and they forget that he who battles for the right always wins the esteem of his fellows, be they of one kind or another.

The diminution of faith that follows the tampering with forbidden things cannot be charged to education.

Some students, while in pursuit of truth, fall into immoral practices. Unless quick and sincere repentance follows, they are certain to fall into unbelief. The unclean life poisons faith. As a rule, the person who has lost his faith because of sexual impurity, becomes an enemy of spiritual truth, and seek to find occasion against the Church. He displays an evil type of self-justification.

Here then are four of the factors that have contributed to loss of faith among a small proportion of those who seek or have sought higher education: (1) Starvation of faith through lack of study and practice of gospel principles; (2) imitation of persons who have acquired improper habits of life; (3) immorality; and (4) the failure to understand the real relationship that religion bears to all truth.

These are among the most important causes of unbelief. The unbelief or gratuitous judgment of the gospel by those who are guilty of one or more of these things is really unworthy of discussion. Let one set his own house in order before he passes judgment upon the abodes of others.

Behind all these causes lie the desire and the will to retain and develop faith. Without a strong desire for faith, the cause is helpless. There is no personal progress in any activity, scientific or religious, except upon the condition of desire coupled with a determined vigorous will.

Education, higher or lower, does not diminish faith; but the lives and attitudes of those who seek education do determine the nature and the degree of faith.

11. WHAT IS A LIBERAL RELIGION?

The word *liberal*, correctly used, has a noble meaning. The true liberal hates slavery of every kind. He battles for human freedom. He wants liberty in thought and action. He is tolerant, free from bigotry, and generous in all his deeds. He places truth above all else and hungers for full truth. He welcomes all new improvements and calls for more—the telegraph, electric light, telephone, printing press, typewriter, railroad, airship, radio. He insists that every new invention must be used for human welfare, with full respect to civil and moral law. In short, the liberal seeks to make better the day in which he lives, and he becomes therefore a crusader for the betterment of the human race.

Such a liberal, to accomplish his purpose, holds fast, without the least concession, to the convictions of his soul. He is anchored to the rock of truth, as he may see it. He never wavers from the basic, underlying principles of the cause, whether of church or state, to which he is committed. All the world knows how and where he stands.

His liberalism lies in his constant attempt to make the underlying unchanging principles of the cause he represents serve the changing conditions of the day. He may differ with the superficial conventions of the past, but not with its established truths. He may refuse to continue the church architecture of the past but will insist that the ancient truths of the gospel be taught in every building dedicated to worship. He may be forever seeking, under changing conditions, to make the doctrine of human brotherhood more effective in behalf of the needy. He is a believer who seeks to use his beliefs in every concern of his life.

Unfortunately, the word liberal is not always properly used. It has been used, or misused, for so many purposes that its original meaning has largely vanished. Word-juggling, making a good word cover a doubtful or an ugly cause, is an age-old pastime. Words are too often used as shields to hide or disguise truth. Many men are inclined to hide their true motives behind a word.

It is folly to speak of a liberal religion, if that religion claims that it rests upon unchanging truth. Neither can one be a liberal in religion except in the application of the underlying doctrine to human needs. It would be as preposterous as speaking of a liberal science, since science rests upon truthful observations of nature. It is only in the use of scientific discoveries that the word liberal may be used. One either accepts or rejects truth. There is no middle course.

Under the true definition of liberalism, the Church of Jesus Christ is preeminently liberal. First, it makes truth and love of truth its foundation. The whole latter-day work was initiated by Joseph Smith's search for truth. "In the midst of this war of words and tumult of opinions, I often said to myself: What is to be done? Who of all these parties are right . . . ?" Thus came the first great vision of Joseph Smith; and as a consequence of his search for truth came the other revelations, and the enduring light-giving structure of the Church. In his differences with the beliefs of the churches of his day, he did not seek cover under the name of an existing church. Instead he frankly formed another Church and fought out the issue on the basis of his own fundamental doctrine. It is understood that every worthy member of the Church must likewise seek and find truth for himself. Then, the Church insists that its truths must be used for human good. The gospel has value only as it fosters the welfare of those who have accepted it. Further, the Church recognizes that there is constant change on earth but insists that every change must respect and use the basic doctrine of the Church. It declares that men "live and move and have their being" under the law of progress. Change steps upon the heels of change in the unfolding of a progressive universe. The simple eternal truths of existence are combined and combined again, in different ways, but progressively, to serve man on his never-ending journey. It is much as the endless combination of the few numerical digits from simple to increasingly larger numbers. Members of the Church of Jesus Christ of Latter-day Saints do not need to look elsewhere for a liberal Church.

12. IS THE GOSPEL CHANGING?

Definite principles and ordinances constitute the gospel of the Lord Jesus Christ.

The first of these principles is faith. It is the beginning of all wisdom. The second is repentance: the sorrow of the man of faith for his past errors, and the resolution to commit them no more. Following these two principles are two ordinances: first, baptism by immersion, the outward sign or witness of a person's readiness to accept Jesus Christ, and to conform to the laws of the gospel; second, the laying on of hands for the reception of the gift of the Holy Ghost, to enlighten, protect, and bless all who enter the Church of Christ. It is the reward to all who by faith, repentance, and obedience prepare themselves for membership in the Church of Christ, whether on earth or in heaven.

These basic, eternal principles and ordinances are made as one by the authoritative Priesthood committed to the Church, which on earth holds the gospel in its keeping. Not by a "jot or tittle" may these principles and ordinances be changed. They will ever remain the foundation stones of the Church of Christ.

Then, there are other principles and ordinances designed for those who have won membership in the Church. Such, among others, are the law of sacrifice, temple service for the living and the dead, and missionary work. These are equally permanent. They cannot be changed or abrogated; they are eternal.

This view is verified by the leaders in this dispensation. For example, Joseph Smith said, "[Jesus] set the ordinances to be the same forever and ever." (*Teachings of the Prophet Joseph Smith*, p. 168.) "Ordinances instituted in the heavens before the foundations of the world, in the priesthood, for the salvation of men, are not to be altered or changed." (*Ibid.*, p. 308.) Brigham Young: ". . . from the day that Adam was created and placed in the Garden of Eden, to this day, the plan of salvation and the revelations of the will of God to man are unchanged. . . ." (*Discourses of Brigham Young*, 1941 Edition, p. 103.) John Taylor: "God is unchangeable, so are also his laws, in all their forms, and in all their applications." (*The Gospel Kingdom,* p. 103.) Wilford Woodruff: "The gospel . . . consists of the simple principles taught by the Savior and contained in the New Testament, which principles never deviate one from another." (*Discourses of Wilford Woodruff,* p. 19.) Joseph F. Smith: "The principles that underlie the organization of the Church of Jesus Christ are irrevocable, unchanging and unchangeable." (*Gospel Doctrine,* p. 12.)

This then is the answer to the question at the head of this article. The gospel is not changing, nor can it change if it is to remain the gospel of Jesus Christ.

However, at various times and in various places people have lived and live under different conditions. In the early days of the restored Church, pioneer conditions prevailed. Nearly all were tillers of the soil or husbandmen. Transportation was by ox or horse team. Communication was by slow mail. Little money was in circulation. Education was not easy to secure.

Today, many members of the Church follow other arts than that of agriculture. The continent is crossed in a few hours by railroad or airplane. By telephone, telegraph, or radio, communication with distant places is accomplished almost instantly. Much money is in circulation. Halls of learning are within reach of every one.

The gospel, founded in intelligence, must meet such changing conditions. Indeed, could it not do so, it would fail of its saving purpose. It must help all men under every condition. Sometimes changes are required, but only in applications or outward forms. Baptism was first performed in out-of-door ponds, lakes, or streams; now, very often in beautiful fonts in meetinghouses. In earlier days tithing was paid in kind; now, more often the new day makes it simpler for the farmer to sell his crop and pay tithing in cash. Formerly, all missionaries went out without purse or scrip; now, many are obliged because of new conditions to pay their way in the mission field.

Some people, noting such outward changes, fail to recognize that the law itself is not affected. The ordinance is unchanged whether one is baptized in the open or indoors. The law of sacrifice is fully respected whether tithing is paid in kind or in cash. To bear witness of the restoration of the gospel is not dependent upon whether the missionary travels with or without money. Yet, it often happens that thoughtless people confuse eternal, unchanging principles and ordinances with their applications in a changing world.

President Brigham Young understood this condition. At the laying of the cornerstones of the Salt Lake Temple, he told the people that in vision he had seen the completed temple. It would have six towers he said, three at each end. Then he warned those who confuse principles with their applications, "Now do not any of you apostatize because it will have six towers, and Joseph built only one." He understood of course that the sacred temple ordinances may be performed in a building properly dedicated, whether it has one or many towers, or has none.

It is really a glorious thought that the Church may meet any emergency, any new demand, any legitimate human aspiration by the use of everlasting gospel principles. It opens the door to individual as well as to Church progress; yet preserves the stability of the Church and its members. The experience of more than a century shows that by gospel truth every problem confronting humanity may be solved.

Some people allow themselves to be disturbed by new, often necessary, applications of gospel principles. By brooding upon their views, the spirit of apostasy may creep into their hearts. A little prayerful reflection will show that there has been no violation of basic law. In the steady growth and progress of the Church that is the one thing that needs to be watched.

The Church in its growth employs the unchanged principles underlying the gospel but applies them freely in meeting the needs of any time or place. In its essence the gospel is unchanging; in its applications it is everchanging to fit the needs of the day.

II. The Godhead

1. WHY ARE THE TERMS "GOD" AND "FATHER" APPLIED TO SEVERAL PERSONAGES?

The supreme, personal intelligence and power in the universe is God. That is his name in the English tongue. He is the Organizer of the universe. He is the one and only God to whom we pray and whom we worship.

We speak of Jesus Christ also as God. He is frequently referred to in sacred writ by that term. On the title page of the Book of Mormon he is called the "Eternal God." The personage known as the Holy Ghost is also called God. Thus, there are God, the Father; God, the Son; and God, the Holy Ghost; the two latter are under the direction of God the Father.

It is evident, therefore, that since the Father, Son, and Holy Ghost are distinct personages, the word "God" is not only a name, but may be used also as a title describing an attainment or office. Such application of titles is not unusual. In the Book of Mormon it is stated that the Redeemer of man "shall be called Jesus Christ, the Son of God, the Father of heaven and earth, the Creator of all things from the beginning." (Mosiah 3:8.) These are titles that refer to Christ's relationship to the Father and to his mission under the Father.

In the same manner the title "God" may be applied to anyone who has attained to Godhood, that is, who has risen so high as to partake sufficiently of the essence of divinity.

Joseph Smith the Prophet declared that there is a plurality of gods. An indication of such plurality runs through the scriptures, ancient and modern. In the very beginning of time Adam and Eve were promised that they should "be as gods" (Genesis 3:5); and Jesus reminded the Jews that in their scriptures it was written "ye are gods." (John 10:34.) Paul spoke of "lords many and gods many." (1 Cor. 8:5.) Modern revelation presents the same truth when it says "according to that which was ordained in the midst of the Council of the Eternal God of all other gods before this world was." (D. & C. 121:32)

This implies that many personages may have attained

the power and place of Godhood. This does not make them in any sense coequal with God, or with his Son, or the Holy Ghost. Those who are denominated gods have a rank in the eternal councils, with corresponding power to help foster the purposes of the Father. There may be many generals in an earthly government, but only one commander-in-chief. Even so in the government of heaven.

This doctrine is familiar to Latter-day Saints. The gospel teaches that the hosts of intelligent beings here and in the spirit world may progress forever. The condition is obedience to eternal law. These personages are in various stages of progression, some beginning, others far on the way. Some, through the eternities, may already have won sufficient of the attributes of divinity to be spoken of as gods. The destiny of all who are faithful is godhood. Modern revelation makes the promise to all who comply with certain requirements: "Then shall they be gods, because they have no end; therefore shall they be from everlasting to everlasting, because they continue; then shall they be above all, because all things are subject unto them. Then shall they be gods, because they have all power, and the angels are subject unto them." (D. & C. 132:20)

The conditions under which Godhood may be attained have not been set forth fully. Necessarily so high a place can be obtained only by rigid obedience to God's laws. Those who aspire to such exaltation must be sealed as man and wife for time and eternity. Then they may continue the work of the Father in behalf of the waiting intelligences in the spirit world. Their "glory shall be a fulness and a continuation of the seeds forever and ever." (D. & C. 132:19)

This doctrine explains why the word "god" is applied in the holy scriptures to various personages. There is no need to stumble over such use of divine titles, if this is understood.

The word "father" is also applied to different personages. God is the father of the spirits of all men. They were begotten spiritually by him in the pre-existent state. The relationship between God and man as father and son is real. Jesus Christ himself was the First Begotten of the Father. (D. & C. 93:21) Therefore, we speak of God, the Father, to distinguish clearly among the Father, the Son, and the Holy Ghost. But, the title "Father" is used also in behalf of Jesus

Christ, who was commissioned by his Father to create the earth and all things on it. Mosiah, a Book of Mormon prophet, speaks of Jesus Christ as "the Father of heaven and earth" because he was the creator of "all things" as pertaining to the earth. (Mosiah 3:8; also Helaman 14:12; Ether 4:7; 2 Nephi 25:12) Adam likewise, being the first man, has been called the father. (D. & C. 29:34) This is not an uncommon use of the word. George Washington is called the father of his country. A man who creates a great business is called the father of the institution. The Indians are said to speak of the great father in Washington. The leader of any cause is frequently referred to as its father.

Some students, noting this use of the word "father," have become confused. They have thought that Jesus is really God, the Father. Others have attempted to identify Adam with God, the Father, or with Jesus Christ. That these are distinct personalities is made clear in numerous passages in holy writ. For example:

> But God . . . called upon our father Adam by his own voice, saying: I am God; I made the world, and men before they were in the flesh. And he also said unto him: If thou wilt turn unto me, and hearken unto my voice, and believe, and repent of all thy transgressions, and be baptized, even in water, in the name of mine Only Begotten Son, who is full of grace and truth, which is Jesus Christ, the only name which shall be given under heaven, whereby salvation shall come unto the children of men, ye shall receive the gift of the Holy Ghost, asking all things in his name, and whatsoever ye shall ask, it shall be given you. (Moses 6:50-52.)

If God, the Father, Jesus Christ, the Holy Ghost, and Adam, irrespective of their titles, are not distinct personages, the above words become meaningless and absurd.

Readers should distinguish carefully between specific and general meanings of words, as may appear in the sacred books or in gospel discourses. If this is not done, much confusion of thought may arise. In fact, many who have failed to do so, have been led astray from the truth.

A good example of the unfounded foolish notions that may arise from careless reading is the famous discourse of Brigham Young, used by apostates and enemies of the Church. (*Journal of Discourses,* 1:50) In this address, Brigham Young spoke of Adam as our father and our God. Reference to the preceding and following paragraphs of the sermon makes clear the intention of the speaker. President Young used the words as titles. The apostate world had long taught that Adam and Eve were the basest and most sinful of the human race. They had brought sin into the world. President Young, in contravention of this false teaching, pointed out that Adam, a son of God of high degree, was called to be the progenitor of the human race. What he did was in harmony with a preordained plan. Adam was in reality the noblest of mankind and would ever stand at the head of his earth family as the presiding officer and patriarch, even as a god. These were the clear ideas of Brigham Young. Every contemporary commentator, and there were several, speaking from personal knowledge of President Young, made this intention and doctrine clear. (See *Millennial Star,* 15: 801)

In the sermon referred to, President Young places Adam unequivocally as a separate character, "Michael," under the dominion of the Trinity. "The earth was organized by three distinct characters, Elohim, Yahovah, and Michael." There was no substituting of Adam for the God to whom we pray. Likewise, the term "father" was constantly applied by Brigham Young to Adam, because Adam was associated with Jesus Christ in the making of the earth; and also in a more literal sense, because, as the first man, he was the father of the race. Yet there are those who have nursed the irrational conclusion that President Young implied that Adam and God, the Father, are one and the same individual.

Brigham Young's much-discussed sermon says that "Jesus was begotten in the flesh by the same character that was in the Garden of Eden, and who is our Father in heaven." Enemies of the Church, or stupid people, reading also that Adam is "our father and our God," have heralded far and wide that the Mormons believe that Jesus Christ was begotten of Adam. Yet, the rational reading of the whole sermon reveals the falsity of such a doctrine. It is explained that God the Father was in the Garden of Eden before Adam, that he was the Father of Adam, and that this same personage, God the Father, who was in the Garden of Eden before Adam, was the Father of Jesus Christ, when the Son took upon himself a mortal body. That is, the same personage was the Father of Adam and of Jesus Christ. In the numerous published sermons of Brigham Young this is the doctrine that appears; none other. The assertion is repeatedly made that Jesus Christ was begotten by God, the Father, distinct by any stretch of imagination from Adam. This is a well-established Latter-day Saint doctrine.

Absurdities of the first order may arise unless the meanings of words are carefully sought. And any statement in doubt should be compared with other statements on the same subject by the same speaker. Then the true meaning will be revealed.

Again, the warning: Read the scriptures with care; do not become mystified by words; remember that the same word is often used in several ways; and defeat the evil one who is the lover of confusion. And there is no profit in dealing with those who deliberately and usually unscrupulously "wrest" the scriptures. They do not love the truth.

2. WHY IS JESUS THE CHRIST SOMETIMES CALLED THE ETERNAL FATHER?

Three distinct personages, the Father, the Son, and the Holy Ghost, constitute the Godhead, or Presiding Council in the heavens. That is the settled doctrine of the Church. In the first vision of Joseph Smith, he saw "two Personages," the Father and the Son. Each one spoke to the boy. There was no confusion of form or substance. Two separate individuals stood before him. (*Writings of Joseph Smith* in Pearl of Great Price 2:17, 25) In the revelations that followed, there is always a clear distinction made among the three members of the Godhead.

In numerous references in the Book of Mormon, the members of the Godhead stand out as distinct personages. The Bible, if read fully and intelligently, teaches that the Holy Trinity is composed of individual Gods.

The early Christian Church, on its way to apostasy, departed from this truth. Several church councils, in which men fought for their own theories, foisted upon the Church the incomprehensible and unnatural doctrine of "one in three and three in one." They twisted the doctrine of unity of nature and of purpose among the Trinity into a oneness of personality. They would quote Jesus' prayer to his Father, that his disciples "may be one; as thou, Father, art in me, and I in thee, that they also may be one in us." (John 17:21) Yet at the same time they ignored the clear evidence in the prayer that Jesus was on earth, at that time, speaking to a Being elsewhere; and the equally clear meaning of the prayer that he did not propose that his disciples should be fused into one personage, but that they should be of one mind with him and his Father. This false doctrine, which has been nurtured through the centuries, is an excellent illustration of philosophical-theological error and nonsense. Latter-day Saints prefer to cling to the revealed word, and to read the word of God intelligently. Only that which we can understand can be used safely by mortal men; that which is incomprehensible is useless to us.

A definite purpose with respect to humankind emanates

from the Godhead. It was clearly stated to Moses: ". . . Behold, this is my work and my glory—to bring to pass the immortality and eternal life of man." (Moses 1:39) To accomplish this purpose, a plan, the plan of salvation, was proposed by the Father.

In full conformity with the eternal law of free agency, the plan would not be attempted without the consent of those concerned. Consequently, the great council in the heavens was called. So vast a "work" would be of wide extent and manifold requirements. Someone would be needed to supervise and carry to conclusion the divinely formulated plan. Organization belongs to heaven as to earth. The chief episode in that famous event, after the plan had been proposed, is simply told in the words of the Lord to Moses: ". . . Satan . . . came before me, saying—Behold, here am I, send me, I will be thy son, and I will redeem all mankind, that one soul shall not be lost, and surely I will do it; wherefore give me thine honor. But, behold, my Beloved Son, which was my Beloved and Chosen from the beginning, said unto me—Father, thy will be done, and the glory be thine forever." (Moses 4:1, 2)

Thus, by the will of the Father, the leadership of the plan was entrusted to Jesus. He was appointed the head of the execution of the plan on earth. He was to organize the earth, place man upon it, atone for human errors, and bring men back to God, all according to the plan. By this appointment he became the maker or creator of the earth, the Savior and Redeemer of men, our advocate with the Father—in short, the member of the Godhead in charge directly of affairs and people on earth.

The scriptures declare this commission of Jesus Christ. In ancient Nephite days it was stated that he is the creator of the heavens and the earth. (Mosiah 3:8) When he visited the American continent, he declared, "I am Jesus Christ, the Son of God. I created the heavens and the earth, and all things that in them are." (3 Nephi 9:15) To the Prophet Joseph Smith he said, "I am Jesus Christ, the Son of the living God, who created the heavens and the earth." (D. & C. 14:9) Jesus is the central figure of the plan of salvation. It was Jesus the Christ who at sundry times revealed himself to prophets of former and latter days.

Necessarily, all that Jesus Christ has done and will do in behalf of the earth and its inhabitants, is in conformity with the plan of salvation, with the consent and under the direction of the Father. Jesus cannot rise above his Father; Jesus is, in these matters of man's salvation, not only one with the Father, but also in a sense his agent. The time will come, when the plan has been completed, that Jesus, his mission ended, will present the results of his stewardship to the Father, the presiding authority in the council of the Godhead.

The commission thus given to Jesus explains why, for example, we pray to the Father in the name of the Son. It explains also why the revelations to Joseph Smith, after the first vision, were received through Jesus the Christ; that is, he was the speaker. That explains many a saying in the scriptures which otherwise would be difficult of understanding. It makes clear why, in pursuit of his assignment, he may be called the Father of the earth and all upon it.

Whenever or wherever in the history of the world, the gospel has been taught in its fulness, the place of Jesus Christ in the plan of salvation has been understood. With that knowledge in mind, writers have often spoken of him as the Eternal Father, or God of this world. Thus Isaiah, in his famous prophecy concerning the coming of Jesus, says, "For unto us a child is born, unto us a son is given: and the government shall be upon his shoulder: and his name shall be called Wonderful, Counsellor, the mighty God, the *everlasting Father*, the Prince of Peace." (Isaiah 9:6) The ancient Nephite prophets, who understood well the mission of Jesus, called Jesus the "Son of the Eternal Father." (1 Nephi 13:40) They also, speaking of the mission of Jesus, gave Jesus the title Eternal Father. Ether speaks of him as "the God of this land." (Ether 2:12.) Mosiah says that he is the "Father of all things;" (Mosiah 7:27) and the "very Eternal Father." (Mosiah 16:15) Alma relates that Zeezrom asked Amulek bluntly, "Is the Son of God the very Eternal Father?" Amulek answered, "Yea, he is the very Eternal Father of heaven and of earth, and all things which in them are." (Alma 11: 38, 39)

In the use of the title *Father* for God, the Father of Jesus and of us all, the presiding authority of the Godhead, and in the use of the same title for Jesus, with reference to his mission of earth, there need be no confusion. One need only understand which Being is discussed. Then the term may as properly be applied to one or to another. The word *eternal*, of course, denotes Godhood, and the everlasting nature of the plan of salvation.

In the light of the mission of our Elder Brother, the appellation to him by prophets of old, of the title of the Eternal Father, is understood, and is found fully justified. Only those who know not the fulness of the gospel fail to comprehend it.

3. HOW DOES GOD HAVE CONSTANT KNOWLEDGE OF THE WHOLE UNIVERSE?

It is an established doctrine of the Church that God is in constant communication with the whole universe, and every person therein. He may, himself, as he has done at various times, appear to men. But, since God is a personal being, he must use helps and helpers to secure complete, constant contact with all creation. His associates in the spirit world, angels and other personages, may be sent out to administer God's purposes. There may also be other means beyond man's present knowledge.

While little has been revealed on the subject, it would appear that the Holy Ghost, the third member of the Godhead, is, as it were, in charge of the divine system of communications. It is one of his functions to manifest the will and power of God to the children of men.

Joseph Smith, the Prophet, speaking of the Priesthood says that, "The Holy Ghost is God's messenger to administer in all those priesthoods." (*Teachings*, p. 323) Brigham Young speaks similarly of the Holy Ghost: "He is God's messenger that diffuses his (God's) influence through all the works of the Almighty." (*Discourses*, p. 30—1941 edition) James E. Talmage says: "The Holy Ghost may be regarded as the minister of the Godhead, carrying into effect the decisions of the Supreme Council." (*Articles of Faith*, p. 160.) Such a commission is of vast importance, and justifies the dependence on the Holy Ghost, by believers in God and Christ.

The Holy Ghost is a personage of spirit, and of limited dimensions, who cannot, himself, be everywhere present. (D. & C. 130:22) Therefore, President Joseph F. Smith says, "The Holy Ghost as a personage of Spirit can no more be omnipresent in person than can the Father or the Son. . . . The Holy Ghost in person may visit men." (*Gospel Doctrine*, p. 61) Consequently, the Holy Ghost needs must use agents in performing his mission.

The chief agent or agency by which the Holy Ghost accomplishes his work, is usually spoken of as the Holy Spirit or the Spirit of God. It is a universe-filling medium, or influence, by which divine messages may be transmitted to man, and man's desires carried to the powers of heaven. It may be comprehended, to a limited degree, in our day, by recent discoveries and inventions. Any one of us may send messages by wireless or telegraph to persons far distant, or actually speak with them over the telephone. By radio devices, far distant objects may be controlled and directed in their movements, in the air or on land or sea.

This agent is also called the light of truth, as in a revelation to the Prophet Joseph Smith:

> Which light proceedeth forth from the presence of God to fill the immensity of space—the light which is in all things, which giveth life to all things, which is the law by which all things are governed, even the power of God who sitteth upon his throne, who is in the bosom of eternity, who is in the midst of all things. (D. & C. 88:12, 13)

This divine universe-filling medium, which holds all things together, places every soul born into the earth in communication with the members of the Godhead. Through it flow the truth and power that touch the intelligence and conscience of men.

That we understand the nature of the Holy Spirit cannot be claimed. Yet, its effects are well known. Only by analogy with discovered phenomena of nature does it become somewhat understandable. We know the effects of electricity or magnetism, but their nature is yet far from human comprehension.

In summary, the Holy Ghost, a personage who cannot be everywhere at the same time, may at will visit any individual in person; but by the universe-filling influence radiating from God, or the Light of Truth, the Holy Ghost may be in constant touch with all creatures. In reading the scriptures, one should carefully determine whether the writer has in mind the person of the Holy Ghost, or the means by which he performs his mighty work among men.

It has caused some confusion that the terms, Holy Ghost, Holy Spirit, and Spirit of God, as rendered by Bible translators with an imperfect knowledge of the gospel, appear to be interchangeable. In common speech, also, the tendency has been to use these terms loosely, without exact definition. This has confused students of the gospel and has led to frequent questions. With the restoration of the gospel, this confusion vanished. We can now better understand the words of the Prophet Joseph Smith, that, "The place where God resides is a great Urim and Thummim, . . . where all things . . . are manifest, past, present, and future." (D. & C. 130:7, 8) This place is in our poor human words, the control station of God's all-pervading influence.

4. ARE THERE MANY GODS?

The Latter-day Saints believe in one supreme God. He is God the Father, to whom we direct our prayers, in the name of Jesus, the Christ. Associated with the Father are his Son, Jesus Christ, and the Holy Ghost. These three separate and distinct personages constitute the Godhead, the governing council of the universe.

The Church believes and teaches that the personages of the Trinity are distinct personalities but that they are as one because they are united in all things of faith and action.

Undoubtedly, in working out the Father's plan of salvation, the three members of the Godhead may have had different assignments. Jesus was commissioned to organize the earth, to place man upon it, to secure for man eternal association with his body, through his atonement upon the cross, and when the time comes, to present to the Father the results of man's journey on earth so that proper judgment may be rendered.

The Holy Ghost was given the high office to help weak man searching for truth win salvation. This he would accomplish by establishing contact between himself and every person on earth. By that contact he may warn against sin, point out the path to righteousness, give guidance to all who really love the gospel, and become a witness of truth when it is found. Thus, through the influence from the Holy Ghost, man is never alone but may always be in the presence of divinity.

This revealed doctrine of the composition and nature of the Godhead teaches that there are at least three Gods. The Prophet Joseph Smith, challenged by unbelievers that he taught a plurality of Gods, replied in a sermon, "I will preach on the plurality of Gods. I have selected this text for that express purpose. I wish to declare I have always, and in all congregations when I have preached on the subject of the Deity, it has been the plurality of Gods. It has been preached by the elders for fifteen years.

"I have always declared God to be a distinct personage, Jesus Christ, a separate and distinct personage from God the Father, and that the Holy Ghost was a distinct personage and a Spirit: and these three constitute three distinct personages and three Gods. If this is in accordance with the New Testament, lo and behold! we have three Gods anyhow, and they are plural; and who can contradict it?"[1]

However, in the restored gospel the word god does not always refer to the governing council of the Gods: the Father, Son, and Holy Ghost. There are in the universe innumerable intelligent beings, some of whom have come to this earth. These beings, if faithful to the law of the Eternal Father, are steadily progressing toward his likeness. Those who have risen high in their progressive development are often spoken of as gods. This is thoroughly consistent with the doctrine that all are children of God the Father, therefore of his nature, and capable of rising towards his image. This promise is clearly stated in a revelation to the Prophet Joseph Smith, wherein the destiny of the faithful is discussed:

"Wherefore, as it is written, they are gods, even the sons of God."[2]

Likewise, speaking of the faithful, "then shall they be gods, because they have no end."[3]

The plurality of gods is further stated in contemplation of the wonderful laws, things, and properties of the universe.

"According to that which was ordained in the midst of the Council of the Eternal God of all other gods before this world was."[4]

While then, there are many gods there should nevertheless be a clear distinction between the Holy Trinity and those who because of righteous labors have won the title of gods.

With this doctrine in mind, President Brigham Young preached the sermon[5] which has been construed by enemies to teach that Adam is the God to whom we pray and whom we worship. President Young merely followed the sound doctrine taught by Joseph Smith that when the earth story is finished, the heads of all the dispensations will deliver their stewardships to Adam, who in turn will deliver them to Jesus the Christ, under whose commission the earth work has been done. That places Adam, the first man, foremost in the

---

[1] *Teachings of the Prophet Joseph Smith,* p. 370.
[2] D. & C. 76:58.
[3] *Ibid.,* 132:20.
[4] D. & C. 121:32.
[5] *Journal of Discourses,* 1:50.

family of men (Jesus excepted, who was begotten of God the Father). The Prophet Joseph said that:

"The Father called all spirits before Him at the creation of man, and organized them. He (Adam) is the head, and was told to multiply. The keys were first given to him, and by him to others. He will have to give an account of his stewardship, and they to him."[6]

"Adam holds the keys of the dispensation of the fulness of times; i.e. the dispensation of all the times [that] have been and will be revealed through him from the beginning to Christ, and from Christ to the end of dispensations that are going to be revealed." . . .[7]

Certainly, under Christ, Adam stands at the head of the human race; as certainly, he will be blessed with the title *God*.

Moreover, in the sermon referred to, Brigham Young spoke of Adam as Michael, the archangel, the Ancient of Days, so that nowhere can an intelligent reader confuse Adam with either member of the Godhead.

The answer to the question at the head of this writing is that there are many gods.

---

[6]*Teachings of the Prophet Joseph Smith,* p. 158.
[7]*Ibid.,* 167-68.

5. WHAT ARE THE FACTS CONCERNING THE SO-CALLED ADAM-GOD THEORY?

Those who peddle the well-worn Adam-God myth, usually charge the Latter-day Saints with believing that: (1) Our Father in heaven, the Supreme God, to whom we pray, is Adam, the first man; and (2) Adam was the father of Jesus Christ. A long series of absurd and false deductions are made from these propositions.

Those who spread this untruth about the Latter-day Saints go back for authority to a sermon delivered by President Brigham Young "in the tabernacle, Great Salt Lake City, April 9th, 1852." (*Journal of Discourses,* 1:50) Certain statements there made are confusing if read superficially, but very clear if read with their context. Enemies of President Brigham Young and of the Church have taken advantage of the opportunity and have used these statements repeatedly and widely to do injury to the reputation of President Young and the Mormon people. An honest reading of this sermon and of other reported discourses of President Brigham Young proves that the great second President of the Church held no such views as have been put into his mouth in the form of the Adam-God myth.

In the discourse, upon which hangs the Adam-God myth, President Brigham Young discussed the earthly origin of Jesus Christ. He denied that the Holy Ghost was the father of Jesus Christ; and affirmed that the Savior was begotten by God the Father. He explained that "Our Father in Heaven begat all the spirits that ever were or ever will be upon this earth; and they were born spirits in the eternal world. Then the Lord by His power and wisdom organized the mortal tabernacle of man." That is, every human being is in direct descent from God, the Father. In the course of his remarks President Young was led to discuss the high place of Adam among the generations of men, for Adam "helped to make and organize this world," and as first man, the father of us all, Adam stands at the head of the human race, and will ever be the representative of his children before our Father in heaven, the Father of our spirits. It was in connection with this thought that the oft-quoted statement was made about Adam, that "he is our Father and our God, and the only God with whom we have to do."

He spoke of Adam as the great patriarch of the human race, a personage who had been privileged and able to assist in the creation of the earth, who would continue his efforts in behalf of the human family, and through whom many of our needs would be met. All this was in contradiction to the common doctrine the world over that Adam was a great sinner, and not to be held in affectionate remembrance. Nowhere is it suggested that Adam is God, the Father, whose child Adam himself was. On the contrary, in the sermon of April 9th, 1852, itself, there is a clear distinction made between Adam and God the Father, in the following words: "The earth was organized by three distinct characters, namely Elohim, Jehovah, and Michael"—the last previously defined as Adam. There can be no confusion in this passage of the separate personalities of these three great beings. A discourse delivered August 8, 1852, within four months of the discourse in controversy (*Journal of Discourses*, 3:94) contains the following: "The Lord sent forth His gospel to the people: He said, I will give it to my son Adam, from whom Methusaleh received it; and Noah received it from Methusaleh; and Melchizedek administered to Abraham." Clearly, President Young here distinguishes between God, the Father, and Adam, the first man.

The sermon of April 9, 1852, also makes the statement that, "Jesus, our Elder Brother, was begotten in the flesh by the same character that was in the Garden of Eden, and who is our Father in Heaven." The dishonest inference has been drawn and advertised widely that President Young meant that Adam was the earthly father of Jesus Christ. This deduction cannot be made fairly, in view of the context or of his other published utterances on the subject. Adam and Eve were not the only persons in the Garden of Eden, for "they heard the voice of the Lord God walking in the garden in the cool of the day." (Genesis 3:8). President Young undoubtedly had this personage in mind, for he did not say Adam, but "our Father in heaven."

In many discourses, President Young refers to Jesus as the Only Begotten of the Father, which would not have been true, had Adam been the earthly father of Jesus. At one time he declared (*Journal of Discourses,* 1:238), "I believe the Father came down from heaven, as the Apostles said he did, and begat the Savior of the World; for He is the Only Begotten of the Father, which could not have been if the Father did not actually beget him in person." On another occasion (*Journal of Discourses,* 2:42) he said, "And what shall we say of our Heavenly Father? He is also a man in perfection, and the Father of the man Jesus Christ, and the Father of our spirits." It seems unnecessary to offer more evidence that Brigham Young held the accepted doctrine of the Church, that God, the Father, and not Adam, is the earthly Father of Jesus.

In all this, President Young merely followed the established doctrine of the Church. Joseph Smith the Prophet, in discussing the Priesthood, touched upon the position of Adam.

> [The Priesthood] commencing with Adam, who was the first man, who is spoken of in Daniel as being the "Ancient of Days," or in other words, the first and oldest of all, the great, grand progenitor of whom it is said in another place he is Michael, because he was the first and father of all, not only by progeny, but the first to hold the spiritual blessings, to whom was made known the plan of ordinances for the salvation of his posterity unto the end, and to whom Christ was first revealed, and through whom Christ has been revealed from heaven, and will continue to be revealed from henceforth. Adam holds the keys of the dispensation of the fulness of times, i.e., the dispensation of all the times that have been and will be revealed through him from the beginning to Christ, and from Christ to the end of all the dispensations that are to be revealed. . . . This, then, is the nature of the Priesthood, every man holding the Presidency of his dispensation, and one man holding the Presidency of them all, even Adam. (Joseph Smith, *History of the Church,* Vol. 4, pp. 207-209)

On another occasion the Prophet Joseph Smith stated further:

> The Priesthood was first given to Adam; he obtained the First Presidency, and held the keys of it from generation to generation. He obtained it in the Creation, before the world was formed, as in Genesis 1:26, 27, 28. He had dominion given him over every living creature. . . . Our Father Adam, Michael, will call his children together and prepare them for the coming of the Son of Man. He (Adam) is the father of the human family, and presides over the spirits of all men, and all that have had the keys must stand before him in this grand council. . . . The Son of Man stands before him,

and there is given him glory and dominion. Adam delivers up his stewardship to Christ. (Joseph Smith, *History of the Church,* Vol 3, pp. 385-387)

The perspective of years brings out the remarkable fact, that, though the enemies of the Latter-day Saints have had access, in printed form, to the hundreds of discourses of Brigham Young, only half a dozen statements have been useful to the calumniators of the founder of Utah. Of these, the sermon of April 9, 1852, which has been quoted most frequently, presents no errors of fact or doctrine, if read understandingly and honestly.

6. WHAT IS THE MEANING OF THE ATONEMENT?

The universe is dual: spiritual and material, composed of "spirit-element" and "matter-element." These two realms are closely interwoven, perhaps of the same ultimate source; yet they are distinct in their nature. Mastery of the universe means acquaintanceship with and control of both of these elemental divisions of the universe in which we live.

All men had a spirit birth, and, before the earth was created, lived in a pre-existent life, often called the first estate. In that existence, the spirit children of God, later to become the men and women of earth, possessed the faculties we enjoy here. They could learn, choose, grow or retrograde even as on earth. God, their Father, provided means for their development, but did not rob them of their free agency. (D. & C. 29:35)

These pre-existent beings possessed only bodies of "spirit-element." Therefore, they were limited to an intimate acquaintanceship with the spirit world. The material world could not be satisfactorily explored, nor known and controlled by beings having only spirit bodies as their means of communication and labor. Nevertheless, their divine destiny was to know the whole universe to which they belonged—to become like their Father. To do this they needed to acquire bodies of "matter-element"—later to become refined and celestialized. Such material bodies would be tools by which the world of matter might be known, and controlled for man's progress.

When God, the Father of the spirits of men, saw that His children were ready for the experiences of the material world, He called them together to discuss their further education. In the great council which followed (Pearl of Great Price, Moses, 4:1-3; Abraham, 3:22-28; D. & C., 29:36; 76: 25-29), the Father presented a plan for this further education known as the Plan of Salvation, or the gospel of Jesus Christ. This plan was accepted by two-thirds of the council, and rejected by one-third. There was no chance for neutrality. The plan had to be accepted or not accepted. The sorrow of the opponents to the plan is that they cannot acquire matter-bodies which would give them knowledge and power that they must now be without.

The plan provided that "matter-element" should be collected and made into an earth, as a schoolhouse, upon which the spirits of men might dwell with bodies of earth-element, in pursuit of their preparation for the more complete mastery of the universe. The eldest spirit-son of God, known to us as Jesus, the Christ, was chosen to lead in the execution of the plan; and Adam, another among the chief sons of God, and Eve were chosen to be the first to go down on earth to take upon themselves earth-bodies, and to become the earthly parents and heads of the race of men to be born on earth.

The education of the spirit children of God was to be exacting. For a great gift one must give much. They would go to the earth in forgetfulness of the past, depending upon their own free agency, to be clothed in bodies of "earth-element," provided by their earthly parents; subject to the conditions of earth, instead of the perfected state of their spirit home.

More terrifying was another requirement. Sometime in their earth career their earth-bodies would be separated from their spirit-bodies, in a process called death, and they would for a time be so separated until divine forces acting under a higher law, would reunite the earth-body, purified and celestialized for an eternal existence, with the spirit-body, which, because it is a child of God, is also eternal. All this was planned for the education of man, and to insure his eternal progress amidst the elements and forces of the universe.

Clearly, the processes involved in the operation of the plan are beyond the full comprehension of man. Yet enough has been revealed to make the essentials of man's entrance upon earth, and progress in the hereafter, understandable to the human mind.

To subject an eternal being to the dominion of "earth-element"—that is, to forgetfulness, the many vicissitudes of earth, and eventual death—appeared to be a descent in power and station. The first man, to bring himself under such dominion and domination would have to break, or set aside, an established law; but unless this were done, the plan could not be inaugurated. Man, made to walk upright, must bend his back through the tunnel through the mountain which leads to a beautiful valley. Adam and Eve accepted the call to initiate the plan, and subjected themselves to earth conditions. That was the so-called fall of Adam, an act necessary for the winning of bodies of earth-element by man, and for the fulfilment of divine law. (Pearl of Great Price, Moses, 4:7-13; 5:10, 11) Just how this "fall" was accomplished is not known, and probably cannot be understood by the mortal mind. One thing must be kept in mind: The fall was not a sin in the usually accepted sense of that word. It was a necessary act in a series of acts by which ultimately all men will win an eternal possession of their earth-bodies. In the gospel sense, the fall of Adam brought life, not death, into man's eternal existence.

Here then, would be the condition of man after he had acquired an "earthly body" and then was separated from it by the process called death: He was rich in earth experience but without the earth-body to be used by him as an eternal tool to help him win his place among the realities of the universe. The "fall of Adam" had made possible the earth experience, but another act was necessary to restore to the eternal spirit the body of the earth, purified and fitted for eternal life. Someone had to secure this reunion of body and spirit and fit the body for eternal existence. Someone must cancel out the effect of the fall.

It was one of the tasks of Jesus Christ to accomplish this return of body to spirit. He was born of a mortal woman, but begotten by God, an Eternal Being. Hence, He was both man and God, of earth and of heaven. By His death and subsequent resurrection, the bodies of all men, laid in the grave by Adam's act, were or will be raised into eternal life. In this matter he atoned for the "fall."

The death of Jesus, who had immortality within His reach, was not as the death of mortal men. Just how His death brought about the resurrection is not known, and, as with the "fall," is probably beyond human understanding.

Yet, vicarious acts, faintly comparable to the vicarious acts of Jesus and Adam, appear in daily life. One man may for certain purposes cut the wires that supply a city with light, leaving multitudes to find their way in darkness. Another man may reunite the wires, and again flood the city with light. The cutting of the wires, and especially the reuniting of them, is often done with peril to life.

Jesus died that men, all men, may recover their earthly bodies from the grave. Despite our frailties, follies, or sins, our bodies will be raised from the grave and given to the waiting spirits. Every person born into the world will be so resurrected. The effect of Adam's act is cancelled out by Jesus, by His willingness to pass through death and the resurrection.

Men must do many things to win salvation in the kingdom of God. Jesus, the Christ, as head of the plan of salvation, under His Father, has many duties besides the resurrection of the bodies of humanity to perform for the blessing of man; and consequently has many titles. He is known as our Elder Brother, our Redeemer, our Advocate with the Father each title referring to a special service for man and meriting special discussion. His compensation for Adam's necessary act, by which He brought about the resurrection, is the most direct meaning of His title, Redeemer.

The "fall" of Adam and the atonement of Jesus Christ are necessary key concepts of the gospel. Christianity stands or falls with them. Neither of these concepts can be understood except as they are placed in their proper places in the whole plan of Salvation. Yet we know that they were equally necessary, as are the beginning and end of a journey.

Adam and Eve, who began the earth work in sacrifice and courage, are the greatest and noblest of the human race. Jesus, the Christ, our Master and Brother, who gave His very life for man, is the great divine Leader of the plan formulated by God for man's good. In His name, through the appointment of the Father, are done all things pertaining to the earth and the race of men.

(Read President John Taylor's *The Mediation and Atonement of Our Lord, Jesus Christ.*)

7. WHAT IS THE DIFFERENCE BETWEEN THE HOLY SPIRIT AND THE HOLY GHOST?

The Holy Spirit is the agent, means, or influence by which the will, power, and intelligence of God, and the Godhead, personal Beings, may be transmitted throughout space. The Holy Spirit, variously called the Spirit of God, the Light of Christ, the Spirit of Truth, proceeds from the presence of God to fill the immensity of space. It is a spirit of intelligence that permeates the universe and gives understanding to the spirits of men. The phenomena of existence are but expressions of this divine medium.

By the Holy Spirit, the Lord is in communication with all His children and can touch their hearts everywhere. It "giveth light to every man that cometh into the world; and the Spirit enlighteneth every man through the world, that hearkeneth to the voice of the Spirit. And every one that hearkeneth to the voice of the Spirit cometh unto God, even the Father." (D. & C. 84:46, 47) Enlightenment, direction, warning, reproof, and approval come to man from the loving Father of humankind, through the agency of the Holy Spirit.

The phenomena of nature, whether on earth or in stellar fields, are manifestations of the Holy Spirit. The light from the sun, heat, electricity, thunder, lightning, the placidly flowing brook and the raging torrent are expressions of the divine will, through the operations of this holy, universe-filling influence.

> And the light which shineth, which giveth you light, is through him who enlighteneth your eyes, which is the same light that quickeneth your understandings;
>
> Which light proceedeth forth from the presence of God to fill the immensity of space—
>
> The light which is in all things, which giveth life to all things, which is the law by which all things are governed, even the power of God who sitteth upon his throne, who is in the bosom of eternity, who is in the midst of all things. (D. & C. 88:11-13)

The Holy Ghost, sometimes called the Comforter, is the third member of the Godhead, and is a personage, distinct from the Holy Spirit. As a personage, the Holy Ghost cannot any more than the Father and Son be everywhere present in person. Little has been revealed as yet concerning the Holy Ghost; but it is evident that His mission is to bear witness to men of the existence of God and the truth of the gospel of Jesus Christ, and also to fill men with knowledge and power and to inspire them to works leading to happiness. "The Comforter beareth record of the Father and of the Son." The labors assigned to this member of the Godhead are high and holy, and necessary for man's eternal progress. It seems not improbable that He uses the Holy Spirit to perform His labors.

The presence and power of the Holy Ghost are promised all who have faith in God, repent of their sins, are baptized for the remission of their sins, and have hands laid upon them by constituted authority in the Priesthood. The act of confirmation of the newly baptized person always includes the words, "Receive the Holy Ghost." It is the baptism of fire, the great gift, the reward for obedience to the preparatory ordinances of the gospel.

The gift of the Holy Ghost confers upon a person the right to receive, as he may desire and need, the presence, light, and intelligence of the Holy Ghost. It gives, as it were, an official claim upon the mighty assistance and comforting assurance of the Holy Ghost. When the servants of the Lord display a spiritual power beyond the command of man; when the grief-laden heart beats with joy; when failure is converted into victory, it is by the visitation of the Holy Ghost. It is the Spirit of God under the direction of the Holy Ghost that quickeneth all things.

The gift of the Holy Ghost remains inoperative unless a person leads a worthy life. Worthiness determines whether a person shall enjoy the privileges promised when the "gift" is conferred. It is useless to expect this high official assistance unless there is daily conformity to the laws of the gospel. In addition, faith and prayer, out of the heart and unceasing, are required to fit a person for the presence of the Holy Ghost. To such a life He will respond in power. Only those who "hearken" will be enlightened by the spirit.

Latter-day Saints have received, under the hands of those divinely empowered, this inexpressibly glorious "gift," which will lead them if they are fitted, into the companionship of the Holy Ghost, and win for them intelligence and power to win joy in life and exaltation in the world to come. Those who have been so blessed have not always understood the greatness of that which has been given them, or have not earnestly sought its help. So powerful a gift, with such boundless promise, justifies every attempt to cleanse body and soul. Certain it is, that only with the aid of the Holy Ghost shall we be able to rise to the heights of salvation of which we dream and for which we pray.

8. WHY DO WE PARTAKE OF THE SACRAMENT? WHO SHOULD PARTAKE OF THE SACAMENT?

A sacrament means a solemn, sacred religious ordinance. There are many of them. The sacrament as understood by the Church, and discussed here, is the partaking of bread and water (or unfermented wine) as emblems of the body and blood of the Lord Jesus Christ.

The central figure of the plan of salvation is Jesus, the Christ. To Him is committed the supervision of the Plan—from the making of the earth to the final report of work accomplished. His atoning sacrifice makes possible the eternal possession by the spirits of men of their earth-won bodies. All things pertaining to the welfare of the earth and its inhabitants are done through Him. Every commandment for salvation is administered by Him. Therefore, all petitions to God, every prayer, should be offered in the name of the Son of God, Jesus Christ.

Every person who accepts the divine plan for human salvation must accept the leadership of Jesus, and covenant to keep the laws of the plan. As Christ is accepted with all the attendant obligations of the gospel, in spirit and in deed, so man may win salvation (Pearl of Great Price, Moses 5:8-9), and there is no other way.

All this was explained to Father Adam, the first man; and it has been explained whenever a new dispensation of the gospel has been opened on earth. Adam was further taught that to keep constantly alive the knowledge of Jesus and His gospel and man's covenant under the gospel law, he should offer sacrifices in "similitude of the [coming] sacrifice of the Only Begotten of the Father." (Pearl of Great Price, Moses 5:7)

From that time onward, until Jesus Himself came on earth, wherever the Priesthood was present, men offered sacrifices in memory of their acceptance of Jesus, the Son of God, and of their covenants with God. The Mosaic law and ritual were built around the offering of sacrifices, which were the most sacred parts of the system. (Leviticus, chapters 7-9; Exodus, chapters 29, 30)

After the coming of Jesus and His sacrificial death, it continued to be important to keep alive among men the meaning of the gospel of Jesus Christ and man's obligations to God. Yet, since the "sinless sacrifice" had been accomplished, and the old and partial law had been superseded by the more complete law, a new form of witnessing to Christ's supreme place and man's acceptance of Him and His law was instituted.

President Joseph F. Smith said:

> It was instituted by the Savior in the place of the law of sacrifice which was given to Adam, and which continued with his children down to the days of Christ, but which was fulfilled in his death, he being the great sacrifice for sin, of which the sacrifices enjoined in the law given to Adam were a similitude. (Joseph F. Smith, *Gospel Doctrine*, p. 252)

Shortly before His crucifixion, in an upper room in Jerusalem, Jesus ate His last supper with His chosen Twelve. The first three evangelists tell the story. Matthew says,

> And as they were eating, Jesus took bread, and blessed it, and brake it, and gave it to the disciples, and said, Take, eat: this is my body. And he took the cup, and gave thanks, and gave it to them, saying, Drink ye all of it: For this is my blood of the new testament, which is shed for many for the remission of sins. But I say unto you, I will not drink henceforth of this fruit of the vine, until that day when I drink it new with you in my Father's kingdom. (Matthew 26:26-29; also Mark 16:14; and Luke 22:14-20)

Thenceforth, under the "New Testament," this has been the type of memorial of Christ's sacrifice and man's acceptance of Christ and obedience to Christ's law. It is the Sacrament of man's communion with God—a most sacred ordinance

The restoration of the gospel through the instrumentality of Joseph Smith clarified the use and meaning of the Sacrament, which through the dark periods of apostasy had suffered many perversions. In the revelation on Church organization and government it is declared that "the church meet together often to partake of bread and wine in the remembrance of the Lord Jesus." Further, the meaning of the ordinance is made clear in the set prayers to be pronounced upon the bread and water which follow. For the bread it is:

> O God, the Eternal Father, we ask thee in the name of thy son, Jesus Christ, to bless and sanctify this bread to the souls of all those who partake of it, that they may eat in remembrance of the body of thy Son, and witness unto thee, O God, the Eternal Father, that they are willing to take upon them the name of thy Son, and always remember him and keep his commandments which he has given them; that they may always have his Spirit to be with them. Amen. (D. & C. 20:77)

To remember the sacrifice of Jesus, to accept Jesus as the Leader; to keep His commandments—these are the covenants made; and the reward is the guiding companionship of the Holy Spirit. This makes of the partaking of the sacrament a renewal of the covenants we made at the time of baptism into the Church. Thus, by the sacrament we declare repeatedly, ordinarily weekly, our allegiance to the plan of salvation and its obligations. Thus we keep ourselves as one with Christ our Elder Brother in seeking to consummate the purposes of the Father with respect to the children of men.

The Sacrament should be taken with sincere acceptance of all that it means. The partaker should seek to cleanse himself from all evil. Otherwise the expected blessings may not be realized. In the words of Paul,

> But let a man examine himself, and so let him eat of that bread, and drink of that cup. For he that eateth and drinketh unworthily, eateth and drinketh damnation to himself. (I Corinthians 11:28, 29)

The statement that "the Church" meet together often to partake of the sacrament, implies that properly it should be administered in authorized Church gatherings. The meeting may be small in number, for "where two or three are met together in my name, . . . there I will be." (D. & C. 6:32; Matt. 18:20)

The authority to administer the Sacrament is possessed by all holders of the Melchizedek Priesthood and also by priests of the lesser Priesthood. It is customary for two persons to officiate, one for the bread, the other for the water. However, one elder or priest may bless both emblems, if necessary. (D. & C. 20:76)

Early in the history of the restored Church, the question of the use of wine in the sacrament was discussed. By revelation it was learned that "it mattereth not what ye shall eat or what ye shall drink when ye partake of the sacrament, if it so be that ye do it with an eye single to my glory—" (D. &

C. 27:2) Consequently, the Church uses water instead of wine. Should wine be used it should be "made new among you." (D. & C. 27:4)

While only those who have entered the Church can renew their covenants, yet to avoid singling out children who may be present, and to accustom them to the ordinance, they are taught to accept the emblems of the Sacrament.

The Sacrament is intended for the members of the Church. The covenants in the prayer of blessing are those made when entrance into the Church is consummated. Where there are many non-members present in a Sacrament meeting, the presiding officer usually announces that the Sacrament will be administered to members of the Church, without further comment. There should, however, be no attempt to withhold the bread and water from non-members. If such persons partake, it will be upon their own responsibility; and to some extent at least they then accept the meaning and covenants of the ordinance.

President Brigham Young, speaking upon the sacrament, said, "Its observance is as necessary to our salvation as any other of the ordinances and commandments that have been instituted in order that the people may be sanctified." (*Discourses of Brigham Young*, p. 266)

Members of the Church should delight in the privilege of partaking of the Lord's sacred supper, thereby affirming their faith in Jesus the Christ and their allegiance to the Church of Christ.

III. Revelation

1. WHY CAN NOT THINGS OF GOD BE KNOWN EXCEPT BY THE SPIRIT OF GOD?

The Savior while on earth declared that "It is the spirit that quickeneth" (John 6:63); and in modern times, speaking to Joseph Smith the Prophet, He said, "the Spirit beareth record" (D. & C. 1:39; 59:24); and "the Spirit giveth light to every man." (D. & C. 84:46)

The Apostle Paul, interpreting life in terms of this doctrine, wrote "the things of God knoweth no man, but the Spirit of God." (I Corinthians 2:11)

This profound yet almost self-evident truth is the beginning of an understanding of the gospel.

The radio now found in almost every household illustrates the meaning of this doctrine. Broadcast throughout space are countless messages, music or the spoken word—some good, others bad. We are immersed in these radio waves or radiations or whatever they may be; they beat upon our senses as waves upon the ocean shore. Yet, we are not conscious of them unless our receiving set is tuned to catch them. Then they are converted into sound waves that activate our eardrums. That which eluded our senses, suddenly enters our world of hearing.

Similarly, the astronomer must have his telescope to scan the depths of space; the biologist, his microscope to perceive the minute things of life; the physicist, his electron-microscope to bring the world of molecules within his range of vision. There would be no progress unless this were done. If the astronomer should attempt to survey the heavens with a microscope, or the biologist set out with a telescope to make the world of small things visible, only confusion or blackness would result.

This is a universal law. In every department of knowledge the seeker for truth must choose his tools with reference to the field to be explored; and the procedure of his studies must fit the needs of the search. While instruments, aids to the senses, are important, indeed often indispensable, they are of little value unless the senses themselves are in a condition to receive that which the instruments transmit. Eye, ear, and all other sense organs must be normal for dependable observation. Otherwise the observations may be misleading.

In addition, man himself must also be able not only to receive but also to interpret that which comes through his senses. The mental interpretation is as important as the physical observation. Unless he can do this, his knowledge is but as rain splashing upon a granite dome, when it might fall upon friendly, absorbing soil to germinate seed or to induce plant growth. In every pursuit of knowledge, therefore, the fitness and power of the man to observe and to interpret become of first consequence. The inner meaning of phenomena is revealed only to one competent to receive the truth sought.

It is so in the pursuit of spiritual truth. There, the seeker deals with living, personal realities; not primarily with the inert, impersonal things and forces of science. The Holy Spirit, which is in touch with every person born into the world, is the communicating agent. In this field, man, a living being, must be the chief instrument of reception as well as the interpreter of the knowledge offered by the Spirit of God. Therefore, the individual must be properly prepared, tuned, if he is to receive and to comprehend spiritual truth. In short, to understand "things of God," a person, who is the receiving apparatus, must qualify himself spiritually.

Mere knowledge of spiritual truth, information that may be drawn from the encyclopedia, for instance, that there is a God, that prayers may be heard, or that it is wrong to steal, is never really understood unless the person is spiritually prepared. The absence of such preparation explains why many who can glibly recite the Ten Commandments or the Beatitudes may violate them with equal ease; or why, though reared in a religious atmosphere, they are irreligious. Such persons believe that spiritual knowledge may be poured into them with no consideration of their fitness and with no effort on their part. That cannot be done in the lower fields of knowledge and less so in the highest, the spiritual field. It would be in opposition to natural law. Such people are out of spiritual focus, and their impressions are blurred, much as a telescope out of focus gives only indistinct and confused images. Or, to use another figure of speech, there is static in their lives which mars the beauty of life's melody. On the contrary, when a person does fit and qualify himself, spiritual messages, waiting to be revealed, come to him. Then, and only then, is spiritual knowledge quickened into living comprehension leading to activity. When there is such correspondence between an individual and the spiritual world, the real joy of life appears. Otherwise, something is missing from our daily desire. We live incompletely.

What, then, can a person do to qualify himself to receive and to understand things of the spirit, to become an instrument through which spiritual messages may be made intelligible? An answer is given in a glorious latter-day revelation:

> But great and marvelous are the works of the Lord, . . . Neither is man capable to make them known, for they are only to be seen and understood by the power of the Holy Spirit, which God bestows on those who love him, and purify themselves before him. (D. & C. 76:114, 116)

Speaking to the same subject the ancient American Prophet Moroni gave this well-known guide:

> . . . I would exhort you that ye would ask God, the Eternal Father, in the name of Christ, if these things are not true; and if ye shall ask with a sincere heart, with real intent, having faith in Christ, he will manifest the truth of it unto you, by the power of the Holy Ghost. (Book of Mormon, Moroni 10:4)

The formula seems simple: Faith, obedience, and prayer. But, as with all good things, it requires personal effort. The seeker after spiritual truth must first have faith in God, that is, in His existence and His relationship to mankind. This is the beginning of all wisdom. Frequently, the difficulty with those who struggle to believe this or that gospel principle, is that they have not yet found full faith in God. Next, love of God must characterize him who would know the things of the spirit. That means surrender of self to the requirements of the Lord. In other words, obedience to law is required, which is the only way to freedom. Knowledge of itself is never sufficient; it must be made alive by obedience, the fruit of love. By obedience to the law of the Lord, we purify ourselves, and become fitted to approach Him and to win His favor. All the while there must be prayer for help to the beloved Being whom we call God, and whom we are ready to obey to secure the knowledge desired. Such prayer must be sincere, of "real intent," otherwise it becomes a useless gesture. "Pray always, and I will pour out my Spirit upon you" (D. & C. 19:38) is the promise of the Lord. In short, "living the gospel" fits a man to receive spiritual truth. Only then can he receive and understand things of the spirit. Upon that condition alone does the light of truth enter his life.

Is it difficult to obey this formula, to qualify oneself spiritually? Nothing is easier or more enjoyable. When there is harmony between the instrument and the pounding message, there is joy in the heart. The world's confusion roots in discord, lack of harmony. To be out of focus or to live in the midst of static is to be in semi-darkness and chaos. To have control of self, to bid the baser appetites depart, is to walk through life in full light and with full power. They who think the path difficult, have not tried it. "Living the gospel" is the true way to the full and free expression of human powers, to the help that the Spirit of God can give.

It may be added that all who yield such obedience to God's law undergo a real transformation, by the Holy Ghost, which enables them more and more, to receive and understand spiritual messages. Unless that transformation is accomplished, a person is opaque to spiritual truth, and the "things of God" are beyond his understanding.

Great is the effect of such spiritual communication. Human experience as well as the divinely inspired word makes clear the overflowing blessings that follow possession of the "things of God." It transforms life. It makes the weak strong, the strong mightier. Every field of activity is illuminated by spiritual truth. The individual becomes filled with light as the incandescent lamp when the electric current passes through it. Moroni left for all truth seekers this world-sweeping message: "And by the power of the Holy Ghost ye may know the truth of all things" (Book of Mormon, Moroni 10:5). Scientist and philosopher; farmer and tradesman; rich and poor; all will be aided in their life pursuits if they have contact with the inexhaustible intelligence of the spiritual realm. The wealth of eternity will be theirs. They who do not seek to make themselves receivers of spiritual messages, but thrash about for such truth as their unaided powers may reveal, do not learn the meaning and destiny of life, and fail to win the vision of the glory of the universe in which we live.

2. WHY DID JOSEPH SMITH, THE PROPHET, NEED THE HELP OF THE URIM AND THUMMIM?

The Urim and Thummim are mentioned in the Bible in connection with priestly functions. They were to be used in making the will of the Lord clear and comprehensible to the priest. Aaron was instructed to wear the Urim and Thummim "upon his heart," when he went to secure "judgment" from the Lord, and his successors were instructed to use the Urim and Thummim when they asked "counsel" from the Lord. Clearly, the Urim and Thummim were used in official communication with the Lord. Beyond that, little is known of them. (See Exodus 28:30; Leviticus 8:8; Numbers 27:21; Deuteronomy 33:8; I Samuel 28:6; Ezra 2:63; Nehemiah 7:65.)

In modern times the Urim and Thummim reappear. The Prophet Joseph Smith records that the angel Moroni said that "there was a book deposited, written on gold plates . . . also, that there were two stones in silver bows . . . and these stones fastened to a breastplate, constituted what is called the Urim and Thummim . . . deposited with the plates; and the possession and use of these stones were what constituted 'Seers' in ancient or former times, and that God had prepared them for the purpose of translating the book" (Joseph Smith, *History of the Church,* 1:12).

When the actual work of translation began, the Urim and Thummim were found to be indispensable. In various places the statement is made that the translation was made "by means of the Urim and Thummim" (D. & C. 10:1). On one occasion, when the Prophet, through the defection of Martin Harris, lost a part of the manuscript translation, the Urim and Thummim were taken from him, and the power of translation ceased. Upon the return of the sacred instruments, the work was resumed (Joseph Smith, *History of the Church,* 1:23). While the Prophet was undoubtedly required to place himself in the proper spirit and mental attitude before he could use the Urim and Thummim successfully, yet it must also be concluded that the stones were essential to the work of translation.

Most of the early revelations to Joseph Smith were obtained by the use of the Urim and Thummim. Speaking of those early days the Prophet usually says, "I enquired of the Lord through the Urim and Thummim, and obtained the following" (Joseph Smith, *History of the Church,* 1:33, 36, 45, 49, 53). The "stones in silver bows" seemed, therefore, to have possessed the general power of making spiritual manifestations understandable to Joseph Smith.

The Prophet did not always receive revelations by the aid of the Urim and Thummim. As he grew in spiritual power, he learned to bring his spirit into such harmony with divinity that it became, as it were, a Urim and Thummim to him, and God's will was revealed without the intervention of external aids. This method is clearly, though briefly, expressed in one of the early revelations.

> Behold, you have not understood; you have supposed that I would give it unto you, when you took no thought save it was to ask me.
>
> But, behold, I say unto you, that you must study it out in your mind; then you must ask me if it be right, and if it is right I will cause that your bosom shall burn within you; therefore, you shall feel that it is right.
>
> But if it be not right you shall have no such feelings, but you shall have a stupor of thought that shall cause you to forget the thing which is wrong; therefore, you cannot write that which is sacred save it be given from me. (D. & C. 9:7-9)

Similarly, the Book of Mormon sets forth the conditions which enable a person to receive divine communications without special outside means.

> And when you shall receive these things, I would exhort you that ye would ask God, the Eternal Father, in the name of Christ, if these things are not true; and if ye shall ask with a sincere heart, with real intent, having faith in Christ, he will manifest the truth of it unto you, by the power of the Holy Ghost.
>
> And by the power of the Holy Ghost ye may know the truth of all things. (Book of Mormon, Moroni 10:4, 5)

That is, truth may become known when one places himself in harmony or in tune with the requirements of the subject in hand.

The possession of the Urim and Thummim, with their purpose and use, really becomes a strong evidence of the truth of Joseph Smith's message. It is a commonplace of science that the senses of man are so poor as to make them inadequate to discover more than a small fraction of universal truth. Indeed, with unaided senses, man stands helpless before the many phenomena of nature. It is an equally elementary fact that aids of the senses of man, when found, open up large and new vistas of knowledge. Every aid to human sense becomes, in fact, a door to a new field of scientific exploration.

The history of science is largely the story of the accumulation of aids to man's senses. By the use of a glass prism, ordinary sunlight is broken into the many prismatic colors; a sensitive thermometer reveals heat rays above the red end of the spectrum; a photographic plate reveals the existence of different rays at the violet end of the spectrum; uranium glass changes the invisible rays at the violet end of the spectrum into light rays; a magnetic needle makes known the presence of a low tension electric current in a wire; the magnetic currents over the earth are indicated by the compass; by X-rays the bones of the body are made visible; a great telescope is now being built which will enable the human eye to see light, of the intensity of a small candle, forty thousand miles away. Such examples might be greatly multiplied.

Joseph Smith was but a humble, inexperienced lad. He was assigned a tremendous task. His need of help such as the Urim and Thummim, until by mighty prayer and effort his body and spirit became spiritually "tuned," seems both logical and scientific.

It should be noted also that the Prophet does not enter into any argument to prove the necessity of the use of the Urim and Thummim. His simple mention of them argues strongly for his veracity. An impostor would probably have attempted an explanation of the "seer stones."

The Urim and Thummim were aids to Joseph's spiritual senses. How they operated is not known. For that matter, the methods of operation of most of the aids to man's physical senses are not understood. Joseph's claim to the need of such aids becomes an evidence for the truth of his life's labor.

3. TO WHAT EXTENT MAY PROPHECY BE INTERPRETED?

Prophecy, in the sense of the above question, is the foretelling, through divine inspiration, of coming events. Such prophecies have characterized the work of the Lord in all ages. They have been means of comforting, guiding, and warning the children of men. The Church holds fast to faith in the spirit of prophecy as a gift of the Lord.

There appear to be several types of prophecies:

First, there are prophecies which in reality are statements of cause and effect. If certain things are done, certain results will flow therefrom. For example, "he that repents not, from him shall be taken even the light which he has received" (D. & C. 1:33); "where two or three are gathered together in my name, as touching one thing, behold there will I be in the midst of them" (D. & C. 6:32). Holy Writ is filled with such prophecies. They need no interpretation. Their fulfillment is part of the general experience of the Church.

Second, there are occasions when the prophet, looking into the future, is able to localize coming events definitely as to time, place, or person. Such particular prophecies are fairly plentiful in sacred history. The most famous, in modern days, concerns the American Civil War. "Verily, thus saith the Lord concerning the wars that will shortly come to pass, beginning at the rebellion of South Carolina, . . . For behold, the Southern States shall be divided against the Northern States, and the Southern States will call on other nations, even the nation of Great Britain, . . . to defend themselves" (D. & C. 87:1, 3). Here the coming event is linked definitely with place and country. This kind of prophecy has no need of interpretation; we wait only for its fulfillment, which is the evidence of its divine source. (See also, I Kings 13:2, 21-22, 24-30; 14:5-17; 16:34; 20:13-30; 20:35, 36. II Kings 2:3-11; 7:2, 19, 20; 9:10, 33-37; 13:16-25; 14: 25-28; 19:6, 7, 20-37; 20:17, 18; and many others.)

Third, a prophet, looking down the stream of time, sees with spiritual eyes the panorama of future history. Such prophecies are general, in that they do not specifiy times, localize places, though they occasionally name individuals. This is the most common entrance of prophecy into the future. It began with Adam who "stood up in the midst of the congregation; and, notwithstanding he was bowed down with age, being full of the Holy Ghost, predicted whatsoever should befall his posterity unto the latest generation" (D. & C. 107:56). The prophecy of Enoch, the Patriarch, is an excellent illustration of this type of prophecy. In answer to his request, Enoch was shown the future of mankind, generation upon generation, down to the coming of Christ, and beyond to the last days. No time or place limits are set. We may only recognize the periods by the events as they occur (Pearl of Great Price, Moses 7:20-67). Likewise, the Prophet Joseph Smith was given visions of the last days and the events that will characterize them, but fixed time or places were seldom given (D. & C. 5:19; 29:14, 16, 18, 19, 20; 34:9; 43:22, 26, 33; 45:31, 40-42; 49:25; 63:34; 84:118; 88:87, 89, 90, 91, 97; 112:25).

The full recognition of the fulfilment of such prophecies comes as time proceeds and the predicted events appear, unless the interpretation is given earlier by divine revelation. Sometimes foretold events actually occur without being recognized by mankind. As an illustration, when Moroni first appeared to the Prophet Joseph Smith, he "quoted part of the third chapter of Malachi; and he quoted also the fourth or last chapter of the same prophecy" (Pearl of Great Price, Joseph Smith, 2:36), and announced that the events there set forth were about to be consummated.

Human curiosity is intrigued by whatever seems mysterious. Therefore, much effort has been expended to reduce such general prophecies to exact dates, times, and persons, This has been a waste of time and energy, as prophecy uttered under divine inspiration usually contains all that the divine will desires to reveal. It behooves those to whom the prophecy is made to prepare for coming events, to watch for them, and to recognize them when they do appear. If more is needed, the power that gave the prophecy will no doubt furnish the interpretation.

For example, modern revelation declares that these are the last days. This period of the earth's history may be recognized by several signs: The fulness of the gospel will be restored and preached to all the world (D. & C. 39:11; 1:23); work will be done for the spirits of the dead (D. & C. 76:73; 124:29-36; also Sections 127 and 128); mighty, natural events will take place, from the darkened sun to tremendous earthquakes, and the whole earth will be in commotion and many will be destroyed because of wars, pestilence, and fear. (D. & C., Sections 29, 45, 49, 84, 87, 88) These are also signs of the coming of the Lord Jesus Christ. (D. & C. 45:39) All who fear the Lord will anxiously look for these signs as they appear. (D. & C. 45:39) Yet, despite these signs, none shall know the exact time of His coming:

> And they have done unto the Son of Man even as they listed; and he has taken his power on the right hand of his glory, and now reigneth in the heavens, and will reign till he descends on the earth to put all enemies under his feet, which time is nigh at hand—
>
> I, the Lord God, have spoken it; but the hour and the day no man knoweth, neither the angels in heaven, nor shall they know until he comes. (D. & C. 49:6, 7)

The Prophet Joseph Smith at one time prayed very earnestly to know the time of the coming of Christ. He was told that if he lived until he was eighty-five years old he should see the face of Jesus, but he was unable to determine from this whether or not it referred to the final coming of the Son of Man, or whether he should see the Savior in the flesh. (D. & C. 130: 14-17)

In view of such information, attempts to fix the exact date of the coming of Christ are futile, useless, and contrary to the ways of truth. Those who try it are impelled by a spirit not of God.

The futility of reducing general prophecy to exact times or places is well illustrated by the famous visions of Daniel. It is conceded that the stone that broke the image to pieces is the Kingdom of God; but there has been and is interminable debate as to the historical kingdoms and meaning represented by the gold, silver, iron, and clay portions of the image; the horns of the beasts; the thousand, three hundred and five and thirty days; and the several other statements of Daniel. (See the Book of Daniel). Hundreds, perhaps thousands, of books have been published and tens of thousands of sermons have been preached in the attempt to interpret Daniel's prophecies. It has been a fruitless effort, at best a doubtful conjecture. There remains only the general meaning of these glorious visions: that righteousness will triumph in its battle with evil.

The present disturbed condition of the world has impelled many to look for prophecies relating to the last days. Several such compilations have been published. Quotations are made from leaders of the present, as of past dispensations. Carefully read, these statements add nothing to the prophecies recorded in our sacred books. The attempts to make them specific, such as to predict any country's downfall, or to identify certain present-day leaders with prophetic personages, are unjustified and misleading.

Even more dangerous is the attempt to connect some isolated Bible passage with an historical event or structure. The statement by Jeremiah (Jeremiah 32:20) that the Lord "has set signs and wonders in the land of Egypt, even unto this day," has been made to refer to the great pyramid of Gizeh, near Cairo, Egypt. As a result, the pyramid has been measured innumerable times, inside and out; the steps in the passages have been counted; angles calculated and every item thus secured has been correlated with some year or event in the world's history. Thousands of volumes on the subject have been written, with as many varying conclusions. A different starting point in measurement, or an inch more or less in the measure, sets up an entirely new series of conclusions. The great pyramid is an interesting structure. It may have been built with some symbolism in mind. But, there is no good reason as yet to tie it into divine prophecy. Such time-wasting pursuits, leading nowhere, should be avoided.

In conclusion: Prophecy may be interpreted only to the extent that it implies within its own statements that it shall be interpreted. If a prophecy is indefinite with respect to certain things, it is probably so intended. It is always wise to read and practice that which is clear and understandable, and to leave the dim and mysterious until further prophetic revelation is received. Occultism, and all manner of darkness, which too often lead to self-deception, are unacceptable to Latter-day Saints. We concern ourselves only with that which is clear and understandable. We know that with the progress of time, increasing light will come, as we may have need.

Moreover, we know that we should not waste our valuable time and energies on remote and doubtful matters, but rather direct our efforts towards the study and practice of the clearly stated principles of conduct embodied in the gospel of Jesus Christ. That is the direct method of obtaining light and truth, the goal of every Latter-day Saint.

4. WHAT SHALL BE DONE WITH PERSONAL SPIRITUAL MANIFESTATIONS?

The doctrine that the Lord may and does reveal His will to men on earth is a cornerstone of the faith of the Latter-day Saints. The restoration of the gospel in these latter days was initiated by the direct appearance of the Father and the Son to Joseph Smith. Since that time every forward step of the Church has been the result of a revelation of the Lord's will by direct appearance of Himself or of other heavenly messengers or by equally direct inspiration from the Spirit of the Lord. The Church has ever been and is now led by revelation—authoritative guidance from divine sources.

It is a cornerstone of equal importance, that every member of the Church may and should obtain a personal testimony of the truth of the latter-day work. He must not rest his final convictions upon the testimony of others. The humblest member of the Church, if he seeks properly, may know with full assurance that the gospel is true. None need know it better than he. However, to secure such firm knowledge he must receive assurance of it from the Author of truth; that is, he must be guided by the spirit of revelation. The conclusion is clear: Every member of the Church of Christ may be guided by inspiration from the Lord in the affairs of his own life.

This doctrine is beautifully set forth in several of the foundation revelations given to the Prophet Joseph Smith. For example:

> And the Spirit giveth light to every man that cometh into the world; and the Spirit enlighteneth every man through the world, that hearkeneth to the voice of the Spirit. (D. & C. 84:46)

On another occasion the Lord said to the Church:

> But ye are commanded in all things to ask of God, who giveth liberally; and that which the Spirit testifies unto you even so I would that ye should do in all holiness of heart. . . . seek ye earnestly the best gifts, . . . and always retain in your minds what those gifts are, that are given unto the church. . . . To some is given one, and to some is given another, that all may be profited thereby. . . . He that asketh in the Spirit asketh according to the will of God; wherefore it is done, even as he asketh. (D. & C. 46:7, 8, 10, 12, 30)

Apparently every person has a gift, according to his needs or the service he may render.

Revelations are given for a two-fold purpose: to furnish guidance for the Church, and to give comfort to the individual.

Revelations for the guidance of the Church are given to officers of the Church, but only within the limits of their official jurisdiction. Thus, lay members of the Church cannot and do not receive revelations for the guidance of any Church organizations, but only for themselves. The bishop has a claim upon divine inspiration for the direction of ward affairs, but no further. The spirit of revelation directs the stake president in his official stake duties, but no further. The President of the Church alone, who may officiate in all of the offices of the Church, receives revelations for the Church as a whole, to which stake presidents, ward bishops, and all other officers of the Church are amenable. This preserves a full and logical order within all Church activities.

True revelations come from the Lord. The evil one, ever vigilant in his work of destruction, tries to simulate with an evil purpose every gift of God. Therefore, he presents false doctrines of man-made commandments through the suggestions of evil spirits or evil-minded men. To protect the Saints, and to maintain truth within the Church, the power of discerning between truth and error is given to the officers of the Church. The bishop for his ward, the stake president for his stake, and the President of the Church for the whole Church have this gift of discernment given them. Note the clear, beautiful words of the Lord upon this subject:

> And unto the bishop of the church, and unto such as God shall appoint and ordain to watch over the church and to be elders[8] unto the church, are to have it given unto them to discern all those gifts lest there shall be any among you professing and yet be not of God. . . .
>
> That unto some it may be given to have all those gifts, that there may be a head, in order that every member may be profited thereby. (D. & C. 46:27, 29)

By this power and in this order, evil inspirations within the Church are recognized and rejected.

Divine manifestations for individual comfort may be

[8]This revelation was given before the organization of the First Presidency and the calling of the Twelve Apostles. At this time the head of the Church was called the First Elder.

received by every worthy member of the Church. In that respect all faithful members of the Church are equal. Such manifestations most commonly guide the recipients to the solution of personal problems; though, frequently, they also open the mind to a clearer comprehension of the Lord's vast plan of salvation. They are cherished possessions, and should be so valued by those who receive them. In their very nature, they are sacred and should be so treated. If a person who has received such a manifestation by dream, vision, or otherwise, feels impressed to relate it beyond his immediate family circle, he should present it to his bishop, but not beyond. The bishop, then, may decide upon its further use, if any, or may submit it to those of higher authority for action. The gift was a personal one, not for the Church as a whole; and the recipient is under obligation, in harmony with the established order, not to broadcast it over the Church.

It is unwisdom, therefore, for those who have received such manifestations to send copies to others, to relate them by word of mouth in diverse places, and otherwise to scatter abroad a personal, sacred experience. There are times and places where testimony may be borne of our knowledge that the restored gospel is of the Lord, and of the goodness of the Lord to us, and when we may present evidence of our faith. It would be well to remember that the Lord Jesus Christ, while on earth, usually instructed those whom He had healed or otherwise blessed, that they should not tell others of the occurrence. Some things are done for the public good, others for private welfare.

It should also be kept in mind that a message is carried by every spiritual experience. Revelation always has a purpose related to man's eternal progress. The message should always be of more importance to the recipient than the substance or vehicle of the manifestation. Our spiritual experiences, if sound, point the way to our own salvation. Life's efforts should be directed towards the treading of that way to the satisfaction of the Giver of all gifts, from whom the spirit of revelation issues.

5. DOES THE CHURCH RECEIVE REVELATIONS TODAY AS IN THE DAYS OF JOSEPH SMITH?

The answer to this question is a simple, Yes. The Church of Jesus Christ is guided by continuous revelation. The Lord speaks to His Church now as in the time of the Prophet Joseph Smith, or in ages past, whenever the Church has been upon the earth.

The question merits, however, a fuller answer.

There are at least three classes of revelations:

First, there are revelations dealing with the organization and basic doctrine of the Church. Such revelations form the foundation of the Church, upon which is built the superstructure of teaching and practice throughout the years. These revelations are necessary at the beginning of a dispensation, so that the Church may be properly organized and sent upon its way to bless mankind. In this age, these indispensable revelations were given to Joseph Smith who was commissioned to effect the organization of the restored Church. As given to the Prophet, they suffice for the salvation of man in this dispensation. Other such fundamental revelations dealing with organization and doctrine may, at the pleasure of the Lord, be given, for there is a universe of truth not yet known to us, but it will in no way change or abrogate the principles set forth in existing revelations.

Second, there are revelations dealing with the problems of the day. Though the essential doctrine, forming the foundation, framework, and structure of the gospel, has been revealed, the Church, directed by mortal men, needs divine guidance in the solution of current questions. Many of the revelations received by the Prophet Joseph Smith were of this character. There were missions to organize, cities to be built, men to be called into office, temples, meetinghouses, and homes to be constructed. The Prophet presented his problems to the Lord, and with the revealed answer was able to accomplish properly the work before him. It is comforting to know that our Heavenly Father helps in the minor as in the major affairs of life. The revelations directing the building of certain houses in the early days of the Church, are, for example, among the cherished words of God, for they throw a flood of light upon the precious, intimate relationships that may be established between God and man.

Such revelations, directing the Church in the affairs of the day, have been received continuously by the Church, through the President of the Church. One needs only review the history of the Saints to assure himself that such revelations have constantly been vouchsafed the Church. Perhaps more of this type of revelation has been received since, than during the time of the Prophet. Because they are not printed in books as revelations does not diminish their verity.

Third, every faithful member of the Church may be granted revelation for his daily guidance. In fact, the members of the Church can testify that they in truth have and do receive such daily guidance. The testimony of the truth of the gospel, the precious possession of hundreds of thousands, has come through the spirit of revelation. By desire, study, practice, and prayer, one must approach the testimony of the truth, but it is obtained finally only under the spirit of revelation. It is by this power that the eyes of men are opened to understand the principles and the truth of the gospel. Without that spirit, truth cannot be comprehended.

We may go further. Every person born into the earth has claim upon the assistance of the Spirit of God. That is a species of revelation. Consequently, all good achievements of man, in science, literature, or art, are the product of revelation. The knowledge and wisdom of earth have so come.

It must be remembered that revelations usually come as needed, no faster. The Prophet Joseph Smith made this clear: "We cannot expect to know all, or more than we now know, unless we comply with or keep those we already have received." (*Teachings of the Prophet Joseph Smith,* p. 256) The question then should not be, "Do we receive revelations now as in the days of the Prophet Joseph Smith?" but rather, "Do we keep so fully the revelations already given us that we have the right to expect more?"

Another important principle of revelation in the organized Church of Christ is the limitation placed upon those who secure revelations. Every member of the Church may seek and receive revelation, but only for himself and those for whom he is responsible. Every officer of the Church is entitled to revelation to help him in the field into which he has been called, but not beyond. The bishop can claim no revelation except for his ward duties, the stake president for his stake duties only; the President of the Church is the only person who can receive revelations for the guidance of the Church as a whole. These limitations, coming from the Lord, protect the orderliness of the Kingdom of God on earth.

6. WAS THE "MANIFESTO" BASED ON REVELATION?

The October, 1890, General Conference of the Church was history-making. On Monday, October 6, 1890, Wilford Woodruff, President of the Church, presented for the action of the people an "Official Declaration" discontinuing the practice of plural marriage. Upon the motion of Lorenzo Snow, then the president of the Twelve Apostles, and by vote of the conference, the official declaration "concerning plural marriage" became "authoritative and binding" and therefore the law and order of the Church. This official declaration has since been known, in common speech, as the "Manifesto."

The practice of plural marriage had subjected the Church, from the days of the Prophet Joseph Smith, to continuous opposition and severe persecution. Nevertheless, the Saints—only about two percent of whom had practiced plural marriage, as reported by the Utah Commission—continued to teach and defend the principle which had come to them through revelation. At length, acts of the Congress of the United States (1862, 1882, and 1887) made plural marriage an unlawful and punishable offense. The Church, believing these laws to be unconstitutional because they abrogated the right of religious freedom, sought protection from the courts of the land. During this period furious persecution followed those who had entered into this order of marriage. Under a rigorous enforcement of the laws in question, many were fined and given penitentiary sentences, the property of the Church was confiscated, and the cessation of many of the activities of the Church was threatened. At length, in May, 1890, the Supreme Court of the land, with three members dissenting, ruled that the acts prohibiting plural marriage and confiscating Church property were constitutional.

Now the Lord had expressly declared that His people should be obedient to any constitutional government under which they might live. (D. & C. 98:5, 6) Further, the revelations of the Lord declare that if such a government should prevent the practice of any command given to the Church, the people and the Church would be held guiltless.

> Verily, verily, I say unto you, that when I give a commandment to any of the sons of men to do a work unto my name, and those sons of men go with all their might and with all they have to perform that work, and cease not their diligence, and their enemies come upon them and hinder them from performing that work, behold, it behooveth me to require that work no more at the hands of those sons of men, but to accept of their offerings. (D. & C. 124:49)

After the Supreme Court had spoken, there was no further opportunity for appeal. All lawful means had been used. The action proposed by President Woodruff was therefore wholly in keeping with authoritative Church procedure.

Nevertheless, it must be kept in mind that this Church, founded by revelation, is ever guided by revelation. It may be held with certainty that when the President of the Church presents a momentous matter, such as the "Manifesto," to the people it is by the spirit of revelation from God. It is not the product of man's thinking or desire. It must also be remembered that the power which has the right to command, also has the right and power to revoke. The principle of plural marriage was revealed through Joseph Smith, the Prophet, and the "Manifesto" came through Wilford Woodruff, who held the same keys of authority as were possessed by Joseph Smith.

With this in view, Yes, is the unhesitating answer to the question as to whether the "Manifesto" was based upon revelation.

Fortunately, however, there is direct evidence that the "Manifesto" was the product of revelation.

President Woodruff himself declared at the said conference that "to have taken a stand in anything which is not pleasing in the sight of God, or before the heavens, I would rather have gone out and been shot."

The Church had courageously supported what they believed to be a command of God. Any change would have to come from a revelation from God. President Woodruff had prayed about the matter, and had besought God repeatedly what to do. On September 24, 1890, "the spirit came upon him" and the "Manifesto" was the result. This was publicly stated at the time of the conference of October, 1890.

In his journal of September 25, 1890, President Woodruff writes: ". . . after praying to the Lord and feeling inspired I have issued the following declaration [the 'Manifesto'] which is sustained by my counselors and the Twelve Apostles."

On December 19, 1891, in a Church petition for general amnesty, signed by the Presidency and the whole Council of the Twelve, occurs the following statement:

> According to our faith the head of the Church receives from time to time, revelations for the religious guidance of his people.
>
> In September, 1890, the present head of the Church, in anguish and prayer, cried to God for help for his flock, and received the permission to advise the members of the Church of Jesus Christ of Latter-day Saints that the law commanding polygamy was henceforth suspended.

Even with these statements, the nature of the "Manifesto" became a subject of discussion among the people. The question that captions this chapter was asked by many. When these controversies reached the ears of President Woodruff, he proceeded to answer them in public. This was done in unmistakable words, notably on one occasion, on Sunday, November 1, 1891, in Logan, reported in the *Deseret Weekly News*, of November 7, 1891 (Vol. 43, pp. 659, 660).

The report of this sermon, by Elder Arthur Winter, was published in President Woodruff's lifetime, and therefore subject to his correction, if inaccurate.

In Logan, he said among other things:

> . . . This Church has never been led a day except by revelation. And He will never leave it. It matters not who lives or who dies, or who is called to lead this Church, they have got to lead it by the inspiration of Almighty God. If they do not do it that way, they cannot do it at all. . . .
>
> I do not want the Latter-day Saints to understand that the Lord is not with us, and that He is not giving revelation to us; for He is giving us revelation, and will give us revelation until this scene is wound up.
>
> I have had some revelations of late, and very important ones to me, and I will tell you what the Lord has said to me. Let me bring your minds to what is termed the Manifesto. The Lord has told me by revelation that there are many members of the Church throughout Zion who are sorely tried in their hearts because of that Manifesto. . . .
>
> The Lord showed me by vision and revelation exactly what would take place if we did not stop this practice. If we had not stopped it you would have had no use for . . . any of the men in this temple at Logan; for all ordinances would be stopped throughout the land of Zion. Confusion would reign throughout Israel, and many men would be made prisoners. This trouble would have come upon the whole Church, and we should have been compelled to stop the prac-

tice. Now, the question is, whether it should be stopped in this manner, or in the way the Lord has manifested to us, and leave our Prophets and Apostles and fathers free men, and the temples in the hands of the people, so that the dead may be redeemed. . . .

. . . The Lord . . . has told me exactly what to do, and what the result would be if we did not do it. . . . But I want to say this: I should have let all the temples go out of our hands; I should have gone to prison myself, and let every other man go there, had not the God of Heaven commanded me to do what I did do; and when the hour came that I was commanded to do that, it was all clear to me. I went before the Lord, and I wrote what the Lord told me to write. . . .

At the same meeting in Logan, President George Q. Cannon said:

We have striven to the utmost extent of our ability to convince this nation that this is a true principle of religion. I myself have testified before Presidents of the United States, before Cabinet officers, before judges of the Supreme Court, before members of the United States Senate and House of Representatives, and before committees of Congress, that I knew that doctrine was from God. I told them I felt that if I had not obeyed it I would have been damned, because the Lord gave to me a direct command to obey that principle. . . .

Over a thousand have gone to prison to show our sincerity. A prominent official of this Territory said to a gentleman the other day: "They say to me that these people are not sincere." "Why," says he, "I know they are sincere. I went myself to the penitentiary and I labored with all the power I had to convince Lorenzo Snow that he should express his willingness to obey the law; but notwithstanding all my persuasions, and notwithstanding he had a year and a half sentence upon him, I could not move him. I believe he would have gone out and been shot rather than to have said he would get out of prison on such terms. . . ."

God gave the command and it required the command of God to cause us to change our attitude. President Woodruff holds the same authority that the man did through whom the revelation came to the Church. It required that same authority to say to us, "It is enough. God has accepted your sacrifice. He has looked down upon you and seen what you have passed through, and how determined you have been to keep His commandments, and now He says. It is enough." It is the same authority that gave us the principle. It is not the word of man. (*Deseret Weekly News*, November 21, 1891, Vol. 43, p. 689)

Certainly, the "Manifesto" was based on revelation. It has the full effect of a commandment of God. Those who ignore it are breakers of the law of the Church. And, it must be kept in mind that, under divine procedure, whenever the Church of God is established on earth, no legitimate Priesthood power operates outside of the Church.

7 WHAT IS AN ANGEL?

Divine guidance may be communicated to man in several ways. God, the Father, may appear, Himself, as He has done at the opening of dispensations of the gospel. More frequently His Son, Jesus Christ, has appeared. On many occasions, messengers have been sent out from the spiritual domain to help men on earth. Often, mortal men have been delegated to help their fellows. Usually, however, the divine message is conveyed by the Holy Spirit, the influence radiating from God and touching every part and personality in the universe. Any or all of these means of communication have been employed in the wisdom of the Lord.

Numerous references to angels are found in the sacred scriptures, ancient and modern. In the Bible, angels ministered to Abraham, Jacob, Gideon, Elijah, Zachariah, and many others. In the Book of Mormon, angels ministered to Nephi, to the sons of Helaman, to the twelve disciples, and to multitudes of others. In modern days, angels appeared to Joseph and others; and in the revelations to the Prophet, angels and their functions are repeatedly discussed. There can be no question about the important functions of angels in the course of human salvation.

There is, however, much confusion in the use of the term angel. Yet an examination of sacred history makes clear that under the most general definition, angels are personages out of the spirit world, sent to earth as messengers of the Lord. This is in full accord with gospel doctrine. The spiritual, invisible world, out of which man comes and into which he returns, is filled with uncounted hosts of such personages. There can be no reason why the Lord may not use them for His purposes in accomplishing the plan of salvation for His earth-children. Indeed, angels residing in the presence of God (D. & C. 130:7) are waiting to be sent forth in connection with this great work (D. & C. 86:5). Angels were sent to commit the gospel in this as in former dispensations (D. & C. 27:16; 20:10). God calls by the ministering of angels (D. & C. 43:25). They may minister also to personages in heaven (Psalm 103:20). With respect to the earth an angel is a messenger of God, to assist in consummating holy purposes. He is a "ministering spirit" (D. & C. 136:37).

The term *angel* is applied to different classes of beings. Some appear to be spirits who have not yet attained to the earth estate, and do not possess celestialized earthly bodies. Others are personages who have lived on earth, but have not yet been resurrected. A third class are those who have gone through the earth experience and have been resurrected, as Moroni who visited the Prophet Joseph Smith. In all likelihood, personages, known as angels, are used according to their fitness to serve.

A passage in the Doctrine and Covenants gives a more restricted or technical definition of an angel. "Angels, . . . are resurrected personages, having bodies of flesh and bones" (D. & C. 129:1). This is confirmed by the doctrine that persons who have won the right to enter the celestial glory, but have not been sealed in marriage cannot receive the highest exaltation. They "are angels of God forever and ever" (D. & C. 132:17). This may be the most accurate definition of an angel.

The duties of these messengers of God are many and varied, as set forth in Holy Writ. They may announce the truths of the gospel, or convey special messages to individuals or nations. They may act as guardians to protect the righteous, or agents to inflict divine penalties upon the wicked. They may come, as at the beginning of a dispensation, with authority to bestow the Priesthood or to help in the development of the organized Church. In short, they go and do as they are bidden.

The angels of God, or their influence, always come in light. It may be light to the eyes if it be a personal appearance, or the light that leads to righteous works if it be a spiritual message. It is an interesting observation of the Prophet Joseph Smith that "angels who minister to this earth . . . belong or have belonged to it. . . . The angels . . . reside in the presence of God, on a globe like a sea of glass and fire, where all things for their glory are manifest, past, present, and future, and are continually before the Lord" (D. & C. 130:5-7).

Satan also has his messengers. The hosts who fell from heaven in the preexistent council are busily engaged in opposition to God's purposes for man's salvation. They are sent out to lead men into sin. They are angels of untruth, therefore of evil. They feed on lies.

These evil "angels" use deception as their main tool of destruction. They simulate all that is good. They urge the satisfaction of sensual appetites. In the words of Brigham Young, they tell a hundred truths so that the one lie may be accepted. Sometimes they may come as angels of light, in borrowed or stolen raiment. Always they fail to reveal themselves as they are.

Satan and his evil angels are bodiless. That is their heavy punishment. Their power, now and hereafter, is greatly limited by this lack. Therefore, they often seek entrance into human bodies, even bodies of lower animals. Whenever this occurs, the individual thus made to share his body is caused much agonized suffering.

However, one does not really need to fear the angels of evil. They are essentially cowardly. They fear light and truth. Darkness and untruth are their native habitat. Their successes always come when the mind of man is darkened by unbelief or unholy practices. A resolute determination to have nothing to do with them drains their strength. They are mortally afraid of the power of the Priesthood. The command, "Get thou behind me," coupled with righteous living, is sufficient to drive them away. Yet, one must always be on guard against new forms of temptation in which these messengers from evil and with evil may appear to offer transient satisfactions.

Three keys for recognizing messengers out of the unseen world were given by the Prophet Joseph Smith:

> There are two kinds of angels in heaven, namely: Angels, who are resurrected personages, having bodies of flesh and bones—
>
> For instances, Jesus said: *Handle me and see, for a spirit hath not flesh and bones, as ye see me have.*
>
> Secondly: The spirits of just men made perfect, they who are not resurrected, but inherit the same glory.
>
> When a messenger comes saying he has a message from God, offer him your hand and request him to shake hands with you.
>
> If he be an angel he will do so, and you will feel his hand.
>
> If he be the spirit of a just man made perfect he will come in his glory; for that is the only way he can appear—
>
> Ask him to shake hands with you, but he will not move, because

it is contrary to the order of heaven for a just man to deceive; but he will still deliver his message.

If it be the devil as an angel of light, when you ask him to shake hands he will offer you his hand, and you will not feel anything; you may therefore detect him.

These are three grand keys whereby you may know whether any administration is from God (D. & C. 129:1-9).

Deceit is the mark of evil. Even if the evil messenger does not appear in person, the test is the same. Compare the offering with the principles of truth. The sure sign of Satan will then appear.

8. WHENCE CAME THE TEMPLE ENDOWMENTS?

It was inevitable that those who have sought to destroy the truth of the Prophet Joseph Smith's message would misinterpret the temple endowment. They have set up the theory that Joseph Smith merely adapted the temple conception and ritual from the rituals of fraternal, secret organizations.

The charge that the temple endowment is so derived is not confirmed by the evidence at hand.

First, almost from the organization of the Church, Joseph promised the people a higher endowment, a continuation of that received in baptism. It was to be a gift bestowed upon those who had attained a greater maturity in gospel life.

To this end the Kirtland Temple was hurried to completion in 1836, though amidst much toil and sacrifice. Then, at the dedication, some ordinances were given preparatory to the fuller endowment to come. There was nothing new about temple work when it came in its greater completeness. It was expected.

Second, on January 19, 1841, when Joseph Smith had not yet belonged to a fraternal organization, he recorded a revelation which explains in general outline the temple ritual. It says:

"For there is not a place found on earth that he may come to and restore again that which was lost unto you, or which he hath taken away, even the fulness of the priesthood. . . .

"Therefore, verily I say unto you, that your anointings, and your washings, and your baptisms for the dead, and your solemn assemblies, and your memorials for your sacrifices by the sons of Levi, and for your oracles in your most holy places wherein you receive conversations, and your statutes and judgments, for the beginning of the revelations and foundation of Zion, and for the glory, honor, and endowment of all her municipals, are ordained by the ordinance of my holy house, which my people are always commanded to build unto my holy name.

"For I deign to reveal unto my church things which

have been kept hid from before the foundation of the world, things that pertain to the dispensation of the fulness of times.

"And I will show unto my servant Joseph all things pertaining to this house, and the priesthood thereof, and the place whereon it shall be built."[9] From the pulpit the Prophet announced thenceforth the building of the temple and the work to be done therein for the living and the dead.

On May 4, 1842, he administered the temple endowment in rooms in the upper story of his brick store, improvised for the purpose.[10] All the while, before and after, he gave instructions concerning the temple to be built and the endowment therein to be given.

Third, many of the men who joined the Church were brethren in fraternal circles, such as Hyrum Smith, the Prophet's brother, Heber C. Kimball, Newel K. Whitney, George Miller, Austin Cowles, John Smith, Elijah Fordham, and others. Nowhere can a word be found from these many men indicating that they placed temple work in a class with the ritual of the fraternal orders to which they belonged. Had there been such, some of these men would have mentioned it, for not all remained true to the Church.

Fourth, that there are similarities in the services of the temple and some secret organizations may be true. These similarities, however, do not deal with basic matters but rather with the mechanism of the ritual. Moreover, they are not peculiar to any fraternity. They are used and have been used by people throughout the centuries. They belong to the common heritage of mankind. Joseph Smith had the right to employ such commonly used methods and symbols without being charged with plagiarizing from any particular group. The Prophet taught baptism by immersion; but none so far has held that he purloined that type of baptism from the Baptists. Immersion comes down the ages from the days of Jesus Christ and before. The beginnings of such practices are lost in the mists of antiquity.

The temple ritual is essentially symbolic. Its ordinances are not only ancient but also represent profound truths. They may be widely used by others than Latter-day Saints, but they do not have the same meaning in all organizations.

-----

[9]D. & C. 124:28, 39, 41-42.

[10]*History of the Church*, Volume 5:1.

Fifth, women as well as men receive the temple ritual. Only a man and a woman together can receive the highest blessings of the temple. Usually, perhaps always, men only receive the rituals of the many man-made secret societies. The women form auxiliary organizations.

Sixth, there is a great difference between the objective of temple work and those of the many secret organizations, though they no doubt have high ideals of living.

In the temple endowment the final ideal is that by obedience to God's law man may be in association with God. The endowment has the promise of eternal growth, of endless blessings. This is not the ordinary objective of a man-made secret society.

Seventh, finally it may be said that the temple endowment is not secret. All who meet the requirements for entrance to the temple may enjoy it. Since it is sacred, it is not bandied about the streets or in gossiping parlors. It is, in outline: the story of man's eternal journey; instructions to make the endless journey increasing and progressive; covenants that we will so live as to make the journey an upward one; a warning that sometime we shall be called upon to show whether we have kept our covenants; and, the great reward that comes to the faithful and the righteous.

Every member of another organization will know whether this is like his fraternity ritual.

Many members of secret societies have joined the Church of Jesus Christ of Latter-day Saints. They have been faithful to their covenants. But as they have come to the temple of the Lord, they have said, in the words of one former member, "Secret societies have nothing to teach the Latter-day Saints."

Carefully and intelligently studied, the proposition that the Mormon endowment was built upon secret fraternal rituals cannot be accepted by any thoughtful person.

Joseph Smith received the temple endowment and its ritual, as all else that he promulgated, by revelation from God.

IV The Bible

1. IS THE BIBLE TRANSLATED CORRECTLY?

The eighth Article of Faith declares that "We believe the Bible to be the word of God as far as it is translated correctly." This implies that there are mistranslations in the Bible. Moreover, the Prophet Joseph Smith, from the beginning of his ministry, gave some time to revising passages in the Bible which had been translated incorrectly or so rendered as to make the meaning obscure. (Joseph Smith, *History of the Church,* notably Volume 1)

Errors in the translation of the Bible are due primarily to the fact that the original documents are lost. The manuscripts from which our Bible translations have been made are copies, perhaps copies of copies of the originals. Even in our day, with our many modern helps, it is practically impossible to secure a letter-perfect copy of a book, if done by hand. It is not a matter of dishonesty, but of human limitations. The wrong word may be written, or a word so written as to convey a false meaning; for example the accidental absence of a dot converts the Aramaic sign for *rope* into *camel.* Therefore we have long wrestled with the meaning of the Biblical statement, "It is easier for a camel to go through the eye of a needle," which really should read, "It is easier for a rope to go through the eye of a needle" (Matthew 19:24). Likewise, the statement, "Let the dead bury the dead" has been perplexing. The Aramaic word for dead is *metta* and for town, *matta.* It becomes likely, therefore, that the true saying was, "Let the town bury the dead," a very common practice in the days of Christ. (Lamsa, *Gospel Light*)

More serious are the evident attempts by ancient copyists to clarify or correct the text of the manuscripts by inserting personal comments, which, in course of time, have become parts of the sacred record. As an illustration, I John 5:7, 8 reads, "For there are three that bear record in heaven, the Father, the Word, and the Holy Ghost, and these three are one. And there are three that bear witness in earth, the spirit, and the water, and the blood; and these three agree in one." It is said that two hundred and fifty Greek manuscripts exist, containing this section of John's epistle, but do not contain the words in verses 7 and 8. Only four known manuscripts made after 1400 A. D. contain these words, and they are not found in any known manuscript before the seventh century after Christ. The words were evidently added by a scribe and have given rise to much religious misunderstanding. (Sims, *The Bible from the Beginning;* McGavin, *An Apology for the Book of Mormon*)

Earnest efforts, employing every available device, have been made by lovers of the Bible to discover such errors, and thus to purify the text of the Bible. The various existing manuscripts have been compared with minute care to detect differences. Quotations from the Bible by ancient writers, when perhaps earlier copies were extant, have been assembled and compared. The human toil given to such labor is a noble example of the esteem in which the sacred scriptures are held. It is another evidence of his greatness that Joseph Smith was one of the early workers in the so-called textual criticism of the Bible.

Another group of workers has undertaken to discover the origin, authorship, and history of the many parts of the Bible. Their avowed objective is not to discredit the Bible, but to discover truth. To accomplish their purpose, methods of literary and historical criticism have been employed. From dissimilarities in style and contemporary historical sources, and by other means it has been inferred, for example, that certain books of the Bible are composites of several original manuscripts, or have been written by several authors. This is the so-called Higher Criticism. However honest and God-fearing these workers may be, many of their conclusions and explanations remain in the field of inference, not of fact. Whether the Pentateuch and Joshua are made up from four original documents, or the Gospel of John and the Book of Revelation were written by two different writers, or Paul did not write the Epistle to the Hebrews, may ever remain in the region of hypothesis, so far as the findings of Biblical scholars are concerned. The purpose of Higher Criticism may be acceptable; but its limitations must ever be kept in mind. Theories have the same value in Biblical study as in chemistry, but no more; and theories are forever changing. This is well brought out in the "modern trend" in Biblical criticism (Willett, *The Bible Through the Centuries;* White,

A History of the Warfare of Science and Theology in Christendom; Journal of Bible and Religion, Vol. 6, part 2).

How the sacred scriptures were translated from ancient tongues into English and made available to the common man is a most thrilling chapter in human history. Love of God and man was the driving impulse of the translators; disgrace and death were their frequent reward. The names of Wycliffe, Tyndale, Coverdale, and many others, including the makers of the so-called authorized or King James' translation, should be held in reverence by all English-speaking people. Like honor should be shown those who made the Bible available in other tongues: German, French, Scandinavian, etc. The Bible has rendered manifold service to every nation which it has entered. As it formed and fixed the English language, and unified the German tongue from Luther's version, so it has influenced deeply all peoples who have received it. (J. Patterson Smythe, *How We Got Our Bible;* Goodspeed, *The Making of the English New Testament;* Colwell, *The Study of the Bible*)

It should be remarked that the translation of the Bible into several modern languages has helped us to understand the meaning of many passages otherwise obscure. To convert the ideas recorded in Hebrew or Greek into another language is not an easy task. The translator at best is only an interpreter of the text. It is well therefore to compare, say a standard translation in German or French with one in English. The peculiar genius of one lanugage often permits a clearer expression of the original meaning.

In recent years many new translations of the Bible into English have been made, chiefly to render the text in modern, colloquial language, though others have sought primarily to make the rendering correspond more exactly with the text. These modern translators have had at their command for comparison many more manuscripts than were possessed by the translators in 1611. Each such translation has contributed something towards our fuller understanding of the Bible; for example, King James' version says, "Else what shall they do which are baptized for the dead, if the dead rise not at all? why are they then baptized for the dead?" (I Corinthians 15:29) The Smith and Goodspeed translation makes the thought clearer, "Otherwise what do people mean by having themselves baptized on behalf of the dead? If the dead do not rise at all, why do they have themselves baptized on their behalf?"

However, none of these translations surpasses the King James' version of the English Bible in beauty of language and spiritual connotation, and probably in faithful adherence to the text available to translators. It is this version which is used by the Church of Jesus Christ of Latter-day Saints in all of its official work both at home and abroad. The literature of the Church refers invariably to the King James' translation. Other translations are used by the Church only to help explain obscure passages in the authorized version. This translation is recommended to obtain an acquaintanceship with the Hebrew scriptures.

The hundreds of revisions made by the Prophet Joseph Smith, some of them extensive and exhaustive, are very enlightening. Note the following as lesser examples: Genesis 3:8, King James' version, says, "They heard the voice of the Lord God walking in the garden"; the Inspired version reads, "They heard the voice of the Lord God, as they were walking in the garden" (Genesis 3:13); 2 Samuel 24:16, King James' version, says, "The Lord repented him of the evil, and said to the angel that destroyed the people, It is enough: stay now thine hand"; the Inspired version reads, "For the people repented, and the Lord stayed the hand of the angel"; Exodus 10:27, King James' version, says, "But the Lord hardened Pharaoh's heart"; the Inspired version reads, "But Pharaoh hardened his heart"; Luke 9:24, King James' version, says, "For whosoever will save his life shall lose it: but whosoever will lose his life for my sake, the same shall save it"; the Inspired version reads, "For whosoever will save his life, must be willing to lose it for my sake; and whosoever will be willing to lose his life for my sake, the same shall save it."

Latter-day Saints believe that the protecting hand of the Lord has been over the Bible, whether in the ancient manuscripts or in copies of the earliest documents. Modern scholarship and modern revelation have clarified erroneous and difficult passages. How the Bible came to be is unimportant compared with what it says. The real message of the Bible has been preserved, unimpaired, and is confirmed by every new translation. That message continues to be the greatest ever given to man.

2. ARE THE EARLY BOOKS OF THE BIBLE (THE PENTATEUCH AND JOSHUA) HISTORICALLY CORRECT?

Events and personages are of frequent mention in the Bible. The opinion has often been voiced that they are but creations of the imagination—mythical figures and episodes, parts of Hebrew folklore. However, it has always been conceded that if they are found mentioned in contemporaneous documents, outside of the Bible, their historicity may well be accepted.

Just that has been found to be the case. Recent archaeological study has uncovered ancient documents which certify to the correctness of the Bible accounts. Since World War I, such finds have been especially numerous. Every spadeful of earth removed from the buried past, every broken potsherd uncovered, every inscription deciphered seems to have added to the historical authenticity of the Bible, by direct or indirect proof. Indeed, these finds have made Bible times of four thousand years ago better known than English history of one thousand years ago. And, future discoveries may add much to present knowledge.

This does not mean that every Bible historical statement has been confirmed, or that there are no errors in the Bible story. Latter-day Saints have long been taught to believe the Bible "as far as it is translated correctly"; and also that the Lord operates through imperfect human instruments. It does mean, however, that if the major historical statements are found to be correct, the verity of the whole story is enhanced. It has too often been the case that, because historical events in Holy Writ are but vehicles for moral truths, historians have studied the Bible under a cloud of prejudice. That is not the way of true scholarship.

It is not to be expected that all the events recorded in the Bible, often of minor and local historical importance, should be recorded on the monuments of the past in other countries. Kings sought to make imperishable records of their own valor. At no time was Hebrew history of major concern to neighboring countries. It is therefore surprising that so many of the events of Israelitish history stand forth boldly in the recorded history of neighboring lands.

Until a few years ago it was held that the compilation of the early books of the Bible was based upon oral tradition, corrupted throughout the centuries, since the art of writing was not invented in the days of Abraham. Now it is known beyond cavil that writing antedates Abraham by hundreds, if not thousands, of years. It may well be believed, therefore, that the early Bible books are based upon ancient documents written by Moses himself, and others.

The Bible accounts of the creation of the earth and man, the early patriarchal days, the Garden of Eden, the flood, and the Tower of Babel occur in early Chaldean records. It is evident that the stories of these events were carried down from earliest antiquity. Actual deposits implying a great flood have been found in Babylonia. Towers of Babel, ziggurats, formerly crowned by temples, have been excavated in Babylonia. One of these may well be the Biblical Tower of Babel (Smith, *The Chaldean Account of Genesis;* Woolley, *The Sumerians,* and *Ur of the Chaldees*).

Ur of the Chaldees has been found and uncovered. A high degree of culture characterized Ur in the days of Abraham. It is clear now that Abraham might have been a learned man, amply able to write his own memoirs. The people of Ur were polytheistic. Abraham, a monotheist, left Ur in protest against the worship of false gods. The birth and presence of Abraham in Ur and his departure therefrom, as stated by the Bible, may unhesitatingly be accepted. The name Abram was in use in the days of the "Father of the Faithful."

It is now well known that in antiquity there was regular, large intercourse among Babylon, Palestine, and Egypt. The journey of Abraham to the Promised Land does not now seem so difficult an undertaking. Many of the cities of Canaan mentioned in Genesis have been found and identified. "Uru-Salem" (Jerusalem) was a city of importance in Abraham's day. One uncovered story seems to tell of Abraham's coming to Canaan, which was looked upon as an invasion by some of the inhabitants of the land. The narrative of the battle of four kings has been shown to be authentic.

Modern scholarship has revealed that in the days of Abraham, shepherd kings, the Hyksos, Semites of the blood of Abraham, had invaded Egypt and become its rulers. That may account for the friendly reception of Abraham by the then ruling Pharaoh, a shepherd king. The discovered records inform us that neighboring nations came in times of drought to buy foodstuffs from the fertile valley of the Nile, just as the Bible declares was done by Jacob and his sons. A man is mentioned who represented the Pharaoh in hoarding grain in years of plenty and doling it out in lean years as was done by Joseph.

The shepherd kings, Semites akin to the Hebrews, ruled Egypt until the time of Moses. The Egyptian oppression of Israel began about the time the Egyptian rulers, not of Semitic blood, regained control of the country. The Pharaoh of the oppression of Israel was undoubtedly Thothmes III, whose mummified body has been found. The Pharaoh who ruled at the actual time of the exodus from Egypt was Amenhotep II, whose mummy has also been found. There is even some fairly acceptable record of the tenth plague, the slaying of the first born. The princess who found Moses has been identified with great certainty, under the name of Hatshepsut. Dates and persons from the ancient records confirm the Bible story. That Egyptian and Biblical chronologies harmonize is of particular note in establishing the historicity of the Bible.

The Midian to which Moses repaired after his exploit in Egypt was a country of high culture. The worship of Jehovah and Elohim was current there, justifying Joseph Smith's statement that Jethro, Moses' father-in-law, held the true Priesthood. In the Sinaitic peninsula the inscription on a rock has been found giving a date corresponding to the Exodus and a name corresponding to Moses.

Research has revealed contemporary records mentioning the invasion of Palestine by the Hebrews after the long sojourn in Egypt. Even the name Israel, strictly a Hebrew name, has been found carved in a rock. The Canaanitish idolatrous civilization and religion have been shown to correspond thoroughly with the Bible record.

Of especial note is the conclusion, after careful study, that the Hebrew laws, such as the Ten Commandments are more primitive "than the corresponding laws of the Babylonians or Hittites." This confirms the Latter-day Saint belief that the gospel was given to Adam, and in many lands has come down in a corrupted form, but maintained in its purity among Israel (Barton, *The Haverford Symposium on Archaeology and the Bible*).

The forty years' sojourn in the wilderness has been explained by the likelihood that the people settled temporarily in Midian, a friendly country, well known to Moses. This is more credible than a long wandering in the Sinaitic peninsula, covered with roads, mines, and quarries under the Egyptian government.

The long discussions about the actual date of the fall of Jericho and therefore of the occupation of Palestine by Israel have been settled in favor of the Bible date. It has been shown that the walls of Jericho fell under a sudden catastrophe. Parallel walls surrounded the fortress of Jericho; wooden beams were laid from wall to wall upon which houses were built, as Rahab's house, "built upon a wall." The corroboration of the Bible account is then complete.

A group of letters, the Tell el Amarna tablets, written about the days of Joshua, discusses repeatedly the invasion of Palestine of the "Habiru," the Hebrews. Cities and events conforming to the Bible story are there mentioned repeatedly.

These, with many other examples that might be cited, go to show that modern Biblical archaeology supports better than could really be expected the historical claims of the Pentateuch and the Book of Joshua—as well as the other books of the Bible. It must always be kept in mind that in its early history, the Israelitish nation was insignificant compared with the many important neighboring nations. At best, it was only another troublesome group of people to Egypt and other lands. It must be remembered, also, that monuments were built to celebrate the great deeds of king and country. The minor affairs, as then conceived, of the Hebrews, would hardly be expected to be memorialized in costly structures of stone, or in special writings on papyrus or clay.

It may well be asked how the archaeological information of the day has been obtained. In Egypt, Assyria, Babylon, and other countries of antiquity, great stone monuments in the form of men, beasts, or shafts (steles) were built to commemorate the noble deeds of the rulers, notably the kings. On these were cut inscriptions relating historic events. Sometimes the proud monarch would cut the story into the face of a prominent cliff. The Egyptians wrote much on papyrus, which has been preserved under the dry climate of the Nile valley. In Babylonia and Assyria, with a higher rainfall, symbols were pressed into tablets of clay, then dried or baked. Inscriptions on pottery have furnished many a clue. Through romantic and magnificent studies and efforts of scholarship, Egyptian hieroglyphics, cuneiform, and other writing may now be read.

Several recent finds have contributed much to the knowledge of early Biblical days. In 1887, a country woman of Tell el Amarna, a village on the Upper Nile, found in a rubbish heap a collection of inscribed clay tablets, an ancient file of correspondence written chiefly from Egyptian overlords in Palestine to the Pharaoh of Egypt. These letters and dispatches were dated at the time of Joshua, when the Hebrews were settling in Palestine. Invaluable knowledge was gained from these tablets.

In 1929, another collection of historical tablets was found in Ras Shamra in Asia Minor, opposite Cyprus. These are contemporary with the Tell el Amarna tablets, and throw further light on the conquest of Canaan by Israel. They emphasize the Semite culture and religion of that day.

Equally important appear to be the glazed potsherds covered with writing discovered in Lachish, twenty-five miles southwest of Jerusalem, in 1933. These have not all been deciphered, but they date from about 600 B. C., long after the days of Joshua, and reveal conditions of that time. From them may come also new knowledge concerning the early history of the Bible.

The sources of Biblical archaeology are many. The finest and most praiseworthy scholarship has been applied to them. Much has been learned; more will be learned.

The question at the head of this chapter may then be answered: As far as human learning has progressed, nothing has been found to discredit the historicity of the early books of the Bible; so much has been found in support of the historical claims of these books, that we are justified in looking upon them as correct historical documents, more accurate than other like documents dealing with the same period of human history. The Bible is an historical record accurate in its statements far beyond the expectations of scholars a generation ago.

3. DID THE FLOOD COVER THE HIGHEST MOUNTAINS OF EARTH?

This question, really of insignificant importance, is a good example of man-made objections to the sacred character of the Bible, and therefore to faith.

The coming of the flood and its extent and duration, are described in the seventh chapter of the Book of Genesis. The account states that "the waters prevailed exceedingly upon the earth; and all the high hills, that were under the whole heaven, were covered. Fifteen cubits upward did the waters prevail; and the mountains were covered." (Genesis 7:19-20)

A cubit, an ancient and well-known measure of length, is the distance from a man's elbow to the end of his middle finger. The Egyptians fixed the length of a cubit as 20.61 of our inches; the Greeks, 18:25 inches; the Romans, 17.4 inches; the Hebrews, 17.58 inches; and the English, 18 inches. The variation is small, from eighteen to less than twenty-one inches.

If we employ the largest of these values, 20.61 inches, fifteen cubits would be something less than twenty-six-feet. This, then, was the depth of the flood, according to Genesis.

The suggestion has been made that the flood filled every hollow and valley until the earth was a great sphere of water, covering the highest mountain peaks twenty-six feet deep, Mount Ararat, seventeen thousand feet high, "upon the mountains" of which the ark rested, would according to this view have been completely under water. It is doubtful whether the water in the sky and all the oceans would suffice to cover the earth so completely.

Another suggestion is that the earth at that time was so flat that a depth of water of twenty-six feet would cover the highest hill. There is no existing evidence of this supposition; and Mount Ararat did exist then according to the record.

It has also been suggested that a blanket of water twenty-six feet thick lay up and down the sides of every hill, mountain, and valley. This would seem to be in defiance of the law of gravity, though under a long-continued, furious rainfall such a layer, not too thick, might roll down every slope.

The fact remains that the exact nature of the flood is not known. We set up assumptions, based upon our best knowledge, but can go no further. We should remember that when inspired writers deal with historical incidents they relate that which they have seen or that which may have been told them, unless indeed the past is opened to them by revelation.

The details in the story of the flood are undoubtedly drawn from the experiences of the writer. Under a downpour of rain, likened to the opening of the heavens, a destructive torrent twenty-six feet deep or deeper would easily be formed. The writer of Genesis made a faithful report of the facts known to him concerning the flood. In other localities the depth of the water might have been more or less. In fact, the details of the flood are not known to us.

Latter-day Saints know, through modern revelation, that the Garden of Eden was on the North American continent and that Adam and Eve began their conquest of the earth in the upper part of what is now the state of Missouri. It seems very probable that the children of our first earthly parents moved down along the fertile, pleasant lands of the Mississippi valley. The great floods that have often occurred there make the description in Genesis seem very reasonable indeed. And if the historian saw the flood there, it is not unlikely that the waters covered the highest points or peaks, for there the mountains are but hills.

Great floods have visited the earth. That has been amply proved. For example, Professor C. Leonard Woolley, studying through excavations the ancient history of Mesopotamia, has found indisputable evidences of a flood in the neighborhood of Abraham's ancestral city of Ur. Whether that flood is the great flood of Genesis is not certain, for we do not know whether at that time the children of Adam had spread from their original home in what is now America into the lands now denominated Asia. (Woolley, *The Sumerians*)

Latter-day Saints look upon the earth as a living organism, one which is gloriously filling "the measure of its creation." They look upon the flood as a baptism of the earth, symbolizing a cleansing of the impurities of the past, and the beginning of a new life. This has been repeatedly taught by the leaders of the Church. The deluge was an immersion of the earth in water (D. & C. 88:25; Brigham Young, *Jour-*

nal of Discourses, 1:274; *Discourses of Brigham Young,* p. 603; Orson Pratt, *Journal of Discourses,* 1:331).

Though the whole of the earth was covered with water, the depth was immaterial. When a person is baptized, it does not matter how far under the water he is brought, nor whether every part of him is at the same depth. The essential part of the symbolism is that he should be completely immersed.

So with the story of the flood. All parts of the earth were under water at the same time. In some places the layer of water might have been twenty-six feet deep or more; in others, as on sloping hillsides, it might have been only a fraction of an inch in depth. That the whole earth, however, was under water at the same time was easily possible under a terrific, long-continued downpour, such as is described in Genesis. The depth of the layer of water is of no consequence.

Many Bible accounts that trouble the inexperienced reader become clear and acceptable if the essential meaning of the story is sought out. To read the Bible fairly, it must be read as President Brigham Young suggested: "Do you read the scriptures, my brethren and sisters, as though you were writing them a thousand, two thousand, or five thousand years ago? Do you read them as though you stood in the place of the men who wrote them?" (*Discourses of Brigham Young,* pp. 197, 198). This is our guide. The scriptures must be read intelligently.

4. DID THE SUN STAND STILL UPON GIBEON?

In the Book of Joshua, 10:12-14, the following occurs:

> Then spake Joshua to the Lord in the day when the Lord delivered up the Amorites before the children of Israel, and he said in the sight of Israel, Sun, stand thou still upon Gibeon; and thou, Moon, in the valley of Ajalon.
>
> And the sun stood still, and the moon stayed, until the people had avenged themselves upon their enemies. Is not this written in the book of Jasher? So the sun stood still in the midst of heaven, and hasted not to go down about a whole day. And there was no day like that before it or after it, that the Lord hearkened unto the voice of a man: for the Lord fought for Israel.

There is no good reason to doubt the historicity of this event, that during a battle between Israel and the Amorites, daylight was extended far beyond the usual limits of day. The sun and moon seemed to be at rest. It is not the only account in history of similar phenomena.

The explanation of the occurrence made by the writer or some later copyist, implies that the earth ceased its daily rotation and annual course around the sun, to bring about the needed additional daylight for Israel's victory in battle. This may well be questioned. Even limited human knowledge suggests several simpler methods—refraction and reflection of light, for instance, by which the extension of daylight might be accomplished. Divine power may stop the rotation of the earth, let that be clearly accepted, but it certainly may have at its command other means for extending the hours of light in a day.

A miraculous event, properly authenticated, must be accepted as any other occurrence. An explanation of a miracle must however be held in doubt until fully confirmed by acceptable knowledge.

A miracle is an occurrence which, first, cannot be repeated at will by man, or, second, is not understood in its cause and effect relationship. History is filled with such miracles. What is more, the whole story of man's progress is the conversion of "miracles" into controlled and understood events. The airplane and radio would have been miracles, yesterday. All well-informed persons now admit that there may be countless forces in the universe not yet recognized by man. These forces in their operation may produce results baffling to man.

We no longer speak of supernatural events, for the invasion of the unseen world by man has shown that all human experiences are but manifestations of the one world—are natural though perhaps not understood.

In the Old Testament are recorded fewer than one hundred, in the New Testament about half a hundred events that can be called miraculous. That is not a large number for the thousands of years covered by Israel's history before Jesus. Many more uncommon events, that have seemed miraculous, have been recorded in every recent century of easy communication among men.

In view of recent progress, many of these "miracles" do not now seem so strange. The cure of leprosy, making a barren woman fertile, the coming of quails, the plagues of Egypt, and many others, are quite within the limits of present human understanding. The floating of Elisha's ax ceases to be a wonder in a day of magnetism. Others, on the other hand, are yet beyond our comprehension, notably, perhaps, the two greatest miracles of all, the creation of the earth and the coming of man.

It must also be kept in mind that some of the Bible miracles, especially in the Old Testament, may be poorly described by the historians, or incorrectly translated, and therefore confusing to us of a later day. Latter-day Saints will do well to remember that the Lord does His work through mortal men, subject to the weaknesses of the earth. Jonah in the belly of the fish may be such a one, which if fully understood would leave no question behind.

The real quibble in the field of miracles arises over the intervention of divine power in the affairs of men. As to this, Latter-day Saints can take but one side, for they believe in the existence of God, whose intelligence permeates the universe. They believe that divine power and intelligence may and do help weak humanity, true sons and daughters of God. Latter-day Saints do not attempt to limit the extent of the Lord's intelligent power, to muzzle Him, as it were. As the possessor of infinite knowledge and power, the Maker of the heavens and the earth may at will set forces into operation to succor His children or to give witness of His power.

5. WHAT IS THE MESSAGE OF THE OLD TESTAMENT?

The contents of the Old Testament center upon the history of the people chosen of God to accomplish a mighty purpose; a people who because of their own actions passed through periods of progress and degeneracy. In telling the story, the writers have sought to show that obedience to divine laws of conduct leads to joy, while disobedience brings sorrow and defeat. In that respect the teachings of the Old Testament are universal—fitted for any people, at any time.

To drive home the lesson, every literary device is used. History appears, especially of contemporaneous events. There is constant resort to formal preaching and teaching. Poetry, allegory, figures of speech, parables are employed with powerful effect. Everywhere, the knowledge of the day, sometimes limited, is reflected in the telling of the story.

Intelligent readers always separate the message of a book from its form of presentation. That must be done in reading the Bible, if its true meaning is to be caught.

The principles of truth, the gospel, have been taught by the Lord to man from the beginning of the human race. At times, men have been divinely inspired to commit to writing the eternal truths pertaining to human existence. Thus have come the Holy Scriptures.

Nevertheless, though the doctrine contained in the Old Testament has been given by the Lord, the actual writing has been done by mortal men, in their own language. This is always so. The Lord, speaking to the Prophet Joseph Smith, said, "These commandments are of me, and were given unto my servants in their weakness, after the manner of their language, that they might come to understanding." (D. & C. 1:24) That is, the Lord does His work in our behalf through earthly instruments. Naturally, therefore, in outward form there may be errors, or we may misunderstand the writer; but in inner substance the eternal truth is preserved for those who read understandingly. This doctrine has been stated in unusual beauty by Moroni, "Thou hast also made our words powerful and great, even that we cannot write them; wherefore, when we write we behold our weakness and stumble because of the placing of our words; and I fear lest the Gentiles shall mock at our words" (Book of Mormon, Ether 12:25).

Further, it is well known that the original manuscripts of the Old Testament have passed through numerous hands before they reached the form available to us. They were copied by hand. Inaccurate as well as accurate, dishonest as well as honest, unbelieving as well as believing scribes have had access to them. Material may have been added or taken away; mutilations may have occurred; through misunderstandings, or by deliberate act, errors and changes may have crept into the text. In the words of Joseph Smith, the Prophet, "I believe the Bible as it read when it came from the pen of the original writers. Ignorant translators, careless transcribers, or designing and corrupt priests have committed many errors."

The human element in the formation of the Old Testament explains many things otherwise obscure. There are many episodes in the Old Testament that suggest a lack of respect for human life. Undoubtedly, the Giver of life may at His will take it. There may be times when life should be forfeited because of sins committed. Yet, it is probable that in some reported cases the Lord has been credited with commands that came from the lips of the human leaders of the day. It is to be observed also that ancient Israel altogether too often adopted practices of the primitive peoples of the day, rather than those revealed by the Lord. Similarly, there are episodes which suggest low standards of sexual morality, such as characterized the tribal neighbors of ancient Israel. Such immoral episodes and other deviations from the law of the Lord seem to be recorded as warnings. Men were no better then than they are now. But it must always be kept in mind that the God of Israel thundered to the people in the wilderness, "Thou shalt not kill," and, "Thou shalt not commit adultery." Never has there been an abrogation of these commands.

Though allowances must be made for human imperfections, yet the Holy Scriptures have never been wholly at the mercy of man. The essential message of the Lord to His children on earth has ever been preserved. The books of the

Old Testament bring to us the unchanging doctrine of God's nature, eternal destiny of righteous, obedient mankind. They contain the most precious truths of humanity. They give the most complete exposition of God's law for human conduct. As they relate the story of God's dealings with His people, the nature of our Father in heaven becomes better understood. Without the books of the Old Testament, the earth would be poor indeed.

The Hebrew scriptures rise above the folklore of the nations as a sun-bathed mountain peak rises out of the mists. For example, the Babylonian Epic of the Creation centers around the battles of two gods who are both sea monsters. The one monster overcomes the other and from his body the earth is created. This account is translated as follows:

Then took their stand Tiamat and the leader of the gods, Marduk;
For the fight they approached, for the battle they drew near.
The lord spread out his net and enclosed her.
The evil wind from behind he thrust into her face.
As Tiamat opened her mouth to its full extent,
The evil wind he drove in, so that her lips could not close.
With the mighty winds he filled her belly.
Her courage was taken away, and she opened her mouth.
He let fall the spear, he burst open her belly,
He cut through her inward parts, he pierced her heart,
He bound her and her life destroyed;
Her body he cast down and stood upon it.
Then the lord rested, he gazed upon her body,
The flesh of the monster he divided; he formed a cunning plan.
He split her open like a flat fish into two halves;
One half of her he established and made a covering of the heavens.
He drew a bolt, he established a guard,
And not to let her waters come out, he commanded.

(George A. Barton, *Archaeology and the Bible*, pp. 272, 273)

Compare this near nonsense with the stately, clear, and understandable account given in Genesis, first chapter:

In the beginning, God created the heaven and the earth.

And the earth was without form, and void; and darkness was upon the face of the deep. And the Spirit of God moved upon the face of the waters.

And God said, Let there be light: and there was light.

And God saw the light, that it was good: and God divided the light from the darkness.

And God called the light Day, and the darkness he called Night. And the evening and the morning were the first day.

And God said, Let there be a firmament in the midst of the waters, and let it divide the waters from the waters.

And God made the firmament, and divided the waters which were under the firmament from the waters which were above the firmament; and it was so.

And God called the firmament Heaven. And the evening and the morning were the second day.

And God said, Let the waters under the heaven be gathered together unto one place, and let the dry land appear: and it was so.

And God called the dry land Earth; and the gathering together of the waters called he Seas: and God saw that it was good.

And God said, Let the earth bring forth grass, the herb yielding seed, and the fruit tree yielding fruit after his kind, whose seed is in itself, upon the earth; and it was so.

And the earth brought forth grass, and herb yielding seed after his kind, and the tree yielding fruit, whose seed was in itself, after his kind: and God saw that it was good.

And the evening and the morning were the third day.

And God said, Let there be lights in the firmament of the heaven to divide the day from the night; and let them be for signs, and for seasons, and for days, and years:

And let them be for lights in the firmament of the heaven to give light upon the earth: and it was so.

And God made two great lights; the greater light to rule the day, and the lesser light to rule the night: he made the stars also.

And God set them in the firmament of the heaven to give light upon the earth.

And to rule over the day and over the night, and to divide the light from the darkness: and God saw that it was good.

And the evening and the morning were the fourth day.

And God said, Let the waters bring forth abundantly the moving creature that hath life, and fowl that may fly above the earth in the open firmament of heaven.

And God created great whales, and every living creature that moveth, which the waters brought forth abundantly, after their kind, and every winged fowl after his kind: and God saw that it was good.

And God blessed them saying, Be fruitful, and multiply, and fill the waters in the seas, and let fowl multiply in the earth.

And the evening and the morning were the fifth day.

And God said, Let the earth bring forth the living creature after his kind, cattle, and creeping thing, and beast of the earth after his kind: and it was so.

And God made the beast of the earth after his kind, and cattle after their kind, and every thing that creepeth upon the earth after his kind: and God saw that it was good.

And God said, Let us make man in our image, after our likeness: and let them have dominion over the fish of the sea, and over the fowl of the air, and over the cattle, and over all the earth, and over every creeping thing that creepeth upon the earth.

So God created man in his own image, in the image of God created he him; male and female created he them. (Genesis 1:1-27)

The Bible account compared with the Babylonian, in the words of D. Bernhard Stade, is "as a clear mountain spring to the slough of a village cesspool" (Fosdick, *Guide to the Understanding of the Bible*).

What is the message of the Old Testament? From the first to the last, in the Pentateuch, in the historical books, in the poetical books, and in the prophets, it teaches the existence of a personal God, the Maker of the heavens and the earth, the Father of the human race. It teaches that the earth and all things upon it are provided for man's benefit, but that man must obey law, divine law, to secure the blessings he desires. It teaches that obedience to the moral law, given by God for human conduct, involving faith in God, not to be compared with man-made, ethical, selfish codes of action, is the most important concern of man. It is the message of messages for humankind.

That message remains unchanged in essence from the first to the last page of the Old Testament; but the people to whom it was given often fell from that truth, and then by slow degrees found their way back.

In the words of Brigham Young, "In the Bible are the words of life and salvation."

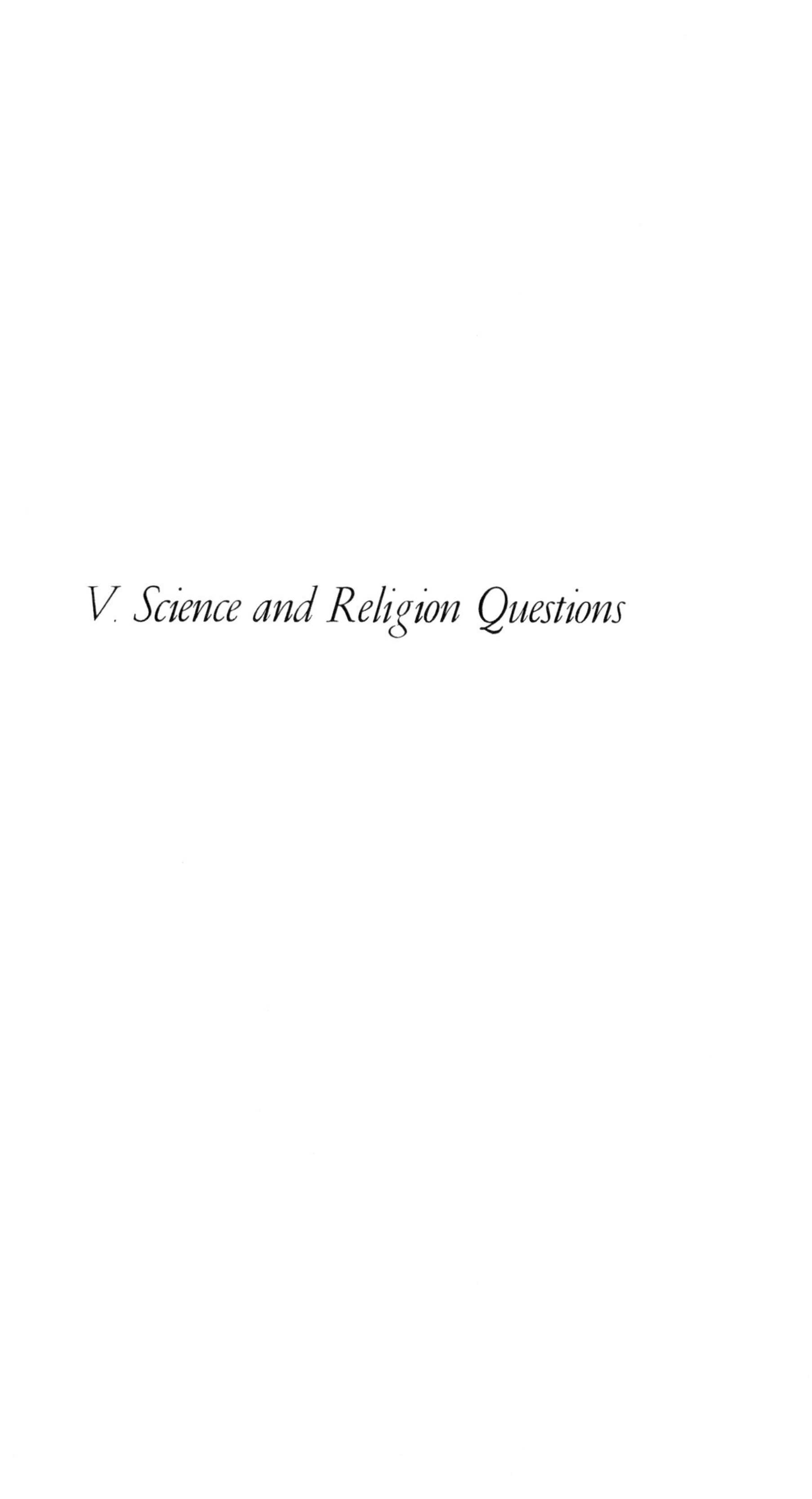

V. Science and Religion Questions

1. WHAT IS THE ATTITUDE OF THE CHURCH TOWARD SCIENCE?

This question, frequently asked, is readily answered.

The Church, the custodian of the gospel on earth, looks with full favor upon the attempts of men to search out the facts and laws of nature. It believes that men of science, seekers after truth, are often assisted by the Spirit of the Lord in such researches. It holds further that every scientific discovery may be incorporated into the gospel, and that, therefore, there can be no conflict between true religion and correct science. The Church teaches that the laws of nature are but the immutable laws of the Creator of the universe.

This view has been held consistently by the Latter-day Saints from the organization of the Church. A revelation given to the Prophet Joseph Smith in 1832, when science was yet in its swaddling clothes, declares:

> And I give unto you a commandment that you shall teach one another the doctrine of the kingdom.
>
> Teach ye diligently and my grace shall attend you, that you may be instructed more perfectly in theory, in principle, in doctrine, in the law of the gospel, in all things that pertain unto the kingdom of God, that are expedient for you to understand.
>
> Of things both in heaven and in the earth, and under the earth; things which have been, things which are, things which must shortly come to pass; things which are at home, things which are abroad; the wars and the perplexities of the nations, and the judgments which are on the land; and a knowledge also of countries and of kingdoms— . . .
>
> And as all have not faith, seek ye diligently and teach one another words of wisdom; yea, seek ye out of the best books words of wisdom; seek learning, even by study and also by faith. (D. & C. 88:77, 78, 79, 118)

President Brigham Young frequently expressed support of the labors of men of science. For example, in one of his sermons he said:

> I am not astonished that infidelity prevails to a great extent among the inhabitants of the earth, for the religious teachers of the people advance many ideas and notions for truth which are in opposition to and contradict facts demonstrated by science, and which are generally understood. . . . In these respects we differ from the

Christian world, for our religion will not clash with or contradict the facts of science in any particular. (*Discourses of Brigham Young*, pp. 397, 398)

President Joseph F. Smith made similar statements:

> We believe in all truth, no matter to what subject it may refer. No sect or religious denomination in the world possesses a single principle of truth that we do not accept or that we will reject. We are willing to receive all truth, from whatever source it may come; for truth will stand, truth will endure. . . . True science is that system of reasoning which brings to the fore the simple, plain truth. (Joseph F. Smith, *Gospel Doctrine*, pp. 1, 6)

The gospel and science have the same objective—the discovery and possession of truth—all truth. Hence follows the attitude of the Church toward science expressed at the head of this chapter. However, science has been content, until recently, to study the material universe, and to leave its findings without reference to their possible effect upon human conduct. The gospel on the other hand is primarily concerned with the manner in which truth is used in the spiritual field, that is, with human conduct. For example, science has discovered explosives of great power, and has shown how by their use rocks may be shattered or projectiles shot through the air, and has left this knowledge without comment as to its proper use. The gospel teaches that this new power be not used in warfare, for wars are evil, but that it be used in the peaceful arts of man. The gospel deals with right and wrong; science as yet has scarcely touched this field. The gospel accepts God as the author of all knowledge; science gathers facts and tries to interpret them, without reference to a Supreme Being. In short, the gospel is the more inclusive; present-day science, less inclusive. In the end, the two must become as one, for their common objective is truth.

The Church holds that the methods used by science to discover truth are legitimate. Indeed, all instruments and means developed for the exploration of nature are welcomed. The Church claims the right to employ, in addition, such processes as are peculiarly fitted to its search for truth in the spiritual domain, which in turn may become tools in the advancement of a future science freed from its present material bondage.

In this wholehearted acceptance of science, the Church makes, as must every sane thinker, two reservations:

First, the facts which are the building blocks of science must be honestly and accurately observed. In science, as in every human activity, dishonesty, carelessness, or aberrations of senses or mind may be encountered. The Church expects science to present accurately observed and fully corroborated facts. Loose methods of study are not acceptable. Indeed, the vast body of scientific facts has been so carefully garnered that it may in the main be accepted without question.

Second, the interpretations of observed facts must be distinctly labeled as inferences, and not confused with facts. The human mind properly attempts to explain or interpret the phenomena of nature, the facts of observation. A pencil looks bent in a glass of water. Why? asks the eager thinking mind. The sun rises in the east and sets in the west. Why? Does the sun move around the earth, or does the earth revolve upon its axis, to give the effect of day and night? The answers to such questions are explanations or interpretations, really inferences, often called hypotheses or theories. These do not have the certain value of facts, for they usually change as new facts are brought forward. For example, with the knowledge at his command, Newton advanced the theory that light consists of particles; later, Young explained the phenomena of light as forms of wave motion; today with increasing knowledge both of these theories are questioned, and another one is in the making. Meanwhile, the phenomena of light remain unchanged; they are the same today as in the time of Newton. Occasionally, but seldom, an inference such as the cause of night and day becomes so well supported by discovered facts that it assumes the dignity of a fact. Most inferences, however, are in a condition of constant change, due to the continuing accumulation of new knowledge.

Dr. Albert Einstein, author of the relativity theory, speaks of scientists as men who seek solutions of the mysteries in the book of nature (Einstein and Infeld, *The Evolution of Physics*, pp. 1, 5). He insists that nature's mystery story is not only still unsolved but may not have a final solution. All that man can do is to collect facts, arrange them in an orderly fashion, and then to make them understandable by "creative thought"—that is, by the formulation of inferences, explanations, interpretations, hypotheses or theories, whatever the name may be.

In this particular do Latter-day Saints, in common with all thinkers, sound a warning to science. There must be a distinct segregation of facts and inferences in the utterances of scientific men. Readers of science should always keep this difference in mind. Even well-established inferences should not lose their inferential label. The facts discovered by an eminent investigator may be safely accepted; his explanations may be of doubtful value.

It is within recent time that Millikan and Compton, both Nobel prize winners, held widely differing explanations of the nature of "cosmic rays." And, recently, also, the discovery of the skull of a prehistoric ape with a set of human-like teeth has overthrown the inference that teeth are always true indications of the place of a fossil in the evolutionary scale. With respect to this latter matter, there was pathos in the remark of the famous anthropologist, Sir Arthur Keith, that "This discovery has destroyed the finer points we anthropologists depend on for drawing the line between anthropoid and man."

In summary: The Church supports and welcomes the growth of science. It asks only that the facts of science be as accurately determined as human powers permit, and that confusion between facts of science and inferences of science be earnestly avoided.

The religion of the Latter-day Saints is not hostile to any truth, nor to scientific search for truth.

2. HOW TRUSTWORTHY IS SCIENCE?

Science is man-made. It consists of facts and the explanations of facts. Facts are gathered by man through his senses. Explanations are the products of the mind. Therefore, the trustworthiness of science may be measured by the accuracy of human senses and the clearness of human thought.

The senses of man are greatly limited. A beloved friend a few hundred feet away is but one of hundreds of indistinct, passing figures. The eye cannot see far, clearly. The common speech of man becomes but a confused murmur a short distance away. The ear cannot hear distant sounds, clearly. Far enough away the eye does not at all distinguish figures, or the ear, sounds. So with the other senses.

Further, no two pairs of eyes see exactly alike. No matter how careful and honest the observers are, the moon is not of the same size to them, nor the length of a measured stick. Knowing this, men of science make repeated observations of the same phenomenon, and then seek other observers to check the findings. Even then, the final result is only an average of observations made, approaching the full truth. Every competent scientist is aware, often painfully, of these limitations placed upon the senses of man.

Moreover, the eye is sensitive only to a small part of the wave spectrum. Above and below the visible spectrum are greater invisible fields. The ear can detect only a small span of sound waves. A more sensitive hearing organ would hear a universe of sound now closed to man. The unaided senses of man at the best can know only a very small part of the universe in which man dwells.

To increase the power of the senses, aids to the senses, instruments, have been devised.

However, all aids to man's senses, instruments made by human hands, lie under definite and often serious limitations. The accuracy of the telescope is decreased by distortions due to the nature of the glass of the lenses; there are disturbing reflections, refractions, and colored fringes that hinder clear vision. The most fundamental constants of science are not absolutely correct. The velocity of light, atomic weights, the force of gravity, and the many other constants from which the pattern of science is woven, are but approximations, often very close, to the true values. There is always a margin of error. The true scientist admits this, and works on with the powers at his command towards a higher degree of accuracy.

Scientific explanations, products of thoughtful reflection and reasoning upon observed facts, are often nothing more than shrewd guesses or good probabilities. That the sun rises in the east and sets in the west is an unchanging fact of human experience. In earlier days, and for centuries, it was held that this observation was due to the daily journey of the sun around the earth. Now, with new facts at our command, we explain night and day by the complete rotation of the earth upon its axis, every twenty-four hours. A straight stick placed in a glass of water looks bent. That is an age-old observation, the explanation of which has been changed several times. The nebular hypothesis long explained the origin of the solar system; now another inference holds sway. In the subatomic world of electrons new discoveries are made almost daily, and the explanations are in constant flux. Chromosomes now hold the center of the stage in the field of heredity, but the explanations of their relationship to the properties of life are the present guesses of the best scholars, which may be overturned tomorrow. Newton was only recently pushed out of his old place by Einstein. No scientific worker worthy of his task attempts to give a scientific explanation a higher standing than that of an intelligent guess, supported by existing facts. New discoveries may modify or upset the explanation (Einstein and Infeld, *The Evolution of Physics*).

The rising and setting of the sun, the bent stick in the pool are safe facts of experience. The exact length of the day or the degree of bending of the stick may not be determined with absolute accuracy by our poor senses. But such facts are immeasureably more trustworthy than the general explanations of such current, well-established facts. Facts of observation are generally more trustworthy than inferences by the mind.

Cocksureness in science is a mark of the immature, often self-deceived, worker with nature. Those who have moved man's knowledge and control of nature forward, and greatly, have always stood humbly before the inexhaustible ocean of the unknown which they are trying to explore.

Science is trustworthy as far as human senses and reason are trustworthy—no more. When the credentials of science are examined, the claims of religion seem more credible than ever. (Cook, *The Credentials of Science, the Warrant of Faith*).

Flower in the crannied wall,
I pluck you out of the crannies,
I hold you here, root and all, in my hand,
Little flower—but *if* I could understand
What you are, root and all, and all in all
I should know what God and man is.

—*Tennyson*

3. HOW OLD IS THE EARTH?

This is an ancient question which has occasioned much controversy. There are at least three prevailing answers among faithful Bible-believing Latter-day Saints. The fact appears to be that no man knows the age of the earth.

The first group believe that the earth was created in six days of twenty-four hours each. That is, the earth was six days old at the coming of Adam. This view is based upon the literal acceptance of the story of creation as given in King James' translation of Genesis. (Genesis, chapter 1; Exodus 20:11) According to this belief there was a succession of sudden or catastrophic creative events during this short period of time which led to the formation of the earth. The catastrophists contend that the Lord is able through His divine power, if He so desires, to form an earth or many earths in short moments of time. They also quote the words of Moses as revealed to the Prophet Joseph Smith, which follow closely the wording of King James' translation (Pearl of Great Price, Moses, 2:1-31).

The second group hold that each day of creation was really one thousand years, and that the earth therefore was six thousand years old at the coming of Adam. Those who uphold this view quote as their support the statement of the Apostle Peter, "one day is with the Lord as a thousand years, and a thousand years as one day" (2 Peter, 3:8). In defense of this view the statement made by Abraham is also quoted:

> The Lord said unto me, by the Urim and Thummim, that Kolob was after the manner of the Lord, according to its times and seasons in the revolutions thereof; that one revolution was a day unto the Lord, after his manner of reckoning, it being one thousand years according to the time appointed unto that whereon thou standest. This is the reckoning of the Lord's time according to the reckoning of Kolob (Pearl of Great Price, Abraham, 3:4).

The third group believe that the creation of the earth extended over immensely long periods of time, not yet correctly known by revelation or by man's scientific advance, and that the earth therefore is very old. In support of this view they marshal several arguments:

First. It is admitted that the Lord has power to accomplish His work in His own way and time. "But nature and scripture both teach us that it has pleased the Lord to work gradually. His purpose was to fill the earth with inhabitants, and yet only a single pair was created. . . . It is His will that the whole earth shall be filled with the knowledge of Himself; but the diffusion of the knowledge has been left to gradual preaching and human instrumentality. So in nature, trees, animals, and men have small beginnings, and require time to attain to perfection" (A. McCall, "The Mosaic Record of Creation," p. 213 in *Aids to Faith*).

Second. The word translated "day" in Genesis really means, in the original, an age or undefined period of time, and is so rendered in several translations of the Bible. Further, the first three "days" could not have been days such as we have, for the sun and the moon had not yet been placed in the firmament. (Genesis, 1:5-19) Moreover, the word "day" is used frequently throughout the Bible in a general sense as "the day of the Lord," "the day of vengeance," "the night is far spent, the day is at hand."

Third. Scripture revealed in modern days to the Prophet Joseph Smith indicates that the word "day" should be understood to mean periods of time, for in the Abrahamic record of creation, each creative act is followed by the statement "this was the first, or the beginning, of that which they called night and day," "and this was the second time that they called night and day," and so on until "and they numbered the sixth time." (Pearl of Great Price, Abraham, chapter 4) Then, "And the Gods concluded upon the seventh time." (Abraham, 5:3)

Fourth. Genesis opens with the phrase "in the beginning God created the heavens and the earth." It is quite agreed by students that the word "beginning" is indefinite in its significance and may mean previous time or previous eternity, according to subject—as in the gospel according to John "before the world was." (John 17:5) This is placed by the side of Alma's words "all is as one day with God, and time only is measured unto men." (Alma 40:8) as indicating that our measurement of time, with its short days and hours came only with man.

Fifth. The slow processes of nature, as known to man, must long have been in operation to lift the mountains from lake and sea bottoms, and to carve out the valleys. All human experience points to the need of periods of time far beyond six thousand years, to fashion the earth as it appears today, or as it seems to have been throughout recorded history.

Sixth. Recent discoveries in the field of radio-activity have furnished a "time-clock" which compels the belief that the earth is very old, far beyond the former, accepted limits.

Those who upon the above and other views hold that the earth is very old, have attempted to estimate the age of the earth in years. The method is always based on a common principle. The rate at which some process is going on at the present day is measured as accurately as possible, and the average change produced in say one year, is compared with the total effect produced by that process during the interval that has elapsed since its commencement. (Arthur Holmes, *The Age of the Earth*, p. 29)

The earliest method of estimating geological time was to discover the maximum thickness of the stratified formations in the earth's crust and to determine the amount of sediment carried annually into the ocean. Geological study indicates that the thickness of the earth's stratified formations is at least 360,000 feet (Holmes, p. 79), and that the annual discharge of sediments into the ocean is such as to require millions of years for the deposition of the strata in question. It is admitted that this method can indicate only long periods of time, and not definite measurements in years.

A somewhat more satisfactory method deals with the salt in ocean water. It is assumed that the first ocean water was fresh. The sodium chloride or salt that it now contains has been dissolved from the soil through which the water has passed or from the sediments brought down into the ocean by the rivers. The water has been evaporated and condensed into rain over and over again, but the salt which is not volatile has remained to increase the saltiness of the ocean. Estimates have been made of the annual discharge by the rivers of earth, their load of materials, and the probable amount of salt in the water and the sediments. Similar estimates have been made of the amount of salt in the ocean. Then by simply dividing the annual addition of salt into the total amount of salt in the oceans, the number of years of the accumulation is obtained. By this method, acknowledged to be subject to many corrections, salt has been added to the oceans for a period of about 330 million years. According to this calculation, the earth must be at least that old.

The discovery of radioactivity and the element radium, furnished an unexpectedly accurate geological hourglass that has been used in estimating the age of the earth.

The element uranium is radioactive. That is, it emits spontaneously, continuously, and uniformly various radiations. As it does so it is degraded, passing from one form to another, including radium, until the final residue is lead. That is, there is a life-limit to uranium, radium, and several other elements. Methods have been developed by which the rate of this degradation may be measured accurately. The amount of lead, or radium in association with uranium will then point to the length of time since the uranium was formed.

It has been found that the age of uranium, determined as above suggested, is lowest in the more recent rocks and highest in the oldest rocks. This is a confirmation of much previous geological work on the relative ages of rock deposits. The age of the oldest rock approaches, by this method, 2,000 million years. The earth must then, by this form of study, be at least that old.

It is a curious fact that studies by modern methods of the age of the solar system have yielded similar results, that is, about 2,000 million years. It is a most interesting chapter in modern exploration (Holmes, *The Age of the Earth,* 1937; also F. J. Pack, *Science and Belief in God*). Those who hold to the long-time age of the earth point out that present scientific data indicate "an epoch of creation," 2,000 million years ago.

Every person must decide for himself, on the basis of the evidence produced, which of these three opinions as to the age of the earth, before Adam, seems most reasonable to him, whether (1) six days, or (2) six thousand years, or (3) many millions of years. Clearly it does not matter to one's daily welfare or ultimate salvation which view he adopts, except that every Latter-day Saint must seek and cherish truth above all else.

4. HOW DID THE EARTH COME INTO BEING?

The earth came into being by the will and power of God. Upon that proposition the accepted scriptures of the Church and their authoritative interpretations agree. Chance is ruled out. Latter-day Saints believe that the earth and the heavens and the manifold operations within the universe are products of intelligent action, of the mind of God. There is nothing haphazard about the universe in which we live. (Genesis 1:1; Pearl of Great Price, Moses 2:1; Abraham 4:1; D. & C. 93:9)

Further, Latter-day Saints believe that the Lord formed or organized the earth from existing universal materials. That it is impossible to create something from nothing is a spiritual as well as a scientific axiom. It is an established doctrine of the Church that the ultimate elements which constitute the universe are eternal, indestructible, everlasting. Whether these ultimate realities be, in the language of present-day science, molecules, atoms, electrons, or pure energy is of little concern. Whatever is the ultimate reality is eternal. Matter as we know it, and which forms the earth, is made from eternal elements. In that sense the formation of the earth was an organization rather than a creation. (D. & C. 93:33; Pearl of Great Price, Moses 1:38)

Just what forces were brought into operation, or what process was used, to organize the "elements" into an earth is not known. Latter-day Saints are inclined to hold that forces about us, known in part through common human experience, especially in the field of physical science, were employed in the formation of the earth. The progress of science may yet shed much light on the origin of the earth.

During human history numerous mystical and mythical ideas have been advanced concerning the origin of the earth. These may be ignored. During the course of science, three main theories have been set up to explain how the earth came into being.

First came the nebular hypothesis, elaborated upon the suggestions of others by the famous French mathematician and physicist, Laplace, nearly one hundred and fifty years ago. This assumes that the sun was formed from the condensation of a nebula, a gaseous body. As the gaseous, rotating sun contracted, gaseous rings would be thrown off from the sun, much as drops of water fly off a grindstone. Each such ring would become a planet revolving around the sun. One such ring of gas after gradual cooling and contraction became the earth. This hypothesis was universally acclaimed; those who would not accept it were long looked upon as "unscientific." Yet, the relentless growth of knowledge seemed to show the nebular hypothesis erroneous, and now it has long been discarded. (D. H. Menzel, *Stars and Planets*)

The planetesimal theory followed. This was proposed by the eminent geologists, Chamberlain and Moulton of the University of Chicago. A star might have come so near the sun as to cause tremendous gravitational pulls upon each other, causing tidal waves, as it were, and erupting material into space. This material, as meteors or cosmic dust, was built up into planets such as the earth. (T. C. Chamberlain, *The Origin of the Earth*)

This theory was modified, as its weaknesses were discovered, notably by Sir James Jeans, of Cambridge University, England. He retains the thought of the tidal effect of the sun and a star in immediate proximity but believes that large masses, the size of the planets, were torn out of the sun. The earth, then, is an original part of the sun, thrown out through the gravitational pull of a star that wandered too near the sun. This theory seems, for the present, to have the right of way (James Jeans, *The Universe Around Us*).

Scrutiny of the tidal theory has led many investigators to reject it and to set up substitutions. R. A. Lyttleton, for example, has suggested that if the sun were a double star at the time the wandering star came too near, many of the difficulties of the tidal theory might be avoided. There is also the theory, proposed by Rev. Georges Lemaitre, that some billions of years ago all universal matter was in the form of a gigantic radioactive atom. For some unexplained reason this atom burst, scattering suns, stars, planets, satellites, and nebulae throughout the universe.

By slow, often painful progress, usually by the method

of trial and error, science reaches its haven of truth. As to the origin of the earth, man knows only that it was organized by divine intelligence and power from existing eternal materials. Speculations about the method or process, however honestly offered, or by what eminent authority, must not be taken too seriously.

5. WHAT IS THE ORIGIN OF LIFE ON EARTH?

This question has occupied the best minds since the beginning of human history. The answer has not yet been found in the halls of science.

From the earliest time, many men of sound thought have believed in the spontaneous generation of life. Aristotle (384-322 B. C.) for example taught that decaying matter, under the influence of moisture and the sun's heat will produce living things. He even went so far as to teach that the higher forms of life were spontaneously generated. St. Augustine (354-430 A.D.), made the doctrine one of the church. His reasoning was simple: As the Lord could make wine from water, so life could be made from the soil and water and air of earth. In his opinion, spontaneous generation was but a manifestation of the will of God. Even such minds as that of Newton (1643-1727) could see no inconsistency in the doctrine. Up to the middle of the last century, the doctrine was very generally accepted.

However, as the more exact methods of science were developed, doubt was cast upon the theory. For example, van Helmont, great scientist as he was, had explained that dirty linen, mixed with grain, would, in twenty-one days, produce mice. Subjected to scientific scrutiny, the folly of this formula was revealed.

Finally came Louis Pasteur, who, in the middle of the last century by a series of brilliant experiments, laid low the doctrine of spontaneous generation. It was, however, only after a terrific battle with his contemporaries that he set up the law that only life can beget life. For a number of decades now, the world has rested secure in the correctness of his conclusion.

Recently, however, it has been suggested that, while, under the conditions now prevailing on earth, spontaneous generation of life is impossible, there may have been times, under different conditions, when living organisms might have been produced from lifeless matter. The reasoning is somewhat as follows: As the molten earth cooled, conditions were such as to form large quantities of the substance cyanogen, composed of carbon and nitrogen, essential constituents of living tissue. As the new-born atmosphere gradually changed to its present conditions, complex chemical compounds were formed from the cyanogen, which, as the earth cooled, increased in complexity, approached the nature of living tissue, and at last acquired the properties that characterize life. From these simple units of life, the theory holds, have developed the forms of life now known to man. It is added that life cannot be so formed today, for conditions are so different. It requires an abnormal faith in science to accept this theory (Oparin, *The Origin of Life*, 1938).

The question has been raised with respect to the viruses, which are so small as to pass through filters: Do they perpetuate life? Existing evidence favors the belief that they also obey the law that life begets life.

If life was not spontaneously generated on earth, if life is necessary to beget life, the first life on earth must have come from some point outside of the earth. So reasoned many men of unimpeachable standing in the world of sound thinking. That raised two questions at once: Does life exist beyond the earth? And if life exists beyond the earth, how can it reach the earth?

Men of the highest standing have believed that the earth is not the only home of living beings—such men as von Liebig, von Helmholtz, and Lord Kelvin.

The existence of life in space is exceedingly difficult to prove by the methods of science for us who live on earth. An attempt was made by the famous bacteriologist, Charles B. Lippman, to discover whether meteorites, which fall from the sky, contain living organisms. Every precaution against error was taken. The best-known technique was followed. Lippman came to the conclusion after this careful work that live bacteria and spores of living things were found in the interior of the rocky meteorites studied by him. Many objections were offered against these findings. The bacteria he found were identical with some known on the earth; the heat generated by the falling body would kill the germs—and so on. The controversy still goes on.

Other workers, assuming that life does exist beyond the earth, undertook to study the possible means by which living germs could be carried through space to the earth. The scientist, Richter, called attention to the fact that it has been shown that germs of life may remain dormant for long periods of time, may exist without food or water, yet may be revivified, as soon as the conditions necessary for active life are available. The eminent physicist, von Helmholtz, followed this up with the proposition that meteorites in their descent through the air are heated only on the surface. Carbon, easily combustible, is found unchanged inside of meteorites—hence life germs could survive any heat that might be generated.

In the progress of science it has been found that light, passing through space, exerts a pressure on the objects it encounters. This principle was seized upon to explain how life might have been brought from other heavenly bodies to the earth. The world-famous physicist, Arrhenius, suggested that miscroscopic germs of life might be carried by atmospheric currents and electrical disturbances into space and, under the pressure of light, be carried within reach of other bodies in space. Arrhenius even subjected the hypothesis to mathematical treatment, and showed that such particles, leaving the earth, would pass beyond the limits of our planetary system in fourteen months, and in nine thousand years would reach the nearest star, *Alpha Centauri.* He also showed that the heat attendant upon such a journey would not exceed 100°, and that only for a short time (Arrhenius, *Worlds in the Making,* 1908). A barrage of objections was pointed upon this hypothesis. The chief weakness, it was claimed, was that the ultra-violet light and cosmic rays of space, not softened by the atmosphere, would destroy quickly any life germs floating in space. There the matter stands today.

Now, from the very beginning of thinking on the subject of the origin of life on earth, a group of powerful thinkers have insisted that life is one of the eternal realities of the universe, uncreated, eternal, as eternal as any other of the ultimate elements of the universe. One school of Greek thought held that the universe, the solar system, and the earth itself were living organisms.

The doctrine of the eternity of life implies that "things" become alive when the life force enters them. Thus came the doctrine of vitalism, or vital force, which has met such fierce opposition from the school of materialism. Under this doctrine all living things are dual in their composition; they are of matter and of life. Those who so believe declare that either life is spontaneously generated, or it is of eternal existence. The majority of them also are believers in God, and inclined to hold that things are made alive by His power, through means not understood by man, or perhaps beyond his understanding.

The corollary of the doctrine that life is eternal is the doctrine of pre-existence. The essential part of any living being is its life. If life is eternal then the living thing is eternal also. Driven by such logic, schools of thought, from the Greeks to our own day, have harbored more or less completely the doctrine of pre-existence.

As far as the data of science or the speculations of philosophers go, no light is shed upon the origin of life on earth.

The teachings of the Prophet Joseph Smith leave the conviction that life is eternal, or at least that it had a pre-existent life, not of spontaneous origin on earth. For example:

> . . . these are the generations of the heaven and of the earth, when they were created, in the day that I, the Lord God, made the heaven and the earth;
>
> And every plant of the field before it was in the earth, and every herb of the field before it grew. For I, the Lord God, created all things, of which I have spoken, spiritually, before they were naturally upon the face of the earth. . . . And I, the Lord God, had created all the children of men; and not yet a man to till the ground; for in heaven created I them; and there was not yet flesh upon the earth, neither in the water, neither in the air;
>
> . . . all things were before created; but spiritually were they created and made according to my word. (Pearl of Great Price, Moses 3:4, 5, 7; see also Abraham 5:2-5)

One may read into these sayings that individuality itself is eternal. With respect to man, that is a well-settled doctrine. "Man was also in the beginning with God. Intelligence, or the light of truth, was not created or made, neither indeed can be" (D. & C. 93: 29). This doctrine is confirmed in the Book of Abraham:

> Now the Lord had shown unto me, Abraham, the intelligences that were organized before the world was; and among all these there were many of the noble and great ones;
>
> And God saw these souls that they were good, and he stood in

the midst of them, and he said: These will I make my rulers; for he stood among those that were spirits, and he saw that they were good; and he said unto me: Abraham, thou art one of them; thou wast chosen before thou wast born.

And there stood one among them that was like unto God, and he said unto those who were with him: We will go down, for there is space there, and we will take of these materials, and we will make an earth whereon these may dwell;

And we will prove them herewith, to see if they will do all things whatsoever the Lord their God shall command them;

And they who keep their first estate shall be added upon; and they who keep not their first estate shall not have glory in the same kingdom with those who keep their first estate; and they who keep their second estate shall have glory added upon their heads for ever and ever (Pearl of Great Price, Abraham 3:22-26).

From the organization of the Church to the present day, the pre-existence of man has been taught as a necessary element in the plan of salvation.

Whether the references in sacred writ concerning the pre-existence of all life, plant and animal, justify the belief that individuality is preserved even in the lower orders of creation, must remain, until further light is obtained, a matter of personal opinion. The wording of the above quotations from the Pearl of Great Price seems to imply the pre-existence of individual life everywhere. Certainly, the earth on which we live is an imperishable, living organism:

And again, verily I say unto you, the earth abideth the law of a celestial kingdom, for it filleth the measure of its creation, and transgresseth not the law—

Wherefore, it shall be sanctified; yea, notwithstanding it shall die, it shall be quickened again, and shall abide the power by which it is quickened, and the righteous shall inherit it. (D. & C. 88:25, 26)

That man, as perhaps all creation, is a dual being, is an equally certain doctrine. Man is composed of the eternal spirit residing in a mortal body. The gospel centers upon the conversion of a perishable into an imperishable body to be possessed by the everlasting spirit. "The spirit and the body are the soul of man" (D. & C. 88:15).

Science stands at present helpless before the mystery of the origin of life on earth. It offers guesses which have no precedence over theological inferences. Through revelation we know that life existed before the earth was, and that "man was in the beginning with God." Life was placed upon earth by God, through His power. That doctrine satisfies the inmost need of man. In time, that doctrine will be confirmed by the accumulation of human knowledge. The method by which life was brought upon earth is not known by anyone.

6. TO WHAT EXTENT SHOULD THE DOCTRINE OF EVOLUTION BE ACCEPTED?

The answer to the above question depends on the meaning assigned to the word *evolution*. Among people generally, as well as by a group of scientists who should know better, the word is used with unpardonable looseness. Especially should the difference between the law of evolution and the theory or theories of evolution be stressed whenever the word is used.

In its widest meaning evolution refers to the unceasing changes within our universe. Nothing is static; all things change. Stars explode in space; mountains rise and are worn down; men are not the same today as yesterday. Even the regularities of nature, such as the succession of the seasons or of night and day, cause continuous changes upon earth. Everywhere, a process of upbuilding or degradation is in evidence. The face of nature has been achieved by continuous small and slow degrees. This has been observed by man from the beginning, and must be accepted by all thinking people. Darwin knew it no better than the peoples of antiquity. The law of change, an undeniable fact of human experience, is the essence of the law of evolution (H. F. Osborn, *From the Greeks to Darwin*).

The great champion and amplifier of the doctrine of evolution, the philosopher Herbert Spencer, defined the law of evolution by saying, in substance, that whatever moves from the indefinite to the definite, is evolving; while that which moves from the definite to the indefinite, is dissolution or the opposite of evolution. Nebulae passing into stars are evolving; stars broken into cosmic dust are dissolving (Herbert Spencer, *First Principles*). When simple units are used to build up more complex structures we have evolution. When any structure is broken down into constituent elements, we have its opposite, dissolution. Evolution in this sense is the same as progression or growth.

From this point of view the law of evolution, representing eternal change upward, becomes a basic, universal law, by which nature in her many moods may in part be explained. Indeed, it has been one of the most useful means of interpreting the phenomena of the universe. The first and most notable deduction from the law of evolution is that, in the words of Spencer, "We can no longer contemplate the visible creation as having a definite beginning or end, or as being isolated" (Herbert Spencer, *First Principles*). That is, existence is eternal.

The noisy babble about evolution, often disgraceful to both sides, since Darwin wrote *Origin of Species,* has been confined almost wholly to speculations or guesses concerning the cause, methods and consequences of the law of evolution. The law itself has not been challenged. It is so with every well-established, natural phenomenon. Inferences are set up to explain observed facts. Such hypotheses or theories, which are often helpful, become dangerous when confused with the facts themselves. There are now many theories of evolution, all subject to the normal scrutiny to which all theories should be subjected; and until their probability is demonstrated, it is well to remain wary of them.

The foremost and best-known theory of evolution is that all living things on earth, whether fish, insect, bird, beast, or man, are of the same pedigree. All creation, it declares, has come from a common stock, from a cell formed in the distant past. Man and beast have the same ancestry. In support of this theory numerous well-established observations are presented. These may be grouped into five classes:

First, the fossil remains of prehistoric life on earth show that in the oldest rocks are remains of the simplest forms of life; and as the rocks become younger, more complex or more advanced life forms seem to appear. The scale of life appears to ascend from amoeba to man, as the age of the particular part of the earth's crust diminishes.

Second, each group of living things has much the same bodily organization. In the case of mammals, all, including man, have similar skeletons, muscular arrangements, nervous systems, sense organizations, etc. In some species the organs are merely rudimentary—but they are there.

Third, the embryos of man and higher animals, in the earlier stages, are identical, as far as the microscope can reveal. This is held to mean that embyronic development summarizes or recapitulates the stages of man's development through the ages of the past.

Fourth, all organic creatures may be so grouped, according to structure and chemical nature, as to show gradually increasing relationships from the lowest to the highest forms of life. Similarities in blood composition are held to indicate nearness of kinship. The blood of the great apes is very similar to the blood of man.

Fifth, it has been possible, within historic times, to domesticate many animals, often with real changes in bodily form, as the various breeds of cattle, sheep, or dogs. Besides, isolated animals, as on the islands of the sea, have become unique forms, differing from those on connected continents.

These facts, so claim the proponents of the theory of evolution, all point to the common origin, and an advancing existence, of all animal forms on earth. To many minds these observations, upon which in the main the theory of evolution rests, are sufficient proof of the correctness of the theory of evolution. It is indeed an easy way of explaining the endless variety of life. All life has grown out of a common root. The ease of explaining the origins and differences among life forms has won much support for the theory of evolution (Sir Arthur Keith, *Concerning Man's Origin,* and *Darwinism and What It Implies;* H. H. Newman, *Evolution Yesterday and Today*).

Yet, at the best, the doctrine of the common origin of all life is only an inference of science. After these many years of searching, its truth has not been demonstrated. To many competent minds it is but a working hypothesis of temporary value.

Many weaknesses in the theory of evolution are recognized by its adherents. Two are especially notable.

First, many reported similarities are far-fetched and not well enough established to be acceptable as the foundation of a world-sweeping theory. It is surprising how many such cases have been found. (Douglas Dewar, *Man a Special Creation;* Sir Ambrose Fleming, *Evolution or Creation;* E. C. Wren, *Evolution, Fact or Fiction*) Moreover, many actual similarities may be interpreted in more than one way. The theory of a common origin is only one of several possible explanations of the mass of biological facts.

Second, the theory fails utterly to explain the emotional, reasoning, and religious nature of man, which distinguishes him so completely from the lower animals. One defender of the theory declares that the brains of man and monkey are identical anatomically, but that the larger size of the human brain accounts for the higher intelligence of man. This suggestion falls to the ground in face of well-known facts such as that the ant shows greater intelligence than the cow. Many notable advocates of the theory, such as Darwin and Huxley, have stood helpless before the mental, emotional, and moral supremacy of man over the ape, the animal most like man in body. Conscience is peculiar to man. Evil, sin, goodness, truth, love, sacrifice, hope, and religion separate man from the highest animal by a gulf not yet bridged by any scientific theory.

The doctrine of the common origin of life on earth is but a scientific theory, and should be viewed as such. Clear thinkers will distinguish between the general law of change or evolution accepted by all, and the special theories of evolution which, like all scientific theories, are subject to variation with the increase of knowledge. Honest thinkers will not attempt to confuse law and theory in the minds of laymen. The man, learned or unlearned, who declares the doctrine of the common origin of life on earth to be demonstrated beyond doubt, has yet to master the philosophy of science. The failure to differentiate between facts and inferences is the most grievous and the most common sin of scientists.

This is the trend of thought in the best scientific circles. In the words of Professor Punnett of Cambridge University, scientists "still hold by the theory of evolution, regarding the world of living things as dynamic, and not a static concern." But the interpretation of Darwinism has changed greatly. The theory of evolution "is released today from the necessity of finding a use for everything merely because it exists." More interesting, the glib talk about changing species is subdued. "Species are once more sharply marked off things with hard outlines, and we are faced once more with the problem of their origin as such. The idea of yesterday has become the illusion of today; today's idea may become the illusion of tomorrow" (Punnett, "Forty Years of Evolution Theory," in *Background to Modern Science*). That is the spirit of science. By slow degrees, among many changes, accepting, rejecting, striving, it may in the distant future reach the correct understanding of final causes.

The majority of the advocates of the theory that all life came from one stock believe that the primeval cell originated by the chance assembling under favorable conditions of the constituent elements of cellular substance. That means that life is only an accidental intruder into the universe. The immediate logical weakness of this view is that if life on earth began by the fortuitous assembling of inorganic materials in a slimy, primitive pool, other equally favorable pools for the generation of life may have existed, thus providing more than one origin of life.

Those who insist that all life on earth has come from one source are almost obliged to rule God out of the picture; for, if a Supreme Being is allowed to create a living cell in the beginning, He may at will create other life at different periods of time. Even believers in God who accept the theory of evolution as a final explanation of the origin of life forms, are inclined to insist that the theory represents God's only method of creation. Nearly always, those who so believe refuse to admit that any other process may also be in operation. They would limit God to one method of operation. Fettering God, or unbelief in Him, or making Him merely a universal super-force, have been usual companions of the theory of evolution (W. W. Keen, *I Believe in God and Evolution*).

Latter-day Saints accept every scientific fact, but rate theories based upon the facts as human explanations of the facts, likely to change as new facts appear. They do not deny that an evolutionary process, a reflection of the gospel law of progression, may be one of the methods of the Lord's labor in the universe. That does not mean, however, that the Almighty cannot perform other acts of will for the promotion of His plan, as, for example, the special creation of man. God is a purposeful Being; whatever is on earth or in heaven has been designed for the accomplishment of the divine purpose—the welfare of man. The spirit of man, itself intelligent, purposeful, is an eternal pre-existent being. He reaches beyond the confines of earth. He was with God before the earth was made. The theory of evolution does not explain the external man.

Any theory that leaves out God as a personal, purposeful Being, and accepts chance as a first cause, cannot be accepted by Latter-day Saints. The evidence for God is yet greater than for the chance creation of the earth and its inhabitants. Mind and thought shape a work of art from the marble block. More marvelous than any human work of art is man. However he may have risen to his present high estate, it has been by the operation of mind and thought. That man and the whole of creation came by chance is unthinkable. It is equally unthinkable that if man came into being by the will and power of God, the divine creative power is limited to one process dimly sensed by mortal man. The great law of evolution may have many forms of expression, far beyond man's present comprehension.

In fact, the whole squabble about evolution centers upon two questions. Did life on earth come by chance or by divine will? If by divine will, is God limited to one process? These questions are as old as history. The ancients asked them; and those who come after us will ask them.[1]

Here, then, is the answer to the question at the head of this chapter: The law of evolution or change may be accepted fully. It is an established fact so far as human power can determine. It is nothing more or less than the gospel law of progression or its opposite. Joseph Smith taught that men could rise towards Godhood only "by going from one small degree to another, and from a small capacity to a great one; from grace to grace; from exaltation to exaltation." Modern revelation also says, "For I, the Lord God, created all things of which I have spoken, spiritually, before they were naturally upon the face of the earth" (Pearl of Great Price, Moses 3:5), and further that each creation "remaineth in the sphere in which I, God created it" (Pearl of Great Price, Moses 3:9). This last statement suggests limitations placed upon development under the general law of progressive change. The theory of evolution which may contain partial truth, should be looked upon as one of the chang-

-----

[1]The real problem of evolution has been well stated by H. F. Osborne: "The Greeks left the later world face to face with the problem of causation in three forms: first, whether intelligent design is constantly operating in Nature; second, whether Nature is under the operation of natural causes originally implanted by Intelligent Design; and third, whether Nature is under the operation of natural causes due from the beginning to the laws of chance, and containing no evidences of design, even in their origin." (*From the Greeks to Darwin*) Latter-day Saints accept the first of these alternatives. Evolution then is but a part of the "intelligent design constantly operating in nature." The intelligence operating in Nature is left free to use other means of carrying out its purposes.

ing hypotheses of science, man's explanation of a multitude of observed facts. It would be folly to make it the foundation of a life's philosophy. Latter-day Saints build upon something more secure—the operation of God's will, free and untrammelled, among the realities of the Universe.

7. WHAT DOES EVOLUTION TEACH TODAY?[2]

All living things, plants and animals, are subject to change. Every observer of nature, certainly all plant and animal breeders, know this to be true. It is an unchanging fact of nature. Living things are not static. This is the *law* of evolution.

In the meaning of this law, Latter-day Saints are the foremost evolutionists in the world. They believe that the immortal spirit of man may eternally approach the likeness of God himself.

The *theory* or *theories* of evolution are man's explanations of the multitude of changes observed in nature. Such theories may or may not be correct. They are always subject to changes as new facts are discovered.

Until recently one of the theories of evolution based largely upon the work of the great scientist, Charles Darwin, was that man was only a product of changes in organic life, throughout long periods of time. So vigorous was the battle over the proof of this theory, that in the minds of men the law of evolution, a fact of nature, and the theory, man's explanation of the fact, became as one. An evolutionist in those days was a person who held that man descended from the lower animals.

The battle over the evolutionary origin of man became so unseemly that each side looked upon the intelligence of the other with distrust. After many years of swaying opinions more temperate views now prevail in this field of science. Leading scientists, those of unquestioned authority have expressed their views upon the matter today.[3] These appear to be quite different from the views of yesterday. Quotations might be made from other numerous students, but the following from distinguished workers well known in the scientific fraternity, will have to suffice.

1. Dr. Clark Wissler of the anthropographic section, U. S. Museum of Natural History:[4]

———

[2]Read *The Improvement Era,* July 1939 issue.

[3]Most of the quotations were assembled by Arthur I. Brown, M.D., in his pamphlet, *Must Young People Believe in Evolution?*

[4]Clark Wissler, *The Case Against Evolution,* p. 344.

As far as Science has discovered there always was a man, some not so developed, but still human beings in all their functions, much as we are today. . . . Man came out of a blue sky as far as we have been able to delve back.

2. Vernon Kellogg, eminent biologist, trustee, Rockefeller Foundation and other philanthropic, scientific and educational organizations:[5]

The fair truth is that the Darwinism selection theories considered with regard to their claimed capacity to be an independently mechanical explanation of descent, stand today seriously discredited in the biological world.

3. Professor L. T. More, Dean of the Graduate School of the University of Cincinnati:[6]

Unfortunately for Darwin's future reputation every one of his arguments is contradicted by the facts.

4. Dr. D. H. Scott, eminent British botanist:[7]

A new generation has grown up which knows not Darwin. Is even then evolution not a scientifically ascertained fact? No! We must hold it as an act of faith because there is no alternative.

5. Dr. Henry Fairfield Osborn, foremost champion of evolution in America:[8]

If living today, Darwin would be the first to modify his theory. Darwin was brave but wrong.

6. Douglas Dewar, zoologist, Indian Civil Service, Barrister, South Eastern Circuit:[9]

The breeder, no matter on what animal or plant he experiments, after he has effected a number of minor changes in any given direction, is suddenly brought to a standstill. In a comparatively short time he reaches a stage at which he cannot accomplish more, no matter how much he try. . . . This fact is fatal to the evolution theory.

7. Dr. David Starr Jordan, first President of Stanford University, educator, author and naturalist:[10]

None of the created "new species" of plant or animal I know of would last five years in the open; nor is there the slightest evidence

---

[5]Vernon Kellogg, *Darwinism Today*, p. 5.
[6]L. T. More, *The Dogma of Evolution*, p. 194.
[7]Arthur I. Brown, *Must Young People Believe in Evolution?*, p. 11.
[8]*Ibid*, p. 11.
[9]Douglas Dewar, *Difficulties of the Evolution Theory*, p. 91.
[10]David Starr Jordan, *Science*, October 22, 1922, p. 448.

that any 'new species' of field or forest or ocean, ever originated from mutation, discontinuous variation or hybridization.

8. Sir Ambrose Fleming, internationally famous physicist, President of the Philosophical society of Great Britain:[11]

Note certain qualities in the human species, not the smallest trace of which appears in the animal species. Thus, no animal has ever made any weapon or tool to help its bodily endowments. It fights with teeth and claws, horns, tusks, or hoofs. But it makes no military weapon of any kind. Nor has any animal made a tool,—spade, rake, knife, hatchet, axe, or saw. No animal makes itself artificial dress, hat or coat, shoes, or ornament to improve its appearance; nor does it dress or arrange the hair on its head. But all of the very earliest humans do these things. No animal had discovered how to produce fire or even to maintain it. . . . The animal mind or intellect is static or limited. It never progresses beyond a certain point. On the other hand, the human mind is extremely progressive, self-educative and assimilative. Uncultured races of men brought into contact with more advanced races, quickly adopt their achievements, customs, modes of thought, and habits. . . . Animals have not developed the powers of speech or rational thought.

9. T. H. Morgan, zoologist, educator and a member of the National Academy of Sciences, and numerous other organizations:[12]

It seems to me that the idea that ancestral stages have been pushed back into the embryo, and that the embryo recapitulates in part these ancestral adult stages, is, in principle, false.

10. Dr. Karl Vogt, of Geneva, German zoologist, associated with Agassiz in preparation of his work on fishes:[13]

This law which I long held as well founded, is absolutely and radically false.

11. Professor Adam Sedgwick, eminent embryologist of England:[14]

After fifty years of research and close examination of the facts of embryology, the recepitulation theory is still without satisfactory proof.

12. Sir Arthur Keith, President, Royal Anthropological Institute:[15]

---

[11]Sir Ambrose Fleming, *Evolution or Creation?*, p. 75.
[12]T. H. Morgan, *Evolution and Adaptation*, p. 83.
[13]Arthur I. Brown, *op. cit.*, p. 17.
[14]Adam Sedgwick, *Darwinism and Modern Science*, p. 174.
[15]Sir Arthur Keith, *The Human Body*.

Now that the appearance of the human embryo at all stages is known, the general feeling is one of disappointment; the human embryo at no stage is anthropoid in appearance.

13. Herbert Spencer, philosopher:[16]

The facts of paleontology can never suffice either to prove or disprove the developmental hypothesis.

14. Charles Darwin:[17]

The belief in natural selection must at present be grounded entirely on general considerations. When we descend to details *we can prove that no species has changed*: nor can we prove that *supposed* changes *are beneficial, which is the groundwork of the theory.*

In his *Origin of Species,* Darwin wrote:

Geology assuredly does not reveal any such finely graduated organic chain; and this, perhaps, is the most obvious and serious objection which can be urged against the theory of Natural Selection.

15. William Bateson, English zoologist:[18]

So we went on talking about evolution. That is barely forty years ago; today we feel silence to be the safer course. . . . Discussion of evolution came to an end because it was obvious that no progress was being made. . . .

16. Dr. J. A. Thompson, scientist, educator and author:[19]

We are more keenly aware than in Darwin's day of *our ignorance* as to the origin and affiliation of the greater classes. . . .

Clearly the theory of evolution has added nothing to our understanding of the beginning of things. The ancient view that God is the creator of all things is still the best, because it is true.

-----

[16]Herbert Spencer, *Illustrations of Universal Progress,* p. 376.
[17]Major E. C. Wren, *Evolution Fact or Fiction?,* pp. 93-94.
[18]*Ibid.,* pp. 91-92.
[19]*Ibid.,* p. 89.

8. DOES SCIENCE CONTRIBUTE TO RELIGIOUS FAITH?

It is a cardinal doctrine of our religion that the gospel of Jesus Christ embraces all truth. Truth may well be another name for the system of faith professed by the Latter-day Saints. In the words of Brigham Young: "Our religion is simply the truth. It is all said in this one expression—it embraces all truth, wherever found, in all the works of God and man that are visible or invisible to mortal eye . . . whether religious, political, scientific, or philosophical." (*Discourses of Brigham Young*, 1941 edition, p. 2)

Such a doctrine eliminates any conflict between science and religion. Every statement must be tested for its truth. If found to be true, it is incorporated into the gospel structure. If found to be false, it is rejected and forgotten. That places factual knowledge high and inferences or theories much lower. Latter-day Saints must be certain of the truth they accept. To be ever searching for truth, and of course practising it, is the real business of Latter-day Saints.

When man sets out to discover truth for himself, he must rely on the evidences drawn from a study of the external world. The whole of nature is a witness of the truth of things not visible to the naked eye, and of the directly revealed word of the Lord. Truth is always truth and must of necessity support its parts.

That great truths may be found or confirmed by a study of the things about us, is verified by the scriptures. When Jesus faced unbelief in his divinity and mission on earth, he declared that his works would bear witness of the truth of his claims.

> Believe me that I am in the Father, and the Father in me: or else believe me for the very works' sake. (John 14:11)

Later, the Apostle Peter made the same statement in emphatic words:

> . . . the invisible things of him (God) from the creation of the world are clearly seen, being understood by the things that are made, even his eternal power and Godhead. . . . (Romans 1:20)

It could not be otherwise in the minds of all who believe that the visible and invisible worlds are but manifestations of the one universe in which we have our being. In one sense, every worker in science, in any branch thereof, is contributing to the truth of revealed religion, and adding to our understanding of the words of revelation.

The history of man's progress in knowledge shows that science may contribute to religious thought and faith.

By recognizing our universe as one of law, order, and intelligence, science has driven fear from the hearts of men. Intelligence acts in intelligent ways. The intelligence at the head of all things may be trusted to act intelligently. There arises therefrom a trust in the things about us. The age-old horror, called fear, which has so long distracted humanity, vanishes. Superstition is laid low. Men come to understand better the love of God, and his offerings of goodness. Certainly, in so doing, science has contributed to religious faith.

Likewise, faith in a world not visible to our natural eyes, another basic principle in religion, has been confirmed by the advances in science. The molecules from which all matter is made are in most cases far beyond the ordinary limits of human powers of observation. The atoms from which the molecules are made are in a world beyond human senses. They shall probably never be seen. They are known only by their effects. Yet they have been weighed and measured. The atoms in turn are composed of much smaller particles, the electrons, protons, and others of immeasurably small dimensions, and occupying a space utterly beyond human direct reach. Nevertheless, we know much about them. They also have to some degree been weighed and measured, marvelous as it may seem. Science has explored the invisible atomic and sub-atomic worlds. That has confirmed our faith in the invisible, spiritual world, the effects of which we have often been happy recipients. The discoveries of science have established more firmly our faith in the world from which we came and to which we shall return. That is another real contribution to religious thought.

Many prophecies, often ridiculed by careless thinkers, are made to seem possible by the advancing front of science. For example, bearers of God's word in ancient and modern times have discussed the end of the earth. They have agreed that after the Lord's work on earth is finished, the earth shall pass away, and be consumed as by fire. Then, there shall arise a new heaven and a new earth. Science, while not entering into the prophecy, does seem to make such events possible. It is now well known that within every particle of matter are inconceivably great forces. In some substances these may now be released, as in the recent atomic bomb. There is good reason to believe that by some methods, probably never to be in the hand of man, the hidden energies of the whole earth might be released. The earth then would be consumed by its own fearful fire. Such a conflagration would be a complete cleansing process.

To restore the earth again, to rebuild it from its own released energy, a creative process comparable to that which at first built the earth, must be employed. That of course is far beyond human power. The explanations of science point to the possibility of such events. Again science contributes to faith.

Science contributes help in numerous corners of religion. The fields of prayer, eternity of man, the resurrection, life hereafter have been made clearer to the human understanding by the facts of science. Indeed the progress of knowledge by the scientific method has been a handmaid to faith.

It is a fascinating activity to check the truth discovered by man against the larger and more comprehensive truth which has come by revelation. No conflict will be found, if one uses only the facts of science. Instead, a series of confirmations of sound religious truth will be discovered. Faith will largely increase in such a study.

So, the answer to this query is that science does contribute, helpfully, to religious faith.

9. DOES THE PROGRESS OF SCIENCE DIMINISH THE CHALLENGE OF RELIGION?

Half a century ago science walked with lifted head, very proud. She had peered into many a dark recess of nature and had found precious truth there. She had won much mastery over nature's hidden powers. She had learned enough of the properties of matter to control some of the forces that act upon matter. The results in possible invention made the seven wonders of the world seem as child's play.

Then, many of her followers, drunk with a sense of greatness, set up their own explanation of life. Blasphemously, they declared that all the wonders of heaven and earth, of the mind as well as the body, of the whole universe, seen and unseen, were but the operations of matter in motion. They lifted up the ancient evil of materialism; and worshiped at the feet of matter, force, and energy. God was not, nor was he needed.

This was an evil day for mankind. It was the "dark age" of science. It was as if the sun had been blotted out of the sky. Men walked as never before in darkness. There was no intelligent direction of the universe. There was no hope for men who were at the mercy of lifeless, unintelligent forces, often unknown, and beyond description. That law prevailed did not give comfort, for the law was without a goal. Chance seemed to rule the world.

This unholy doctrine, which tore at the hearts of men, could not continue, because it was untrue. Its death was inevitable. It did at last pass out, and is now as a memory of a moment of disorderly thought. It was killed by science, which had mothered it.

This was the end also of the conflict between science and religion. Science is nothing else than a search for truth. When truth is found, it must be accepted, else the search fails in its purpose. With clearer eyes and better spirit, unprejudiced men saw in science nothing out of harmony with the more encompassing field of religion. If former beliefs crumble under the power of truth, it does not matter. Truth alone matters. So, God was restored in scientific thinking. The fog before man's eyes was lifted.

As science advanced, new wonders appeared. The atom was opened, and infinitely small particles moved within it according to unchanging law. The heavens were opened; stars and planets of illimitable numbers were found, were weighed, measured, and analyzed. The earth became but as a particle of star dust in the cosmic assembly. By new helps to the senses the processes of life in living things—plants and animals—were revealed and elucidated. With every day, in laboratories far and near, science grew, and revealed a new world to our human eyes. Knowledge was multiplied until the mind wavered before its comprehension.

The wonder grew, for wherever students turned, from the infinitely small to the immeasurably vast, whether to dead or living objects, the forces involved moved in orderly operation. A harmonious system was revealed in which every part moved with precision along with every other part. Whether in sky or atom, there was concord, not discord. There was no reading back in nature. Every law seemed overshadowed by a universal law of laws—the law of united action.

It became apparent that the multitude of phenomena were fitted into one another as to a common end. The picture of nature became more and more that of an immense purpose in which man played an important part. Such universal harmony could not come from the operation of blind forces. The mind refused to believe it. The harmony of nature could not come by chance.

Scientists, who above all else are honest, saw this harmony, this direction of discovered truth towards a definite goal. They acknowledged that to the best of their powers, they observed purpose in nature, else there would be clashes in everyday phenomena. Where there is a purpose, there must be a purposeful thought. The universe, with its contents, emerged in human thinking as a great thought. And, where there is thought, there must be someone who thinks! Thus in our age, with the help of science, an ancient truth again took its proper place in the minds of the body of truth-seekers. There is intelligence dominating the universe. There is a God.

So, materialism in science was laid low. Thoughtful men turned again to faith in God. True, all did not define

God alike. But all agreed that he is, that he is intelligent, and that his intelligence explains the metes and bounds, and the forms of operation of the forces of nature within the unbounded universe. When men come to a belief in God, the beginning of wisdom is reached. It is then easy to reconcile any new truth with true religious principles or practice.

Science did more in this time of increasing knowledge and clearer thinking. Theories or inferences drawn from discovered facts, were no longer placed first. It was recognized that, though necessary for scientific progress, they were but tentative explanations of observations made, subject to change with every new discovery. The observations themselves, the facts of science, were given first place, for, under like conditions, they do not and cannot change. This has relieved science of much controversy. Science now admits that its theories are but guesses until reinforced by more facts, and no longer casts derision upon those who will not swallow them holus-bolus.

The conduct of man among the innumerable forces of nature is the objective of religion. Science stops short, at present, with the discovery of the phenomena of nature. It has touched only lightly upon the proper use of its discovered facts—whether powder, for example, shall be used to secure a foundation for a home, or to destroy life. Yet, a short while ago a number of scientists concluded that the work of science is not complete until it considers the proper use of its hard-won knowledge—for the good of man. That conclusion was published to the world.

Progressive science has steadily confirmed and is confirming the claims of religion, the basic one of which has been discussed here. It cannot gainsay them; but only fortify them. Whenever there seems to be a conflict, it is not in the facts discovered, but in man's feeble changing explanations of them.

There was never a time when religion was so well equipped as now to serve humanity, for every available truth is as a tool in the hands of those who labor for human good, and there is more known today than at any other time on earth. So, the question propounded at the head of this writing may be answered with certainty: The progress of science *increases* the challenge of religion—the science which includes all lesser sciences.

10. IS RELIGION NEEDED IN AN AGE OF SCIENCE?

We live literally in an age of science. In every factory, farm, and home are helps undreamed of a century or two ago. On every man's table today are things beyond the reach of kings or potentates before science began its onward march. The change in human life, in comforts and luxuries, since the scientific age began, is beyond understanding. All this is received gratefully by the people of the world.

This has come about because about three hundred years ago men began to search out the laws of nature. With every new discovery came other discoveries. The knowledge of man grew so rapidly that many new sciences were born. Today the multiplicity of knowledge won from the study of nature is bewildering. No one man can know all that has been discovered. The best a person can do in our day is to occupy some little corner of human knowledge and make himself strong therein.

It was a great day for human welfare when people began to replace traditions and imaginations with answers of nature herself to questions asked by man. Since that time we have seen the universe with clearer vision, and now we refuse to accept any statement which has not been tried out by the powers with which nature has endowed man.

Through the advancement of science man has not only learned to understand the laws of nature, but he has also obtained great power over the surrounding forces of nature. Trees are blown out of the ground; rock is blasted out of the mountain; falling water now turns turbines and motors to perform much of the work that man formerly had to do with his hands.

These great achievements filled men with a sense of pride. They were masters of nature. They forgot the higher power—God. They sought more knowledge and paid little attention to the proper use of increased knowledge. Unfortunately, therefore, as powers multiplied, they were not always used for the best interests of humanity. Powder, for example, useful in clearing forests or tunneling in mountains for coal or valuable minerals, became also a tool in the hands of evil. Guns and cannons were made to destroy human beings. The release of atomic forces with their promise of tremendous service to mankind was first used only in terrible, unspeakable destruction of life. The wars of the present are a thousandfold more horrible than those of past ages when men fought with simple instruments, each one against his opponent.

It must be confessed that, while science has brought ease into man's daily work, it has also often reduced man to beast-like conditions. This misuse of new discoveries has become so grievous as to make man wonder if science is really an unmixed blessing; for example, the discovery of how the atomic forces of certain elements may be released has therefore been received with fear rather than joy.

The situation has become so serious that many scientific men have at least accepted their full responsibility and have set up the dogma that a man who makes a discovery in science must thereafter concern himself with its proper use among men. It must be watched over so that it may help advance the welfare of men. Gradually, this conception is moving in upon all workers in science. Scientific men are being held responsible, in part at least, for the use to which their discoveries are put.

What are the standards of right and wrong? What is the common good? To these questions science is silent. There is but one field, the field of religion, in which the standards of right and wrong of human behavior, are set up and where the seeker may find courage to cling to the right and eschew wrong in discoveries made.

The doctrine of the common good, which is the essence of religion, is a basic principle in the plan of salvation, laid out by the Lord for his children on earth.

It is left to man to apply facts as they may be discovered, for human benefit. That is a religious process, for the common good implies the existence and purpose of God, and man's relationship to him.

Religion is able to answer the question that may be asked by delvers of science into the mysteries of nature. Religion asserts that all men are the children of God; that they were placed on earth to become acquainted with the elements of earth; and to learn to control themselves, by directing the laws of nature to the good of man.

Every discovery of science should be used for the good of man, in harmony with his divine plan. That is a thought greatly needed by science. The vastness of the discovered universe is an evidence of the fathomless nature of the supreme Intelligence who made this universe possible. Science may become a faith-promoting subject of consideration if tied in with the spirit and practice of religion. Standing alone, it is cold, lifeless, inert, soulless; placing itself under the direction of religion it becomes warm, helpful, inspiring, a means of blessing to the human soul.

As science advances and increases, as new discoveries are made, as more complete command is obtained over the forces of nature, the more necessary it becomes that we have a religion to guide us in employing these discoveries. To save the world from science, and to make science the builder of a good world, we must hasten our progress towards the fuller acceptance of God. So, the answer to the question at the head of this article is very simple. In an age of science we have greater need than ever before of religion. A conscience of science is a present need.

11. ARE WE PROGRESSING?

The determining law of the gospel is the possibility of eternal progression. The plan of salvation was formulated to enable those present in the pre-existent great council to progress.

Progress means a moving forward from place to place, from knowledge to knowledge, from action to action. It is a process of adding to that which we now possess, by the elimination of errors, by the actual accretion of new truth, and by the development of greater self-mastery. It is a process by which increased power of every faculty is gained. It is a process of growth and development, a movement towards greater maturity. It is a steady approach to the likeness of God.

Progress is active and increasing. That which is static does not come within the province of advancement. They who are satisfied with the past, or who hesitate to toil for added knowledge, or who are unwilling to give life to their possessions by constant use, are not in a state of progress. Effort is required to lay by the errors of the past, to invade the kingdom of increasing truth, and to set every new gain into action. Such persons alone are progressing. Activity in conforming to and using truth, God's commandments, is the first condition for joining the advancing hosts.

Progress must be rounded. Some choose one corner of the field of life, and progress in it to the exclusion of all else. That is not true progress. If the seven primary colors are painted in proper proportion on a revolving disk, it appears to be white. Remove one of the colors, or change its proportion, and the result is a reddish, blueish, or yellowish disk. Or, a beam of the white light of our existence passed through a glass prism is broken into its constituent colors. In just such a manner progress in several fields is necessary for the complete progress which will win divine approval. Unhappiness, and often misery, follow the failure to recognize the necessity of complete progress in life.

The spectrum of parts of rounded or complete progress has often been given by revelation. One of the most direct and inclusive is found in section four of the Doctrine and Covenants.

The primary principles of progress there given, which "qualify a person for the work" are: 1. Faith; 2. Hope; 3. Charity; and 4. Love. A person in a state of progress has faith in the existence of an unseen world in which God and other beings dwell; a faith which makes him ready to yield obedience to the requirements which issue from that world. He has the hope or certain trust that God's purpose overshadows all the acts of man. He proceeds to help his frail fellow men in their attempts to progress; thus becoming a partner with God in working out the plan of salvation. His every act is directed by the spirit of love for God, the divine gospel with its requirements, and all the creatures of the Lord. These are cornerstones in a progressive life.

These basic principles are in turn broken down into secondary propositions derived from the primary ones: 1. Virtue; 2. Knowledge; 3. Temperance; 4. Patience; 5. Brotherly Kindness; 6. Godliness; 7. Humility; 8. Diligence. That is, the person who really desires to progress, keeps himself clean morally; he is a seeker after knowledge; he is master of himself; he is able to wait until the Lord gives results; he is kind to all men, who, like himself, are children of God; he strives in all things to do God's will, to keep his commandments; he recognizes his own limitations and the limitations placed upon all children of the earth; and in all righteous endeavors he is constantly active.

Combine these in a human life, and new paths to progress will be seen, constant development will follow, and the white light of full progress will shine brightly and steadily. Those who so live are the elect of God who shall receive a fulness of glory, have eternal increase, and be as the Gods.[21]

There is nothing difficult about this program for progress. They who follow it, find it easy, for when they ask, they shall receive, when they knock, it shall be opened unto them.[22] Besides, the test of progress is whether we do earnestly seek to comply with this program. Our actual achievements count for little compared with the efforts for progress we put forth.

Under this program the individual is of foremost impor-

-----

[21]D. & C. 132:19, 20.
[22]D. & C. 4:7.

tance. How the man behaves, how he uses the facts or forces at his command determines his progress.

It is a wholesome exercise to test oneself, at regular times with these and other divine tests of progress. It gives courage to go on.

The frequent question, "Are we better than in the past?" really means "Have we progressed since the past?" The answer is not easily found, since it lies in the heart and actions of each individual man. Moreover "comparisons are odious," because so many things involved can not be clearly seen.

Our problem is, the unending one, to keep in the path of progress, as stated by Brigham Young:

"The principle of increase, of exaltation, of adding to that we already possess, is the grand moving principle and cause of the actions of the children of men."[23]

---

[23]*Discourses of Brigham Young,* p. 87.

12. WHAT IS ETERNAL PROGRESSION?

Latter-day Saints find great joy in the doctrine that man will retain eternally the power that he possesses on earth. Forever he may learn. Forever he may accept or reject any offering. As he uses these endless gifts of personal existence he will progress, or retrograde.[24]

The doctrine of eternal progression was a tremendous addition to Christian belief and thought. For centuries the churches had promised man eternal existence; but Joseph Smith promised man through the restored gospel possible endless activity and development. That gave heaven, often conceived as a static psalm-singing place, a new and desirable definition.

Man's powers, after his earth journey, may be keener, sharper, than here. There he may see and understand more clearly. That is granted. But, his right to exercise his powers or to choose remains inviolate. He may ascend or descend. He may rejoice in or scoff at the offerings of the Lord. Therefore, the retention of his powers does not necessarily protect him. Lucifer, high in the councils of heaven, fell to the low estate of Satan.

To insure progress the powers of man must be exercised for the achievement of the great objective of existence. He must become by every act more and more like the Lord of heaven. That is the highest hope and highest conception of joy by every thinking person. In a small degree this is attainable by man, through strict obedience to the laws of the Lord.

They who so employ their time and talents properly, whether here or hereafter, increase in knowledge. That is the beginning of wisdom. There is no end to knowledge. The field of available knowledge is much like the ten digits, from 0 to 9, the combinations of which are infinite in number. By using or combining simple principles he may likewise multiply knowledge, without limit.

But, as knowledge is gained, whether here or in the infinities, it must be used. Man must not only learn, but he must also apply his learning to a worthy purpose. The uses

---

[24]See *Discourses of Brigham Young,* 1941 edition, p. 90.

to which knowledge may be put are also infinite. Knowledge unused is dry and tasteless. Use gives it life and value. When knowledge is used correctly, properly, righteously, towards the great objective, it enables man to progress. The law of God ever rises above the desires of man.

This then is eternal progress: To add truth to truth; and to use truth, insistently and persistently for the accomplishment of the Lord's plan for the perfection of his willing children. That is how progress is attained.

Now, such progress can with full propriety be called growth.[25] Eternal progress is really eternal growth. To progress forever a man must eternally grow in power to develop the plan of salvation. Then he moves towards the likeness of the Lord. That is growth; that is progression.

In the path of eternal progression there are, of course, degrees of achievement. Though the powers of every living soul will remain undiminished, they who have won an exaltation in the celestial kingdom alone will have the blessing of increase of their kind. That is the great blessing vouchsafed to those who learn most, do best, and bend their will to the purposes of the Lord.[28]

What then is eternal progress? It is an eternity of active life, increasing in all good things, toward the likeness of the Lord. It is the highest conceivable form of growth.

---

[25] *Ibid.*, p. 95.
[26] John 11:25.
[27] Moses 1:39.
[28] See D. & C. 132:19-20.

13. IS THERE PROGRESS IN HEAVEN?

During the long centuries of apostasy after the time of Jesus the Christ, many misleading beliefs had fastened themselves upon the people. Among them was the doctrine that those who won salvation in the hereafter would be in a state of eternal, inactive joy. In the presence of God they would worship him and sing praises to him eternally, but nothing more.

In a world of struggle and sickness such a promise was hailed by unhappy humanity. But it seemed incomplete. It did not conform to the laws of existence. As far as human experience knows, life is always active. Inactivity spells death. Associated with life, in the higher realms of existence, is the power to progress or retrogress. Among human beings this is called the power of choice or free agency.

The question forced itself upon thoughtful people that eternal worship of the Almighty must mean more than an everlasting placid life of psalm singing. The life hereafter promised by the Savior must be as life is on earth; active, achieving, and purposeful. So it seemed to many, though teaching and tradition remained silent on the subject.

The restoration of the gospel of Jesus the Christ by the Prophet Joseph Smith cleared up the subject. He taught that on the "other side," in the hereafter, the individual retains the power to learn, think, and act, and to use or to ignore that which has been learned. That means that the right of choice is everlastingly an attribute of life and intelligence. Therefore, the possibility of progress is eternal.

The question then arises: Since active men in the hereafter are grouped according to their works on earth in one or the other of three ascending glories,[30] is there the possibility of progress in each group or glory?

Since those assigned to each glory are living, intelligent beings, the answer must be yes. In each glory, the power of free agency remains. For them the field of truth is open. The spirit of man is never fettered in his search for truth.

-----

[29]See John A. Widtsoe, *Discourses of Brigham Young,* p. 378; also Joseph F. Smith, *Gospel Doctrine,* p. 432.

[30]D. & C., Section 76.

It may be that they are self-fettered by the deeds that brought them into a lower glory.

It does not follow, as some have suggested, that the possibility of progress in all the glories might enable the inhabitants of the lower glories to overtake those in the higher glory. Righteous living gives power greater than that possessed by those who were assigned to the lower glories. The deeds of those of the lower glories were less in harmony with God's law, hence they possess less power. Therefore, with lesser power to progress they cannot overtake those who travel with more power in the path of progress; for example, it is common practice to set the maximum speed at which an automobile may travel. If two automobiles start out together, the one set at twenty-five, the other at seventy-five, miles an hour, the slower cannot overtake the faster machine, if both travel at full speed. It is so with progress.

What may happen if the man with less power uses it steadily in the spirit of repentance through the eternal years is not known to man. That knowledge rests as yet in the bosom of God.

One thing is known through the revelations of God. Those in the higher, the celestial glory, the one that we all hope to achieve, are in full activity. Their worship of God manifests itself in doing the will of God, hence the works of God.

Those of the celestial kingdom or glory will be occupied in building their own kingdoms as parts of God's greater kingdoms. They will have "increase." Not so in the lower glories; progress they may, but increase will not be theirs.[31]

There is also a difference in possible achievement in the different glories. Granite cannot be carved with wooden tools. So it is in the glories of the hereafter. Those of the celestial kingdom have so lived as to achieve Godhood itself. Those of an inferior glory cannot reach that far. The deeds on earth become tools of achievement in the heavens.

-----

[31]Joseph Fielding Smith, *Teachings of the Prophet Joseph Smith*, p. 301. See also D. & C. 132:19-20.

VI. Salvation

1. WHAT IS THE MEANING OF SALVATION?

Before the Church was organized, the Lord said to the Prophet Smith, "there is no gift greater than the gift of salvation." (D. & C. 6:13) This was repeated in several later revelations. On another occasion, also while the young prophet was receiving his preparatory training, the Lord further declared that "eternal life . . . is the greatest of all the gifts of God" (D. & C. 14:7). It would appear, therefore, that salvation is eternal life; or that to obtain salvation, one must win eternal life. In the Bible and Book of Mormon, also, eternal life, or everlasting life, is promised those who accept the Lord and His Son Jesus Christ. Life and salvation are forever intertwined. Indeed, our own Church leaders have spoken and speak of the "gospel of life and salvation."

The conception of the meaning of salvation requires a definition of life. Man had a pre-existent state, and will live on throughout eternity. He is immortal. It becomes necessary therefore to distinguish clearly between life as mere existence, and life as something greater that may issue from existence.

Brigham Young has furnished a definition in thrilling words: "Salvation is the full existence of man, of the angels, and the Gods; it is eternal life, the life which was, which is, and that which is to come." Life, then, is more than mere existence; it is "full existence." Life is active, existence is static. Life is warm; existence, cold. Life uses its powers to secure progress; it moves upward. Existence is today where it was yesterday, or lower. Life is the increasing realization of man's highest ideals. The Lord Himself has made clear the distinction, for He said to Moses, "This is my work and my glory—to bring to pass the immortality and eternal life of man." (Pearl of Great Price, Moses 1:39) And Jesus, the Christ, made the same distinction when He said, "I am the resurrection, and the life." (John 11:25) Life in contradistinction to existence has always been the objective of Latter-day Saints. Life, implying a future of endless development, is the ultimate goal of the Church.

The Prophet Joseph Smith in his discourses gave added meaning to this definition of salvation. "Salvation," he said, "means a man's being placed beyond the power of all his enemies" (*Teachings of the Prophet Joseph Smith,* p 301), and "Salvation is nothing more or less than to triumph over all our enemies and put them under our feet. And, where we have power to put all enemies under our feet in this world, and a knowldge to triumph over all spirits in the world to come, then we are saved, as in the case of Jesus, who was to reign until he had put all enemies under His feet, and the last enemy was death" (*Teachings of the Prophet Joseph Smith,* p. 297). There is no thought of inertia, mere existence, in such words. Instead, these statements imply action, a battle for triumph over enemies without and within.

The conditions which enable man to win eternal life are included in the plan of salvation. In fact, the plan is but a series of invariable, unalterable laws, obedience to each of which increases man's power to triumph over evil. That means that there is knowledge to be acquired (*Teachings of the Prophet Joseph Smith,* p. 297); principles of action to be accepted; ordinances to be received (*Teachings of the Prophet Joseph Smith,* pp. 12, 331); duties to be performed through life; and the complete acceptance of Jesus, the Christ (John 17:3); that is, full health of body, mind, and spirit to be won. All this that man "might be raised in immortality unto eternal life" (D. & C. 29:43)

The man who uses his powers in obedience to law to fight all enemies of progress, whether ignorance, temptation, appetites, or personalities, rises above existence; he lives; he is on the way to salvation. For him who does not so use his powers, though he exist, life does not function fully; the light of truth is blotted out; the enemy may defeat him; he is retreating from salvation. Salvation then is conditioned under the divine plan and with divine help, upon the proper exercise of the will of man. Complete salvation, which is full and eternal life, results from man's full endeavor to conform to the laws of life, the gospel of the Lord Jesus Christ. That is why we often say that men save themselves with the aid of the Lord (D. & C. 29:44, 45).

Since men differ in their obedience to law there must be stages of salvation. Mankind may win any degree of salvation, from mere inert existence, beyond a kingdom of glory, to the celestial kingdom or highest glory. "In my Father's house are many mansions [kingdoms]." (John 14:2) They who use only a part of their pomers, or use them improperly, do not live life fully. Only those who render obedience to all the duties required of them, who are in process of full living, can expect complete salvation. (*Teachings of the Prophet Joseph Smith*, p. 332) They become the sons of God. They will be where God and Christ dwell.

If salvation is eternal life as here defined, it may begin on earth, or may have begun in the pre-existent state of man. To the degree that a person uses his powers for progress on earth, and lives fully under the law, he is daily achieving salvation and in a state of salvation. But, the summation of our efforts will be made on the great day of judgment, and will determine the degree of our salvation, our final place in the hereafter.

This meaning of salvation is simple, easily understood. If the body is to be kept healthy, and fit for the work of life, certain definite laws must be obeyed. If the mind is to render full service, it must be properly fed and exercised. If the spirit is to lift man into joy, spiritual tasks must be performed. Only under such conditions of fully functioning powers can full life be lived. If salvation is to be gained, all the powers of life must be used, under the laws of truth, so far as in man's power lies. There must be a coordination of these powers for steady progress. As we seek salvation, an active eternal life, we must prepare ourselves for it by proper activity on earth.

This conception of salvation explains why the activities of the Church on earth enter into every phase of man's life, and why activity must characterize the life to come.

2. WAS THE "FALL" INEVITABLE?[1]

According to the plan of salvation, accepted by the hosts of heaven in the great pre-existent council, Adam and Eve were placed on earth to become the parents of the human race. They could not, however, perform this mission, unless they themselves became subject to mortality. Why, then, did the Lord command them not to partake of the tree of good and evil, the gateway of mortal life? There has seemed to be a contradiction between God's purpose as embodied in the plan of salvation, and this command to Adam and Eve.

Perhaps a full explanation is not possible with our present knowledge, yet modern revelation has shed light upon the subject.

First, there is the certain knowledge that without the "Fall," Adam and Eve would have remained in a condition in which children with earthly bodies, for whom the earth was made, could not have been begotten by them. The plan of salvation would have been defeated.

This is the emphatic view of the prophet Lehi. His terse statement leaves no other meaning. "Adam fell that men might be." (2 Nephi 2:25)

Equally direct are the words of Alma: ". . . if it had been possible for Adam to have partaken of the fruit of the tree of life at that time, there would have been no death . . . they would have been forever miserable, having no preparatory state; and thus the plan of redemption would have been frustrated" (Alma 12:23, 26).

Further evidence is supplied by Adam and Eve themselves. After their expulsion from Eden into the earth as it is, Adam exults: ". . . Blessed be the name of God, for because of my transgression my eyes are opened, and in this life I shall have joy, and again in the flesh I shall see God." And Eve seemed almost jubilant: ". . . Were it not for our transgression we never should have had seed, and never should have known good and evil, and joy of our redemption, and the eternal life which God giveth unto all the obedient." (Moses 5:10-11)

[1]For the story of the "Fall" read Genesis, chapter 2; Moses, chapters 3-5.

These were not the words of sinners or of repentant sinners. This was spoken by people who had met and accepted a great challenge, with which, as they imply, God was pleased.

President John Taylor recognized that the "Fall" resulted in good for Adam and Eve, and the whole human family: "They would have been incapable of increase; and without that increase the designs of God in relation to the formation of the earth and man could not have been accomplished; for one great object of the creation of the world was the propagation of the human species, that bodies might be prepared for those spirits who already existed, and who, when they saw the earth formed, shouted for joy." (*The Gospel Kingdom,* p. 96)

In the joy of Adam and Eve after the "Fall" lies hidden, perhaps, a principle which disputants about this subject have not understood, and which may not as yet be full comprehended. However, in modern revelation, a clue to understanding of the "Fall" is given, which may be the key to the apparent contradiction.

After Adam had been supplied with a body made "from the dust of the ground," and placed in the garden of Eden, instructions were given him:

"And I, the Lord God, commanded the man, saying: Of every tree of the garden thou mayest freely eat, But of the tree of the knowledge of good and evil, thou shalt not eat of it, *nevertheless, thou mayest choose for thyself, for it is given unto thee;* but, remember that I forbid it, for in the day thou eatest thereof thou shalt surely die." (Moses 3:16-17)

Though a command had been given, Adam was permitted to exercise his free agency. "Thou mayest choose for thyself." The eternal power of choice was respected by the Lord himself. That throws a flood of light on the "Fall." It really converts the command into a warning, as much as if to say, if you do this thing, you will bring upon yourself a certain punishment; but do it if you choose.

Such was the problem before our first parents: to remain forever at selfish ease in the Garden of Eden, or to face unselfishly tribulation and death, in bringing to pass the purposes of the Lord for a host of waiting spirit children. They chose the latter.

This they did with open eyes and minds as to consequences. The memory of their former estates may have been dimmed, but the gospel had been taught them during their sojourn in the Garden of Eden. They could not have been left in complete ignorance of the purpose of their creation. Brigham Young frankly said: "Adam was as conversant with his Father who placed him upon this earth as we are conversant with our earthly parents." (*Discourses*, p. 104) The Prophet Joseph taught that "Adam received commandments and instructions from God; this was the order from the beginning." (*Teachings*, p. 168)

The choice that they made raises Adam and Eve to pre-eminence among all who have come on earth. The Lord's plan was given life by them. They are indeed, as far as this earth is concerned, our loving father and mother. The "Fall" and the consequent redeeming act of Jesus became the most glorious events in the history of mankind.

In the heavens above, as in the earth below, law prevails. No one can escape the consequences of the acceptance or rejection of law. Cause and effect are eternally related. The Lord had warned Adam and Eve of the hard battle with earth conditions if they chose to eat of the tree of the knowledge of good and evil. He would not subject his son and daughter to hardship and the death of their bodies unless it be of their own choice. They must choose for themselves. They chose wisely, in accord with the heavenly law of love for others.

In life all must choose at times. Sometimes, two possibilities are good; neither is evil. Usually, however, one is of greater import than the other. When in doubt, each must choose that which concerns the good of others—the greater law—rather than that which chiefly benefits ourselves—the lesser law. The greater must be balanced against the lesser. The greater must be chosen whether it be law or thing. That was the choice made in Eden.

This view of the "Fall" is confirmed by the scriptures. For example, ". . . if Adam had not transgressed he would not have fallen, but he would have remained in the garden of Eden . . . forever . . . And they would have had no children; wherefore they would have remained in a state of innocence, having no joy, for they knew no misery; doing no good, for they knew no sin." (2 Nephi 2:22-23)

The role of Satan in this drama is not difficult to understand. He seeks to overthrow the work of God. By inducing Adam and Eve to disobey the Lord, he thought to have them in his power. He forgot, or did not know, that by their very "disobedience" the purposes of the Lord with respect to his spirit children would be accomplished. The temptation of Eve turned upon him to the defeat of his evil designs. This often is the fate of evil.

The Lord himself in these latter days has spoken of the place and mission of Adam: ". . . Michael, or Adam, the father of all, the prince of all, the ancient of days." (D. & C. 27:11; 88:112; 116:1) "The Lord God . . . hath appointed Michael your prince, and established his feet, and set him upon high, and given unto him the keys of salvation under the counsel and direction of the Holy One." (D. & C. 78:15-16) These are eloquent words, which could not well have been spoken of a sinner; only of one who has filled his mission well. Indeed, in the true gospel of Jesus Christ there is no original sin.

It is a thrilling thought that Adam and Eve were not coerced to begin God's work on earth. They chose to do so, by the exercise of their free agency. It is the lesson for all their children: Seek the truth, choose wisely, and carry the responsibility for our acts.

Considering our full knowledge of the purpose of the plan of salvation, and the reason for placing Adam and Eve on earth, the apparent contradiction in the story of the "Fall" vanishes. Instead the law of free agency, or individual choice, appears in distinct view. God's command is qualified by his great purpose to bless his children. Adam and Eve rise to the position of helpers in initiating the divine purpose on earth. They become partners with the Lord in making eternal joy possible for the hosts of heaven.

We, the children of Adam and Eve, may well be proud of our parentage.

3. WHAT IS THE NEED OF ORDINANCES?

If a person has faith in God, is repentant, and tries to live the moral code, why does he need to be baptized and receive other ordinances of the gospel? That is an old question.

To this query, usually honestly made, there are several answers.

First: The Church of Christ is divinely organized. It is not man-made. The conditions for membership have been clearly defined by the Lord. Among the requirements are several ordinances, baptism being the basic one. Ordinances are necessary because the Lord has so decreed. The Lord himself while on earth, as an example to us, submitted to ordinances, as in baptism. There is no other way to membership in Christ's own organization.

This, of course, should be a sufficient answer to those who believe that the Church was founded by the Lord, and that in all we do, we conform to his will. We cannot go beyond or around the Lord's plan.

Members of the Church who ask about the need of ordinances should begin with a consideration of God, his existence, his hand-dealing with man, and his laws for human salvation. If these fundamentals are found to be secure, ordinances become a welcomed activity in achieving the high gifts of the Lord.

There are two first principles, faith and repentance, and two first ordinances, baptism and the laying on of hands for the gift of the Holy Ghost in the Church of Christ. These are closely interwoven. Faith is the first principle, upon which other principles rest, and in the end all ordinances are derivatives of faith. But faith must be expressed in human actions, else it cannot be known. A man proves his faith by his works; he has no other means of doing so. The ordinance of baptism for example may be viewed as man's signature to his compact with God, as an acceptance of the leadership of Jesus the Christ, and as a promise to live the law of the Lord—the things that would be expected from one who has acquired faith. Baptism is a logical sequence of faith. Every ordinance becomes in like manner a necessary tangible outward evidence of some phase of that inward conviction called faith. Each ordinance, in its place, becomes a logical acquiescence with some part of the vast territory covered by faith. Each ordinance becomes a witness to man's surrender to his Heavenly Father.

> Being baptized into this Church is only like learning the alphabet of our mother tongue—it is the very first step. But having received the first principles of the gospel of Christ, let us go on to perfection.[2]

Third: Ordinances give life to faith because they require a covenant from those who participate. Faith is a principle that demands action. Whether it is faith in a law, doctrine, or plan relative to human affairs, it fails unless it leads to a practice, rite, or ceremony. Otherwise it remains an idle belief, an abstract conviction, a theory. The moment it is used, as in an ordinance, it flames into life, and leaps into the world of practical affairs, becoming a positive power, helpful in the world of men.

Everyone who receives an ordinance must make a covenant, else the ordinance is not fully satisfactory. He who is baptized covenants to keep the law of the Church; he who is administered to for sickness, and the administrators, covenant to use their faith to secure the desired healings; he who receives the temple endowment covenants to use in his life that which he has been taught; he who is ordained to the priesthood agrees to honor it, and so on with every ordinance.

That places covenants high, as they should be. Knowledge of itself has little saving power. Only as it is used does knowledge become of value. The man who learns and promises to use that knowledge is of value to society. To accept the plan of salvation without promising to comply with its requirements will result in something worse than ignorance. The world moves forward by the efforts of covenanted people —who keep their covenants.

So, whether from the point of view of obedience to the Lord's command, or of logical necessity, or of giving life to human knowledge for the good of mankind, ordinances are necessary and desirable.

-----

[2] *Discourses of Wilford Woodruff*, p. 20.

4. HOW MAY MEMBERSHIP AND EXALTATION IN THE CELESTIAL KINGDOM BE WON?

It is a basic gospel doctrine that every person, except a very few, will be saved. It is an equally basic doctrine that salvation is graded. Every person will be placed in the hereafter according to his works.

These truths had been forgotten in the dark ages of apostasy. It was then commonly believed that the sinner would forever remain in a torturing hell and that all who escaped that place of unending misery would receive equal places in God's kingdom. Soon after the coming of the Restoration a glorious manifestation revealed anew the ancient truths. While Joseph Smith and Sidney Rigdon were engaged in the revision of the Bible, it became "apparent" to them "that many important points touching the salvation of man had been taken from the Bible or lost before it was compiled. It appeared self-evident from what truths were left, that if God rewarded every one according to the deeds done in the body, the term 'Heaven,' as intended for the Saints' eternal home must include more kingdoms than one."[3] While pondering upon this matter, the vision, known as Section 76 in the Doctrine and Covenants, was received. It threw a flood of light upon the nature of God, and his dealings with his children on earth.

In essence, this vision or revelation explains that all except the sons of perdition will be saved. The traditional hell with its threats of fire and brimstone, and of unending torture, has no existence. But the degree of salvation will vary with the just desserts of those who appear for judgment. Those who in life, or in the later spiritual domain, deliberately did evil, or refused to comply with gospel requirements, would not receive the rewards given to the just and obedient. By his own works, every person would place himself in a higher or lower eternal home. "For they shall be judged according to their works, and every man shall receive ac-

[3]*History of the Church,* 1:245.

cording to his own works, his own dominion, in the mansions which are prepared."[4]

These gradations in salvation may be innumerable, since all members of the human family are different. The many gradations are however reduced to three classes: (1) the celestial, the highest, as of the sun in glory; (2) the terrestrial, the next, as of the moon; (3) the telestial, the lowest, as of the stars.[5]

The revelation details somewhat fully, and with much beauty of language, the conditions that place people in each of these kingdoms. Those of the celestial, the place where God and Christ dwell, have accepted Jesus and the ordinances of his Church. Those of the terrestial died without the law, or were not valiant in the testimony of Jesus. Those of the telestial kingdom did not receive Jesus but were content to follow falsehood.

These kingdoms, though very different, are filled with the children of God the Father. Though those of the lower kingdom have not shown themselves worthy of the fulness of salvation, yet the love of the Father envelops them. Even the glory of the lowest, the telestial, "surpasses all understanding."[6]

To an apostate world this was a new conception of God and his relationship to his children on earth. It raised God to a new height in the thoughts of men. It invited a new love of men for their Eternal Father, a firmer response through righteous works to his love for us. The malignant god of apostasy was removed from the fears of humanity.

Nevertheless, there remained the punishment that one in the lower kingdoms might by another mode of life have received and enjoyed a higher glory. The eternal memory, though terrible, is a more reasonable punishment than the fiery furnace taught through generations of time by false teachers.

Moreover, those who are assigned to the lower kingdoms, have so lived, so misused their opportunities, that they could not adapt themselves to the prevailing conditions in the higher kingdoms. Their capacities, by their own acts, have been changed to fit a lower glory. They would not be happy

[4]D. & C. 76:111.
[5]See I Corinthians, 15:40-41.
[6]D. & C. 76:89.

in a higher kingdom. They are unprepared for association with those whose lives have been in accord with God's truth. As we have made ourselves, so shall our judgment be.

It is further recorded that though these kingdoms are separate, yet there is intercommunication among them. Those in the higher may minister to those in the lower kingdoms. But, the reverse cannot be done. Those in the lower kingdom cannot enter a higher one.[7] Wherever a child of God may be placed, he is not forgotten. That is not the Lord's way. It shows again the infinite, never-ending love of God for his children.

Despite this divine mercy, it must be remembered that though we shall in the hereafter find salvation in one of the kingdoms it is dangerous to allow sin to enter our lives.

Now the concern of the Church is to bring all men into the celestial kingdom. It has no interest in the other, lower kingdoms. Every doctrine, principle, and item of organization within the Church pertains to the celestial glory. The manner of entrance into this the highest kingdom, is therefore made clear. Any person who wishes to enter it must have faith and repent from his sins. Then he must be baptized, and receive the gift of the Holy Ghost by one who has divine authority to perform such ordinances. There are principles and ordinances which in their entirety belong peculiarly to the higher kingdom.

After having laid the foundation for his claim to celestial membership and association, he must, to receive all available blessings of this kingdom, comply with the many requirements of life within the Church. He belongs to "those who are valiant and inspired with the true independence of heaven, who will go forth boldly in the service of their God leaving others to do as they please, determined to do right, though all mankind should take the opposite course."[8] All this having been done, he is qualified to enter the celestial kingdom. Indeed, he is then, even on earth, in the celestial kingdom of God.

Naturally, those who enter the celestial kingdom are of various attainments. There is not absolute uniformity anywhere among the children of God. Their innate capacities

[7] *Ibid.*, 76:86-87.

[8] *Discourses of Brigham Young*, 383.

and their use of the law of free agency make them different, often widely so. Therefore, the members of the highest kingdom are also grouped, according to the Prophet Joseph Smith into three "degrees."[9]

To enter the highest of these degrees in the celestial kingdom is to be exalted in the kingdom of God. Such exaltation comes to those who receive the higher ordinances of the Church, such as the temple endowment, and afterwards are sealed in marriage for time and eternity, whether on earth or in the hereafter. Those who are so sealed continue the family relationship eternally. Spiritual children are begotten by them. They carry on the work of salvation for the hosts of waiting spirits. They who are so exalted become even as the gods. They will be "from everlasting to everlasting, because they continue."[10]

To find entrance to the celestial kingdom, and be exalted therein, form the great hope of every true Latter-day Saint.

The fate of the sons of perdition is not known. There will be few of them, for few know so much as to fall so low. The suggestion has been made, by Brigham Young and others, that they will lose all that they have gained in the long journey, from the dim beginning. They must start over again. But their fate is sealed from us. In this matter we must accept God's own declaration: "Eternal punishment is God's punishment. Endless punishment is God's punishment."[11]

-----

[9]D. & C. 131:1.
[10]*Ibid.*, 132:20.
[11]*Ibid.*, 19:11-12.

5. WILL ALL MEN WHO LIVED ON EARTH BEFORE CHRIST BE RESURRECTED BEFORE THOSE WHO CAME AFTER CHRIST?

The Prophet Alma, in a discussion of the resurrection, long before the days of Christ, declared:

> Now, whether the souls and the bodies of those of whom has been spoken shall all be reunited at once, the wicked as well as the righteous, I do not say; let it suffice, that I say that they all come forth; or in other words, their resurrection cometh to pass before the resurrection of those who die after the resurrection of Christ (Book of Mormon, Alma 40:19).

In this statement and its context, Alma bears witness to the basic Christian doctrine that all men shall be resurrected. The atonement of Jesus Christ was for all men, without exception. An express purpose of the plan of salvation was to provide means by which the spirit children of God could win eternal, imperishable bodies to serve them on their unending, progressive journey.

So important an event, none more so in man's endless existence, would certainly be consummated in an orderly manner. All men will not be resurrected at once; but they will arise, under the divine voice, in groups according to their faithfulness in life. There will be the resurrection of the righteous and of the wicked, of the just and the unjust; the first resurrection and the last. Apparently a succession of such group resurrections will occur until all the earth children of the Father have reclaimed their bodies (D. & C. 76:17; 88:95-102; John 5:28, 29).

Alma appears to apply this orderly process of the resurrection to the individuals within each group. After all, resurrection is an individual matter. Who, in a group equally deserving, who have shown equal fidelity in life's journey, shall conquer the grave first? With simple, clear logic Alma seems to indicate that in each group those who finished their earth life first will first be called to arise from their graves. Thus, both justice and order are preserved in the resurrection of the human family.

Meanwhile, little has been revealed concerning the means, methods, and times of the resurrection. With certainty we know only that all will be resurrected, and that the righteous will come forth from their graves first. That is the glorious testimony of Alma, the Book of Mormon prophet.

6. IS IT POSSIBLE TO PROGRESS FROM ONE GLORY TO ANOTHER?

In the final judgment, all the earth children of the Lord will be assigned places in one or the other of the three grand divisions or degrees of salvation, known to us from modern revelation as the three glories. Each assignment will depend upon the use the candidate has made of the opportunities placed before him on earth and elsewhere. "For they shall be judged according to their works" (D. & C. 76:111). By his own acts each person has shown his fitness to participate in the activities of this or that glory. It would be useless to place him higher than his capabilities would permit, and unfair to place him lower. If placed too high, he would not be competent or happy there, nor could he be content if placed too low. The degree of salvation of necessity corresponds, under the merciful justice of the Lord, with the demonstrated worthiness, capacity, and capability of each individual. The final judgment is individual.

Within each glory, however, there may be advancement. The law of progress may be utilized by every intelligence in the universe. Those who inherit the telestial, terrestrial, or celestial glories may progress, and progress eternally. But, let it ever be remembered that the power to progress is greatest in the celestial glory, and is decreasingly smaller in the lower glories. There can be no talk, therefore, of those in the lower places overtaking those in the higher, any more than an automobile traveling at the rate of twenty-five miles an hour can overtake one moving at the rate of fifty miles an hour.

They who inherit the celestial glory will dwell in the presence of the Father and the Son. They are kings and priests. From that glory issues the power of God, known to us as the Priesthood of the Lord. In that glory certain conditions of joy belong which are absent in the other glories. They who have inherited the lesser glories will receive a salvation so glorious as to be beyond the understanding of man—that has been revealed to us—but, "where God and Christ dwell they can not come, worlds without end" (D. & C. 76:112).

7. WHAT IS EVIL?

A library of books has been written on this subject. Philosophers have exhausted their ingenuity in explaining evil. Nevertheless, Latter-day Saints find the answer to be easily understood.

First, there is "an opposition in all things." If there be a south, there must be a north; if there be light, there must also be the possibility of darkness; if a right side, also a left side; if activity, also quiescence; if good, there must be its opposite, which is evil; and so on with respect to every condition and act of existence. This is much like the positive and negative recognized in all mathematical and scientific work. It is because of this eternal "opposition" that man is able to choose, thus doing good or evil.

This doctrine is laid down in much clearness in the Book of Mormon. The Prophet Lehi, explaining man's free agency to his son Jacob, says:

> For it must needs be, that there is an opposition in all things. If not so, . . . righteousness could not be brought to pass, neither wickedness, neither holiness nor misery, neither good nor bad. . . .
>
> And if ye shall say there is no law, ye shall also say there is no sin. If ye shall say there is no sin, ye shall also say there is no righteousness. And if there be no righteousness there be no happiness. And if there be no righteousness nor happiness there be no punishment nor misery. And if these things are not there is no God. And if there is no God we are not, neither the earth; for there could have been no creation of things, neither to act nor to be acted upon; wherefore all things must have vanished away. . . .
>
> And to bring about his eternal purposes in the end of man, after he had created our first parents, and the beasts of the field and the fowls of the air, and in fine, all things which are created, it must needs be that there was an opposition; even the forbidden fruit in opposition to the tree of life; the one being sweet and the other bitter.
>
> Wherefore, the Lord God gave unto man that he should act for himself. Wherefore, man could not act for himself save it should be that he was enticed by the one or the other (Book of Mormon, 2 Nephi 2:11, 13, 15-16).

Second, man is on earth under a plan provided by God, the Father of the spirits of men. This plan is for the good and welfare of man. The ultimate purpose of the plan is to enable every person to develop his every power, and thus to progress eternally. Imbedded in every part of the plan is the right of every man to act for himself, to choose one or the other of the opposites which present themselves before him. If he chooses to do that which is for his welfare, which enables him to progress, he chooses the good. If he chooses that which retards his progress, he chooses the evil. Whatever conforms to the plan of God for His earth children is good; whatever is in opposition to the plan is evil. That is a simple, plain definition of evil.

Third, our Father in heaven, who directs all things pertaining to His children on earth, often deals, and necessarily so, with matters beyond the clear understanding of mortal man. Commandments are sometimes given which at least at first must be accepted through our faith in God and His revelations. In any case, obedience to the will of God is good; refusal to obey the will of God is evil. In every instance evil is "inverted good or a correct principle made evil use of" (*Discourses of Brigham Young*, p. 106).

However, there can be, there is, no good or evil except by the intrusion of an intelligent being possessed of the power and right of free agency. Things and forces themselves are neither good nor bad. A current of electricity is neither good nor evil. Good results, however, when intelligent man uses the current to give light in darkness; and evil results when the current is directed through the human body to the hurt or death of man. Good and evil are not apparent, do not exist, apart from the actions of intelligent man.

Whether the actions of men are good or evil may be determined by their effects on human life, and their conformity to God's will. Warfare, for example, is not for man's good. It destroys life and the products of life. It seeks for good in an incorrect manner. It violates the firm command of God. It is therefore evil. War is not of God.

The Prophet Joseph Smith declared that all evil done by man was voluntary (*Teachings of the Prophet Joseph Smith*, p. 187). Brigham Young taught the same doctrine (*Discourses of Brigham Young*, p. 85). President Joseph F. Smith (Joseph F. Smith, *Gospel Doctrine*, p. 69) and all other leaders of the Restored Church have taught that by the actions of men possessed of free agency, good or evil is referred to the will of man. He who desires good, and seeks to become master of his will, will do good; while he who desires evil, and uses his will for that purpose, does evil. Men who love darkness do so because their deeds are evil.

The great discourse of the Prophet Lehi already mentioned sets forth this doctrine in great plainness. Modern revelation is equally emphatic. "All truth is independent in that sphere in which God has placed it, to act for itself, as all intelligence also; otherwise there is no existence" (D & C. 93:30). Brigham Young declares:

> Evil is with us; it is that influence which tempts to sin, and which has been permitted to come into the world for the express purpose of giving us an opportunity of proving ourselves before God, before Jesus Christ, our Elder Brother, before the holy angels, and before all good men, that we are determined to overcome the evil, and cleave to the good, for the Lord has given us the ability to do so (*Discourses of Brigham Young,* pp. 107, 108).

How man may desire to do good above all else, and so direct his will, is a subject for later treatment.

8. IS THERE A PERSONAL DEVIL?

The devil has not escaped modern attempts to explain away old beliefs. Mormonism, however, has found it easy to answer the baffling question about the existence and nature of the devil.

The beings in the "spirit world"—whence humanity comes—are alike in that they possess the right of free agency; they are unlike in that they do not choose, nor have they chosen, alike. Consequently, the inhabitants of the spirit world, as in our world, with the same beginnings and opportunities, differ in the degree or stage of their development. There is therefore in the spirit world as on earth a gradation among individuals in knowledge and power from the lowest to the highest, from the least advanced to the God who represents all knowledge, power, and good. Those who lag behind in the march towards progression are not necessarily evil. They are chiefly enemies to themselves as they loiter along the highway of eternity, though they do hinder the purposes of the Lord who seeks the ultimate salvation of all His children.

The inequality or gradation among those who dwell in the domain of spirits is clearly set forth in the Book of Abraham:

> And the Lord said unto me: These two facts do exist, that there are two spirits, one being more intelligent than the other; there shall be another more intelligent than they; I am the Lord thy God, I am more intelligent than they all. . . .
>
> Now the Lord had shown unto me, Abraham, the intelligences that were organized before the world was; and among all these there were many of the noble and great ones;
>
> And God saw these souls that they were good, and he stood in the midst of them, and he said: These I will make my rulers; for he stood among those that were spirits, and he saw that they were good; and he said unto me: Abraham, thou art one of them; thou wast chosen before thou wast born (Pearl of Great Price, Abraham 3:19, 22, 23; also, 3:16-23).

Another class of beings, using free agency improperly, are of more serious concern. A being may choose wisely and well, throughout ages of existence, until great progress has been achieved, and then he may turn against truth and actively reject that which made his rise possible and become opposed to those with whom he was formerly associated. This is not an uncommon experience among human beings; it occurs also in the spirit world. Such a change, or apostacy, results from sin—negligence of duty, ambition, greed, selfishness, jealousy, impurity, or any of the many acts that defeat progress. Such persons become enemies of truth, opponents to progress, ready to use evil to defeat good. They become personified evil.

The story of Lucifer is the most terrible example of such apostacy. Lucifer, son of the morning, through diligent search for truth and the use of it, had become one of the foremost in the assembly of those invited to undertake the experiences of earth. But, in that Great Council, his personal ambition and love of power overcame him. He pitted his own plan and will against the purposes of God. He strove to gain the birthright of his Elder Brother, Jesus the Christ. When his proposition was rejected, he forsook all that he had gained, would not repent of his sin, defied truth, and of necessity lost his place among the followers of God. He was no longer Lucifer, bearer of truth, who walked in light, but Satan, teacher of untruth, who slunk in darkness. He became the enemy of God and of all who try to walk according to the Lord's commandments. One-third of the spirits present in that vast assembly supported Satan and became enemies of the truth that they had formerly cherished. With him these rebellious spirits lost their fellowship with the valiant sons of God. What is more, they lost the privilege of obtaining bodies of flesh and blood, without which they cannot gain full power over the forces of the universe. In the face of that defeat, and that curse, they have sought from Adam to the present time to corrupt mankind and defeat the Lord's purposes.

Now, under God's plan, the core of the meaning of human activity is that man, while winning his body, shall progress by overcoming surrounding conditions. He must learn to be master of every improper impulse. His right of choice remains with him; and as he chooses truth he rises toward his ultimate divine destiny. To accomplish this, our Father in heaven makes use of the evil designs of the devil. God allows His fallen son to tempt the children of men, so that they may more deliberately choose between good and evil. The Lord could banish Satan and his angels from earth, and remove temptation from men, but in His wisdom He permits His wayward bodiless children to come upon earth. Thus, despite their intentions, the followers of Satan are so used as to help accomplish the divine purpose. Whether understood by the evil one or not, in his efforts among mankind, he is made an instrument to secure the very plan that he opposed in the Great Council.

And it must needs be that the devil should tempt the children of men, or they could not be agents unto themselves; for if they never should have bitter they could not know the sweet (D. & C. 29:39).

Man may of himself, with no outside temptation, choose between good and evil. The binding of Satan during the millennium means only that he is banished from earth and that no outside temptation is presented to man. Man's agency remains untrammelled. The devil, and his messengers, suggest evil, whisper to their victims, paint sin in glowing colors, make evil seem inviting, urge a momentary thrill against permanent joy—in short, try to deceive, to make a lie appear as desirable as truth. In the words of Joseph Smith, the Prophet, "The devil has great power to deceive; he will so transform things as to make one gape at those who are doing the will of God" (*Teachings of the Prophet Joseph Smith*, p. 227). But, he cannot compel man to do evil. Too many try to place the blame for their evil doing on the devil, when the fault lies within themselves. Touching on this subject the Prophet Joseph Smith declared:

Satan was generally blamed for the evils which we did, but if he was the cause of all our wickedness, men could not be condemned. The devil could not compel mankind to do evil; all was voluntary. Those who resisted the spirit of God would be liable to be led into temptation. . . . God would not exert any compulsory means, and the devil could not (*Teachings of the Prophet Joseph Smith*, p. 187).

That leads to the principle that the devil is helpless, cannot lead men into error, unless his victims are willing. At the best, the devil is an intruder in the world: "The earth belongs to Him who framed and organized" (*Discourses of Brigham Young*, p. 105). If one pursues truth always, seeks for help from the spirit of God, he can bid the devil get behind him knowing that the command must be heeded. Untruth may be blatant, but is always a coward. "The power of the devil is limited, the power of God is unlimited" (*Ibid.*, p. 105).

> Recollect, brethren and sisters, every one of you, that when evil is suggested to you, when it arises in your hearts, it is through the temporal organization. When you are tempted, buffeted, and step out of the way inadvertently; when you are overtaken in a fault, or commit an overt act unthinkingly; when you are full of evil passion, and wish to yield to it, then stop and let the spirit, which God has put into your tabernacles, take the lead. If you do that, I will promise that you will overcome all evil, and obtain eternal lives. But many, very many, let the spirit yield to the body, and are overcome and destroyed (*Discourses of Brigham Young,* p. 107).

In summary: There are many gradations in knowledge, power, and integrity among the personal spirits in the spirit world. They who have learned truth, then oppose it, are evil. As far as this earth is concerned, Satan is the leader of the evil spirits who battle against the Lord's plan of salvation. They are as personal as the spirits who come on earth to assume mortal bodies, but they remain bodiless. If personality in the spirit world is accepted, the personal nature of the devil must be accepted. There is a personal devil.

9. WHO ARE THE SONS OF PERDITION?

The name Perdition was given to Lucifer, a son of the morning. He refused to accept the plan proposed by God the Father, for the salvation of His spirit children. For this defiant rebellion he was "thrust down from the presence of God and the Son," and became Satan or the devil who "maketh war with the saints of God." Those who do likewise, who follow Satan are called sons of perdition. (Pearl of Great Price, Moses 4:1-4). They are they who have known "my power, and have been made partakers thereof, and suffered themselves through the power of the devil to be overcome, and to deny the truth and defy my power." (D. & C. 76:31)

However, Lucifer was "an angel of God who was in authority in the presence of God." He had risen high in knowledge, understanding, and power. He was Lucifer, a son of the morning (of light). For his rebellion there was no excuse. He committed the unpardonable sin, in denying that of which he had full and complete knowledge. He became thereby the father of lies (See D. & C. 76:26, 32-48).

It is probable that only personages who have acquired similar full knowledge, who willfully and deliberately deny the truth, when they know it to be the truth, can commit the unpardonable sin and become sons of perdition. They are sons of perdition because, "Having denied the Holy Spirit after having received it, and having denied the Only Begotten Son of the Father, having crucified him unto themselves and put him to open shame" (D. & C. 76:35). They must have had a fullness of knowledge; a testimony which cannot be destroyed. One must be on a high eminence to fall so low; and few in world's history have attained such a height. It is doubtful if even Judas, who betrayed Jesus, was sufficiently enlightened to become a son of perdition (Joseph F. Smith, *Gospel Doctrine,* p. 545). Cain was called Perdition because of his sin, but it is added "for thou wast also before the world," implying a reason from out of the pre-existent world, for this heavy punishment (Pearl of Great Price, Moses 5:24).

Moreover, the expression, sons of perdition, is often

used in the scriptures to describe disciples of Satan, all who defy God and teach untruth, and who delight in lies, without necessarily committing the unpardonable sin. The many brethren and sisters who have propounded questions about the sons of perdition may rest secure that with their present knowledge they cannot become sons of perdition.

According to Mormon doctrine, the bodies of all who have had a mortal existence upon earth will be resurrected from the grave. The atonement of Jesus Christ knows no exceptions (Book of Mormon, 3 Nephi 19:22). Yet, after the resurrection comes the judgment. The acts on earth may forfeit many of the possible gifts following earth existence (*Ibid.*, 3 Nephi 26:4, 5). The spiritual redemption, which is part of the redemption from the grave, will apparently be denied the sons of perdition. That appears to be the meaning of the statements that "he [the Lord] saves all except them"; and that they are "the only ones on whom the second death shall have power" (D. & C. 76:38, 43, 44). They who will be judged to be sons of perdition will arise from the grave with their bodies, but their bodies will be of no use to them, as the "second death" is meted out to them in the final judgment.

The destiny of the sons of perdition is not known. They shall suffer the "second death"; they shall be subject to "everlasting punishment"; they shall "reign with the devil and his angels in eternity." What this means has not been revealed. The Lord has declared:

> And the end thereof, neither the place thereof, nor their torment, no man knows;
>
> Neither was it revealed, neither is, neither will be revealed unto man, except to them who are made partakers thereof; . . .
>
> Wherefore, the end, the width, the height, the depth, and the misery thereof, they understand not, neither any man except those who are ordained unto this condemnation (D. & C. 76:45-46, 48).

It must be a terrible punishment beyond human comprehension, the greatest conceivable, yet a justified punishment. Since the greatest sin is the unpardonable sin, it would appear that they will forfeit all the gains of the ages of pre-existence and the years on earth. It is no wonder that the heavens wept over Lucifer's rebellion (D. & C. 76:26).

President Brigham Young has suggested that the ultimate punishment of the sons of perdition may be that they, having their spiritual bodies disorganized, must start over again, must begin anew the long journey of existence, repeating the steps that they took in the eternities before the Great Council was held. That would be punishment, indeed! "They will be decomposed, both soul and body, and return to their native element. I do not say that they will be annihilated; but they will be disorganized, and will be as if they had never been; while we live and retain our identity and contend against those principles which tend to death or dissolution" (*Journal of Discourses,* 7:57). "The clay that marred in the potter's hands was thrown back into the unprepared portion to be prepared over again" (*Ibid.,* 2:124).

Little is known of the sons of perdition and their destiny, yet that little known stands as a warning to all men. To deal carelessly with truth, to deny it when once gained, to defy the laws of truth which are the laws of God, must be counted among the greatest sins. Those who deal lightly with truth in their lives, though they may not become sons of perdition, must expect a heavy punishment, which often begins in mortality.

10. WHAT IS THE MORMON MEANING OF HELL?

Joseph Smith grew up at a time when preachers still taught the proverbial hell of everlasting torture. In the textbooks of his day in many nations were pictures of devils with pitchforks pushing sinners into the flames of hell, there to suffer the agonies of being burned but never consumed. With one hand the preacher offered a fragment of God's love, and with the other, the unutterable, never-ending torment from an angry, unforgiving God. Under such a cruel doctrine men would be frightened, so it was hoped, into a righteous manner of living. How men could devise so horrible a future for any one of God's children is a striking evidence of the apostacy from the simple, loving gospel of Jesus Christ.

Naturally the correction of this evil doctrine had to be made. About a month before the organization of the Church, a glorious revelation was received by Joseph Smith which threw into limbo the illogical doctrine of eternal burnings for sins committed.[12]

In this revelation, Jesus Christ affirms that his commission was to carry out the Father's plan for man's salvation. It is explained that the plan includes laws that must be obeyed. In the final judgment every man will be judged "according to his works and the deeds which he hath done."[13] This threw a flood of light on God's treatment of the sinner. The judgment passed upon any man will be great or small according to his works and deeds.

Further, the breaking of any law brings punishment which, however, may be paid for through repentance. If repentance does not follow sin, full punishment inevitably follows. Whatever that punishment may be, under a higher law, the doctrine destroyed completely the unnatural, ungodlike doctrine of past age.[14]

Two great revelations (Doctrine and Covenants, Sections 19 and 76) have completely changed the world's conception

-----

[12]D. & C. 19:1-15.
[13]*Ibid.*, 19:3.
[14]See *Ibid.*, 19:5-12.

of the payment in the hereafter for sins committed on earth, and of the eternal destiny of man.

The word *hell,* when used in these revelations, refers to the abode of the devil and his ugly brood. As used in the Bible, it has the same connotation.

In the Church of Jesus Christ of Latter-day Saints, there is no hell. All will find a measure of salvation; all must pay for any infringement of the law; but the payment will be as the Lord may decide. There is graded salvation, and this may be a more terrible punishment: to feel that because of sin a man is in one place, when by a correct life, he might be in a higher. The gospel of Jesus Christ has no hell in the old proverbial sense.

11. WHY DOES THE LORD PERMIT WAR?

The battle of life is essentially a battle between obedience or disobedience to eternal law; between good and evil; between right and wrong. The Lord desires His children to win salvation; Satan, an apostate son of God, seeks to enslave them in his own dark kingdom.

This warfare in one form or another has been going on since the days of Adam. Sickness and poverty; slavery of man, physical or mental; selfishness, pride, and unkindness; the attempt of man to rule others—all are but phases of the struggle between light and darkness, the culmination of which is bloody warfare, when evil men seek to win their way at the sacrifice of human lives.

All contention follows a departure from truth, gospel truth. Only when men yield to evil can Satan have power over them. War is always of man's making. The Lord abhors war or contention, whether in the household, office, or on the field of battle. The responsibility for war rests upon man, the free agent, not upon the Lord. Those who are the occasion of war may rightly be classed as murderers. Brigham Young said: "Of one thing I am sure; God never institutes war; God is not the author of confusion or of war; they are the results of the acts of the children of men. . . . If the people generally would turn to the Lord, there would never be any war." (*Discourses of Brigham Young,* p. 562)

Since the law of free agency is ever uppermost in the plan of salvation. the Lord who gave the law must respect it, even though He weep at the errors of His children. It would be a violation of His own plan, should He step in, and, by His undoubted power, stop warfare among the children of men. He would then have to interfere in all contention, and ultimately reduce His children to the status of the unintelligent serfdom proposed by Lucifer in the great council in the heavens. Mankind, however sorrowful the condition, must fight its own battles, and win its own victories.

Nevertheless, though the Lord will not deprive men of the right of free agency, even in the last extremity, He may, in His great mercy, ameliorate the terrors of warfare and turn the tide of battle in behalf of the righteous. In this sense do we pray to the Lord for victory. In the long run, the Lord is always the victor. The history of mankind shows that whatever the momentary result of contention and warfare has been, righteousness has ultimately triumphed. This will be so to the end of the world's story.

There are wars and wars. If both contending parties are but seeking aggrandizement, in territory or power, they are both unworthy of divine help. It is a type of blasphemy under such conditions to offer prayers to heaven for relief. However, when human rights and freedom, the plan of salvation itself, are the issues, the raging battle becomes the battle of the Lord, and those who have truth, and fight for it, should then plead with the Lord for help, and in course of time will receive it, for it has been said: "The Lord shall fight for you" (Exodus 14:14).

There would be no wars unless men had forgotten to live righteously. Even the nation that fights for divine principles, the nation on the Lord's side, may have forgotten the Lord in its material prosperity, and thereby have lost wisdom and strength. Thus, it is within the realm of thought that a nation, through war, may bring upon itself deserved chastisement for its own follies.

At times men are justly engaged in war. The eternal battle has been between right and wrong. Whenever evil has girded itself for war, it may be necessary to use the same weapons to secure defeat of evil. Contrary as it may be to righteous feeling, in the fight for the right, cannon must often be used to meet cannon. Certainly, every means must be used to protect truth from the domination of untruth. The injunction of the Savior to turn "the other cheek," does not mean surrender to untruth, but patience, long suffering, before entering into controversy with one's fellow man. This doctrine is clearly taught in modern revelation:

> And again, this is the law that I gave unto mine ancients, that they should not go out unto battle against any nation, tongue, or people, save I, the Lord, commanded them.
>
> And if any nation, tongue, or people should proclaim war against them, they should first lift a standard of peace unto that people, nation, or tongue;
>
> And if that people did not accept the offering of peace, neither the second nor the third time, they should bring these testimonies before the Lord;
>
> Then I, the Lord, would give unto them a commandment, and

justify them in going out to battle against that nation, tongue, or people.

And I, the Lord, would fight their battles, and their children's battles, and their children's children's, until they had avenged themselves on all their enemies, to the third and fourth generation.

Behold, this is an ensample unto all people, saith the Lord your God, for justification before me. (D. & C. 98:33-38)

There is no suggestion here that evil shall be allowed to range unhindered in the world, to the injury of humanity. There comes a time when patience is no longer required. But, the righteous will show forbearance as long as it is possible or proper to do so.

At best, this is a difficult question. It is imperative to remember that it is not given to man to read fully the divine mind. All that we can do is to use such truth as has been revealed for our guidance in our thought and action. Of one thing we may however be certain—whatever happens to those who live righteously is permitted by the Lord. Man's only safety is to walk in faith with the Lord.

12. SHOULD A SOLDIER LOVE HIS ENEMY?

The divinely revealed preface to the Doctrine and Covenants makes the statement that "I the Lord cannot look upon sin with the least degree of allowance" (D. & C. 1:31; Book of Mormon, Alma 45:16).

The nature of sin justifies this unrelenting, final judgment. Sin is untruth, and the misuse of truth. It decries freedom, and fosters tryranny. It deceives and lies. It destroys, but never builds up except for more destruction. It slinks away from light and lurks in darkness. It is in deliberate opposition to the Lord's plan for human progress. Sin is the mark of Satan.

The wide spectrum of sin, laid against a background of selfishness, is everywhere evil. It extends from wilful ignorance to the use of knowledge for unholy purposes; from dishonesty in speech, to deliberate murder; from family and neighborhood contentions, to warfare among nations. Every part of it corrodes, annihilates, is death-dealing. Every part of it, if uncovered, is hideous and found to beckon from slimy, poisonous depths.

Sin cannot be shown love or mercy, however meek and beguiling it may present itself. It cannot be condoned. Were that done the structure of truth would collapse. The battle of the Church is against sin, of every kind; it must be conquered, or the plan of salvation will be defeated; it must be fought to the bitter end. Tolerance of sin is itself a sin.

All human affairs must be measured by the standards of right. If evil is in man's acts, it becomes a sin to support them. The statue totters and falls if clay is mixed with the iron of the feet. The strength of a democracy, more than any other form of government, lies in its adherence to the principles of the plan of salvation.

A war can be called just, only when waged against sin and for the victory of truth; when it battles for the preservation of the principles which make up the plan of salvation, then warfare is righteous. If it is waged to defeat the attempt to enslave men under tyrannical rule, it becomes a war against sin. Such a war should be supported by all who love right above wrong; by all who adhere to the right of free agency, for which the heavenly battle was fought, long ago.

If it be desired to test the righteousness of a war, compare the issues with those of the divinely formulated plan for human happiness. No other test is needed. The standards are all there.

In such a spirit, with such understanding, the soldiers who go out from this Church must go into battle. They are fighting sin; they are fighting for truth; no quarter can be shown the opposing side. The soldiers of the enemy, whether willing or not, represent a sinful, destructive cause. They must be defeated at any cost, even that of their lives. Sin cannot be looked upon "with the least degree of allowance." (D. & C. 1:31) The opposing army must be viewed as a cause, not as a group of men.

The cause must be uppermost. The individual must recede in importance, until the cause for betterment has triumphed. Soldiers of a righteous cause, whether the warfare be great or small, must fix their attention upon that cause, and with determination fight for it. The fate of the enemy as individuals must be set aside in the battle for principle. If right wins, as it must and will, the enemy and all humanity will be blessed.

In sacred history war has often been permitted, to establish the cause of righteousness, or to prevent evil from triumphing among men. Even the Savior when the temple of God, "a house of prayer," had been made into "a den of thieves," overthrew the tables of the money-changers and the merchants, and drove out all who were violating the holy purposes of the temple. The cause of righteousness must be man's first and constant consideration.

Nevertheless, though sin can be given no quarter, nor those who seek to impose sin upon others, yet the soldier must recognize that the sinner, as an individual, remains a child of God, subject to repentance and the Lord's eternal mercy. Since he represents a sinful cause, it may be necessary to use against him the only weapons he recognizes, even though it means his destruction. The coin of Caesar is his; we must render it to him to win the Lord's cause. Yet we may hope and pray that on the endless, eternal journey, he may find his way to salvation.

Love is the first activating force of the gospel. For love of His children the Lord laid out the plan of salvation. It was love for humanity that gave the Savior courage to meet His death upon the cross. It is through love, one for the other, among the children of men, that the brotherhood of man, the aim of the gospel, will arise upon earth. Through love, right will triumph over evil, But, it should ever be borne in mind that love is defeated, unless righteousness is victorious.

Therefore, the love of truth, the gospel which blesses all mankind, must transcend the love of an individual or a group. Usually, the best way to love our enemies is to keep truth from being trodden into the ground by those who are led by evil, designing leaders. Make truth and right triumphant, and love will bear rule among men. There is no other way.

All need to learn that love, as all other virtues, must be exercised with wisdom and in a commonsense manner. Hysteria and emotional outbursts, often for criminals, are not expressions of love, but of diseased conceptions of the right manner of loving our fellow men.

The banner of love will ever be held aloft by the Church. The soldier can and should love his enemy, but not in the sense that he forgets the greater love of the cause by which in the end the enemy and all others will be blessed.

13. WHAT IS THE MEANING OF INTELLIGENCE?

In everyday language we say that a person is intelligent who learns easily, comprehends quickly, or is an apt pupil in school.

Latter-day Saints however are obliged by their religious philosophy to extend and expand the ordinary definition of intelligence. To them, intelligence falls into two parts. First, the possession of knowledge, and, second, the proper use of acquired knowledge for human welfare. That is a higher intelligence than that based upon readiness in learning. It pushes intelligence beyond the field of mere acquisition of knowledge. It includes the voluntary act of using knowledge in harmony with the laws of human happiness. In Mormon discussions of intelligence, knowing and using knowledge are as Siamese twins, fed by the same life stream. . . . A really intelligent person uses well whatever knowledge, however little, he possesses.

Knowledge of itself is very dry. It gives scant comfort to the soul of man. It has no life. It is interesting to understand how dynamite may be made; but that knowledge becomes alive only when the substance is used in blasting the mountainside. It is interesting to know that certain forms of life may be destroyed by carbolic acid, but that knowledge is of living power only when the corruption in a sore on hand or foot is destroyed by the use of the chemical. Use makes knowledge blossom into life. Such intelligence becomes a universal process which builds the house of joy for man on earth and in the eternities.

In this sense do we understand the famous statement in the Doctrine and Covenants that "the glory of God is intelligence." He, above all, has infinite knowledge; he, above all, fits knowledge into processes for man's welfare. His plan of salvation consists of knowledge directed into channels for the eternal blessings of humankind. That means the proper and correct use of knowledge to achieve the high destiny of man, declared in the gospel of Jesus the Christ.

Joseph Smith the Prophet declared that "no man is saved faster than he gains knowledge." That is in full harmony with the Mormon definition of intelligence, for he lays down then the principle that law, the product of knowledge, must be obeyed if it shall serve mankind. Knowledge is the open door to full intelligence.

Knowledge cannot be used until it is possessed. That places the gathering of knowledge high in the lives of men who seek intelligence. That explains the eagerness of the Church for education, throughout life, in schools and by other devices. That explains also why the Church holds a foremost place in educational circles. It is not for the sake of knowledge alone, but as a means to reach the larger intelligence required for acceptable active membership in the kingdom of God, that Latter-day Saints are seekers after truth.

The high position of knowledge in the Church has ever been set forth. At the very beginning of the restored Church the Saints were admonished to "remember knowledge."[15] A little later they were told to "grow . . . in knowledge."[16] Then they were told to "obtain a knowledge of history, and of countries, and of kingdoms, and of laws of God and man."[17] Joseph Smith always urged the Saints to gather knowledge. His successors in office have spoken against ignorance and in praise of knowledge. Leaders of the Church have ever urged the people to gather knowledge.

There are of course many kinds of knowledge; some of lesser, some of higher value. When Joseph Smith said that a man cannot be saved in ignorance, he meant naturally ignorance of the laws which all together lead to salvation. Such knowledge is of the highest value. It should be sought after first. Then other kinds of knowledge may be added to support and amplify the more direct knowledge of spiritual law. For example, it is a duty of the Church to preach the gospel to all the world. This however requires the aid of railroads, steamships, printing presses, and a multitude of other things that make up our civilization. A knowledge of the gospel is the missionary's first need, but the other needs, though lesser, help him perform better the divine injunction to teach the gospel to all people.

In the history of the Church it has not been forgotten to emphasize the proper use of knowledge. Such use is

[15]D. & C., section 4.
[16]*Ibid.*, 50:40.
[17]*Ibid.*, 93:53 (see also 88:79).

commonly spoken of as obedience to knowledge and law. Indeed, obedience in the sense that all knowledge shall be directed to the salvation of man is the very cornerstone of Mormon philosophy.[18] Knowledge must be used for the good of man. Thereby hangs the valuation of man as an intelligent being. The leaders of the Church generally have emphasized as they have discoursed on knowledge that all truth won must be used in harmony with the requirements of the plan of salvation.

Frequently, members of the Church have thought that the glorious revealed statement "the glory of God is intelligence," means merely the gathering of knowledge. That view must be enlarged in view of the Latter-day Saint definition of intelligence; a compound of knowledge and the proper use of knowledge.

Indeed, this view is implied in the revelation itself, for it reads in full, "The glory of God is intelligence, or, in other words, light and truth."[19] That is, the intelligence here discussed is a compound of light and truth. Sound knowledge is truth. Such truths become a light to guide man on his way, on every road, to meet every need.

In the same revelation this view is further confirmed by the statement that "He that keepeth his (God's) commandments, receiveth truth and light, until he is glorified in truth and knoweth all things,"[20] In the correct life, light and truth travel together and are progressive towards the nature and power of God. Hence the beautiful statement: "That which is of God is light; and he that receiveth light, and continueth in God, receiveth more light; and that light groweth brighter and brighter until the perfect day."[21]

It is this light (intelligence) that Latter-day Saints need. This is the light that makes possible our entrance into celestial glory.

It is the type of intelligence here discussed that has made this Church. Knowledge of the laws of God has been converted into the actions of everyday life.[22]

---

[18]*Teachings of the Prophet Joseph Smith,* p. 217.
[19]D. & C. 93:36.
[20]*Ibid.,* 93:28.
[21]*Ibid.,* 50:24.
[22]See also Taylor, John, *The Gospel Kingdom,* pp. 270-271.

14. SHOULD CHURCH DOCTRINE BE ACCEPTED BLINDLY?

Th obvious and emphatic answer is no. The question is admitted here only because recently it has been asked frequently. Apparently some explanations are necessary.

It seems to be the opinion of some that Latter-day Saints do not think, but accept the doctrines and follow the practices of the Church without an intelligent consideration of what they believe and do. There could not be a more unfounded and erroneous view.

The doctrine of the Church cannot be fully understood unless it is tested by mind and feelings, by intellect and emotions, by every power of the investigator. Every Church member is expected to understand the doctrine of the Church intelligently. There is no place in the Church for blind adherence.

This is indispensable in a Church which rests upon the the individual testimonies of its members, and in which there is no professional ministry. Church government lies in the hands of the membership, every man of which may hold the priesthood. That requires more than a blind following.

A Church member who does not study the gospel and try it out in his life is not really in good Church standing. Such a man cannot intelligently perform the work of the Church. With insufficient knowledge he sees things obliquely and obscurely. Indeed, he is a danger to the progress of the latter-day work.

There is nothing new in this. From the beginning of its history the Church has opposed unsupported beliefs. It has fought half-truth and untruth. It has insisted that its members learn the gospel and its doctrine. It has demanded an intellectual as well as an emotional acceptance of the restored truth. It is today a great educational organization. It has urged and urges today, upon every candidate, a good understanding of the gospel before entering the waters of baptism. Though a person be touched in his heart and is baptized when first hearing the gospel, he must later give it further study, else he cannot become a useful member of the Church nor can he rise to the possible heights in personal joy. The case of President Brigham Young is but an example of the general rule. It took him two years of study, prayer, and reflection, after having the gospel brought seriously to his attention, before he asked for baptism.

It is this open-eyed understanding of the gospel that makes the Latter-day Saints so certain of their faith. A blind acceptance is an incomplete acceptance, and usually leaves a person in doubt.

After his two years of examination, Brigham Young remained throughout his life firm and unshaken in his faith. He knew from his careful study, beyond peradventure of doubt, that the restored gospel is true. Those who in this Church waver in their faith, need to fortify themselves by prayer for truth, further study of the gospel and practice in gospel living. So clearly understood is the gospel and its principles, that there seldom is an apostasy from the Church except by those who have allowed sin to enter their lives.

To understand the gospel a right beginning must be made. If God and Jesus Christ are accepted, the search for the truth of the restored gospel must be initiated by a study of the Prophet Joseph Smith and his work. Were his claims true—that he had conversed with the Father and the Son; that the priesthood was conferred upon him legitimately by personages from the days of Jesus Christ; that he was authorized to organize the Church of Christ; and that a body of revelations was given him for the guidance of the Church?

A certainty of the divine calling of Joseph Smith must be a foundation of faith in the Church.

Then, it must be understood that some Church practices rest upon unchangeable gospel principles. We may not always understand these, but no amount of argument can change them. The strength of the gospel lies in these eternal, undeviating laws.

Some prefer baptism by sprinkling, but the divine law is that baptism shall be by immersion. Some feel that an inward call is sufficient to perform such ordinances, therefore making the transmission of authority unnecessary. This view is beyond argument, since it violates divine law.

Still others even in the Church may question the law of tithing. Why should not the requirement be a fifth or a twentieth? Why should there not be an upper limit for the rich man. Again, the Church is bound by the revelations of God through the Prophet of the Restoration, Joseph Smith.

The labor question is a live issue. Some would have the Church take sides with one or the other of the many propositions of the day. Again, the Church rests its opinion on the eternal law: that the labor confusion will disappear when all men learn to do to others as they would have others do to them. Whatever leads in that direction invites Church support.

All such queries, designed to question the propriety of the basic laws of the gospel, are a waste of time. Every future revelation of the Church will be in the nature of an extension of these spiritual foundation stones of the latter-day kingdom of the Lord. This is accepted open-eyed not blindly by Latter-day Saints.

However, there are practices within the Church of less fundamental nature.

The Saints must gather in meetings. That is a divine commandment. But the time of the meetings is set by the people of the Church upon the recommendation of the sustained leaders. There may in many cases be a justifiable difference of opinion as to the best time.

The Saints must study and learn. That is in the revelations to Joseph Smith. But the value of the various study courses provided by the different Church organizations may with propriety be discussed by all.

Whether tithing shall preferably be paid in kind or in cash, is a question dependent on existing circumstances. It is subject to lawful discussion.

Every open-eyed Latter-day Saint, who refuses to accept things blindly, will distinguish clearly between the fundamental and the derivative, the essential and the non-essential, in the program and practices of the Church.

Those who confuse the two are either immature, perhaps honest seekers after truth, or faultfinders, perhaps enemies of the Church.

But Latter-day Saints who sustain their leaders, are always willing to try out debatable regulations, before passing judgment on them, and then report their objections, if any, to the proper Church officers.

Latter-day Saints should not and do not accept Church doctrine blindly.

VII. Priesthood

1. WHO WAS MELCHIZEDEK?

The ancient history of the priesthood is only dimly known. Especially is this so for the period between Noah and Abraham.

After the flood, Noah, who had himself received the priesthood (D. & C. 107:52; 84:14, 15; Moses 8:19), ordained his son Shem to the same priesthood (Genesis 9:26), and perhaps many others as the generations of faithful men increased. Shem and other priesthood bearers in turn undoubtedly ordained other faithful men who had a claim upon the priesthood. It is likely that whole communities of followers of the gospel which was taught to Adam existed at this time. Modern revelation confirms this view, for Moses received the priesthood from Jethro in Midian; and the descent of the priesthood from Abraham to Jethro is given in names that do not appear at that period in the Bible. (D. & C. 84: 6-13.)

In this period, Melchizedek springs suddenly into view. Abraham, after a victorious battle with Chedorlaomer, calls on Melchizedek, who is king of Salem (a place in or near the present Jerusalem), is entertained by Melchidezek, and finally pays tithing to him. In this act, Abraham recognized in Melchizedek a person of authority among the organized followers of the gospel, for he would not pay his tithing to one not authorized to receive it. This view is supported by Joseph Smith's inspired translation of the Bible, in which the statement is made that Melchizedek, "being the high priest, and the keeper of the storehouse of God; him whom God had appointed to receive tithes for the poor."

Paul, the apostle says, ". . . this Melchizedec, . . . first being by interpretation King of righteousness, and after that also King of Salem, which is, King of peace." (Hebrews 7:1, 2.) The accepted Hebrew meaning of Melchizedek may then be taken as king of righteousness or peace. But, students of language suggested that the word is a title rather than a name, a title implying a high position of spiritual leadership. Linguists, dissecting the word and finding the syllable "el" in it, the Hebrew for God, interpret Melchizedek to mean a servant or king of the supreme God, a "King-priest." Paul tells the Hebrews to "consider how great this man was." (Hebrews 7:4.) Through the ages Melchizedek has been a somewhat mystical figure, but one to whom the highest respect is given.

Not only was Abraham entertained by Melchizedek but he received the priesthood from him. The priesthood which descended from Abraham to his descendants is thus traced back through Melchizedek. (D. & C. 84:14.) His priesthood is the most important thing about Melchizedek. David speaks of himself as "a priest for ever after the order of Melchizedek." (Psalm 110:4.) Paul discourses at some length upon the high priesthood after the order of Melchizedek, and associates it with the mission of Jesus the Christ. (Hebrews 5:6, 10; 6:20; 7:1-21.) We of the restored Church of Christ, following divine revelation to avoid repeating the name of Deity too often, speak of the higher priesthood as the Melchizedek Priesthood or the priesthood of Melchizedek.

A curious illustration of the result of missing or distorted or misunderstood scripture appears in Paul's epistle concerning Melchizedek. In the King James translation it reads, "For this Melchizedec . . . Without father, without mother, without descent, having neither beginning of days, nor end of life." (Hebrews 7:1, 3.) This is an absurd statement about a mortal man. The statement refers, of course, to the priesthood of Melchizedek, which is eternal. The Prophet Joseph Smith rectified the error in his inspired translation of the Bible, as follows: "For this Melchizedek was ordained a priest after the order of the Son of God which order was without father, without mother, without descent, having neither beginning of days, nor end of life."

There is an old Hebrew tradition that Melchizedek was none other than Shem, the son of Noah. As far as the age of Shem is concerned, that is possible. Shem lived five hundred two years after the flood, and Abraham was born two hundred ninety-two years after the flood. Abraham, therefore, must have known Shem. However, doubt is cast upon this claim by the revealed statement that "Melchizedek received it (the priesthood) through the lineage of his fathers, even till Noah." (D. & C. 84:14.)

Fortunately, modern revelation has given us information concerning this man great in sacred history:

"Now Melchisedek was a man of faith, who wrought righteousness; and when a child he feared God, and stopped the mouths of lions, and quenched the violence of fire. And thus, having been approved by God, he was ordained an high priest after the order of the covenant which God made with Enoch, It being after the order of the Son of God; which order came, not by man, nor the will of man; neither by father nor mother; neither by beginning of days nor end of years; but of God; And it was delivered unto men by the calling of his own voice, according to his own will, unto as many as believed on his name.

"For God having sworn unto Enoch and unto his seed with an oath by himself; that every one being ordained after this order and calling should have power, by faith, to break mountains, to divide the seas, to dry up waters, to turn them out of their course; to put at defiance the armies of nations, to divide the earth, to break every band, to stand in the presence of God; to do all things according to his will, according to his command, subdue principalities and powers, and this by the will of the Son of God which was from before the foundation of the world. And men having this faith, coming up unto this order of God, were translated and taken up into heaven.

"And now, Melchisedek was a priest of this order; therefore he obtained peace in Salem, and was called the Prince of peace. And his people wrought righteousness, and obtained heaven, and sought for the city of Enoch which God had before taken, separating it from the earth, having reserved it unto the latter days, or the end of the world; And hath said, and sworn with an oath, that the heavens and the earth should come together; and the sons of God should be tried so as by fire. And this Melchisedek, having thus established righteousness, was called the king of heaven by his people, or, in other words, the King of peace.

"And he lifted up his voice, and he blessed Abram, being the high priest, and the keeper of the storehouse of God; Him whom God had appointed to receive tithes for the poor.

"Wherefore, Abram paid unto him tithes of all that he had, of all the riches which he possessed, which God had given him more than that which he had need." (Genesis 14:25-39, Inspired Version.)

2. WHAT IS THE DISTINCTION BETWEEN THE PRIESTHOOD AND THE KEYS OF THE PRIESTHOOD?

A key unlocks the door to our house, or the cover of our jewelbox, or the ignition of our automobile. Without the key, we cannot have access to the house, possess the jewels, or drive the car. Our property is inactive, awaiting the coming of the key. A man, likewise, holds the Priesthood by which all the work in the Church is accomplished, but he can use it in certain Church activities only when the necessary keys are conferred upon him.

Further, a man who owns a car may not be allowed, because of police orders, to drive down certain streets. Similarly, a man may receive the Priesthood, but can exercise its power, within the Church, only by the authority of the proper officials.

On his own property and on open streets the man may drive his car without question. Similarly, in behalf of himself and his family, and for the general good, a man may exercise his Priesthood without reference to the official body of the Church.

They who have the right to say when, where, and how the Priesthood shall be used for the Church have keys of authority. They may give similar authority or keys to others.

Every priest has the authority to administer the sacrament; every elder has the authority to baptize; but neither can so officiate in the activities of a ward unless called to do so by the bishop who holds the keys of authority for the ward.

Every high priest has the authority to preside, but cannot preside over any stake organization without being called to do so by the stake president, who holds the keys of authority for the stake.

All members of a Priesthood quorum hold equal Priesthood authority, but in the president of the quorum is vested the authority to use the Priesthood for quorum purposes, for he holds the keys of authority for the quorum.

A seventy by virtue of his Priesthood has authority to

preach the gospel, but he cannot fill a mission unless he is called by the proper officers of the Church, and set apart for that purpose—that is, unless the keys of that ministry are conferred upon him, within his specific field, by those who hold the general keys of spreading the gospel abroad, and can confer them on others.

Therefore, it is customary and proper in ordaining or setting apart men to presiding offices to confer upon them the associated keys of authority. If in ordaining a man to the office of elder, seventy, or high priest, the keys of authority are conferred, it means that henceforth he has full right to the use of the power committed to him to meet his own needs, and in guarding and blessing his own family, and all who have need of help. But, when men are called to specific offices of responsibility, the corresponding keys of authority are conferred, even though the man already holds the Priesthood.

President Joseph F. Smith has drawn the clear distinction between the Priesthood and the keys of the Priesthood:

> The Priesthood in general is the authority given to man to act for God. Every man ordained to any degree of the Priesthood has this authority delegated to him.
>
> But it is necessary that every act performed under this authority shall be done at the proper time and place, in the proper way, and after the proper order. The power of directing these labors constitutes the keys of the Priesthood. In their fulness, the keys are held by only one person at a time, the prophet and president of the Church. He may delegate any portion of this power to another, in which case that person holds the keys of that particular labor. Thus, the president of a temple, the president of a stake, the bishop of a ward, the president of a mission, the president of a quorum, each holds the keys of the labors performed in that particular body or locality. His Priesthood is not increased by this special appointment, for a seventy who presides over a mission has no more Priesthood than a seventy who labors under his direction; and the president of an elders' quorum, for example, has no more Priesthood than any member of that quorum. But he holds the power of directing the official labors performed in the mission or the quorum, or in other words, the keys of that division of that work. So it is throughout all the ramifications of the Priesthood—a distinction must be carefully made between the general authority, and the directing the labors performed by that authority (Joseph F. Smith, *Gospel Doctrine,* pp. 168-9).

3. WHEN DOES A PROPHET SPEAK AS A PROPHET?

This is an old question. It was asked of the Prophet Joseph Smith and answered by him. He writes in his journal, "This morning . . . I visited with a brother and sister from Michigan, who thought that 'a prophet is always a prophet'; but I told them that a prophet is a prophet only when he was acting as such" (Joseph Smith, *History of the Church,* 5:265).

That statement makes a clear distinction between official and unofficial actions and utterances of officers of the Church. In this recorded statement the Prophet Joseph Smith recognizes his special right and duty, as the President and Prophet of the Church, under the inspiration of the Lord, to speak authoritatively and officially for the enlightenment and guidance of the Church. But he claims also the right, as other men, to labor and rest, to work and play, to visit and discuss, to present his opinions and hear the opinion of others, to counsel and bless as a member of the Church.

Whenever moved upon by the Spirit of the Lord, the man called to the Prophet's office assumes the prophetic mantle and speaks as a mouthpiece of the Lord. He may then interpret the word of God, apply it to the conditions of the day, governmental, social, or economic, warn against impending evil, point out the better way, bring to light new truth, or bless the righteous in their endeavors. Such inspired deliverances are binding upon all who believe that the latter-day work came and is directed by revelation. There is no appeal from them; no need for debate concerning their validity. They must either be accepted or be subjected to the dangers of private interpretation. This has been made plain in modern revelation: "Wherefore, meaning the church, thou shalt give heed unto all his (Joseph's) words and commandments which he shall give unto you as he receiveth them, walking in all holiness before me;

"For his word ye shall receive, as if from mine own mouth, in all patience and faith" (D. & C. 21:4, 5). In this commandment there is no limitation upon the prophet, as to subject, time, or place.

Such official prophetic utterances to the Church are usually made in the great general conferences of the Church, or in signed statements circulated among the people. The phrase "Thus sayeth the Lord" may at times be used; but is not necessary. When the prophet speaks to the people in an official gathering or over his signature, he speaks as the Lord directs him. If a new doctrine or practice be involved in the revelation, it is presented to the people for acceptance, in recognition of the free agency of the Church itself, but once accepted, it is thereafter binding upon every member.

Though the prophet may step out of his official role in dealing with the daily affairs of life, he can never divest himself of the spirit and influence which belong to the sacred office which the Lord has placed upon him. The faith and readiness to do the work of the Lord which fitted him for his high office, shape his life in harmony with the eternal principles and purposes of the gospel. Though often humble by the world's measure, in gifts and ability, he lives under inspired guidance, which makes him great among men, and therefore, his unofficial expressions carry greater weight than the opinions of other men of equal or greater gifts and experience but without the power of the prophetic office. It would be wisdom on all occasions and with respect to all subjects in any field of human activity, to hearken to the prophet's voice. There is safety and ultimate happiness in following the counsel that may be received from the prophet.

Men are called to the prophetic office because of their humility and their willingness to be in the hands of the Lord as clay in the hands of the potter. Yet a man called to the prophetic office is almost without exception of high native endowment, often with large experience in life, and possessed of wisdom and sound judgment. That is, the prophet, though but a man, is an able man, rising in ability above the multitude. An examination of sacred history from Adam to the present will show that able men, in the words of Jethro, men "such as fear God, men of truth, hating covetousness" (Exodus 18:21), have been called to the prophetic office. The unoffiicial views and expressions of such a man with respect to any vital subject, should command respectful attention. Wise men seek the counsel of those wiser or abler than themselves.

Every member of the Church, and all men for that matter, would do well to give heed, and indeed should do so, to any public utterance or to the unofficial counsel of the man who has been called to the office of prophet. One cannot limit him by saying that on some subjects pertaining to human welfare he may not speak. The spiritual and the temporal have ever been blended in the Church of Christ. Obedience to the counsels of the prophet brings individual and collective power and joy. Of all men, the prophet of the Lord should, at all times, have most influence with the Latter-day Saints. No other cause can be greater than that of the Church of Christ.

How may the rank and file of the Church recognize the prophetic voice, whether official or unofficial, when it speaks? The answer is simple enough. A person who is in harmony in his life, in thought and practice, with the gospel and its requirements, who loves truth so well that he is willing to surrender to it, will recognize a message from the Lord. My sheep know my voice, said the Savior in the Meridian of Time. In this day, the Lord has given the key for our guidance.

> Verily I say unto you, he that is ordained of me and sent forth to preach the word of truth by the Comforter, in the Spirit of truth, doth he preach it by the Spirit of truth or some other way?
>
> And if it be by some other way it is not of God.
>
> And again, he that receiveth the word of truth, doth he receive it by the Spirit of truth or some other way?
>
> If it be some other way it is not of God.
>
> Therefore, why is it that you cannot understand and know, that he that receiveth the word by the Spirit of truth receiveth it as it is preached by the Spirit of truth?
>
> Wherefore, he that preacheth and he that receiveth, understand one another, and both are edified and rejoice together. And that which doth not edify is not of God, and is darkness. (D. & C. 50:17-23)

Thus the burden of proof is upon the hearer, not alone upon the speaker. Whoever quibbles about the validity of a message of the prophet would do well to engage in a serious self-examination. Is the trouble with him? Perhaps he is not "in tune" with truth. Perhaps he does not live the law of the gospel in such manner as to respond to the message of truth. President Joseph F. Smith declared that those who honor their own Priesthood first, will honor it in those who preside over them (President Joseph F. Smith, *Gospel Doctrine,* p. 207). That doctrine may be applied when the prophet speaks to the Church or to the world.

Acceptance of the teachings of the prophet does not violate the right of free agency; but rather enhances it. The Lord expects every man to solve, as far as possible, his own problems with the knowledge and power given him. Yet, divine help is often offered to mortal man who labors under the severe limitations of earth life. Every revelation from the Lord is for the increasing welfare of mankind. Always, however, men retain the right to accept or reject the offered gift. Membership in the Church itself is voluntary; is never forced upon a person. Nevertheless, such membership includes the acceptance of a series of principles and ordinances, among them the presence of a prophet to stand as the Lord's spokesman to the Church. When therefore, a Latter-day Saint yields adherence to the Prophet's advice, he merely uses the free agency which led him to membership in the Church. He does not thereby renounce his free agency; instead he reinforces his claim upon it. He follows the prophet because he chooses to do so in view of the doctrine and constitution of the Church in which he voluntarily claims membership. When he fails to give his consent to the prophet's teachings, he limits, reduces, and removes the free agency which brought him into the Church.

In the daily lives of Latter-day Saints it is best to listen carefully to the counsel of the prophet concerning any subject upon which he speaks, whether technically official or unofficial. Note the words of Brigham Young:

> The Lord Almighty leads this Church, and He will not suffer you to be led astray if you are found doing your duty. You may go home and sleep as sweetly as a babe in its mother's arms, as to any danger of your leaders leading you astray, for if they should try to do so the Lord would quickly sweep them from the earth. Your leaders are trying to live their religion as far as they are capable of doing so. (*Discourses of Brigham Young*, p. 212)

That is as true today as in the days of President Young.

4. DID THE NEPHITES HAVE THE HIGHER PRIESTHOOD BEFORE THE COMING OF CHRIST?

There is no direct answer to this question in the Book of Mormon. Yet, the events recorded in the Nephite scriptures indicate that the Higher Priesthood was among the Nephites prior to the coming of Christ.

The Nephites were descendants of Manasseh, the son of Joseph of Egypt. (Book of Mormon, 1 Nephi 5:14-16; Alma 10:3) The Nephite Priesthood therefore differed from the Levitical Priesthood which was assigned to the sons of Levi, the brother of Joseph.

Lehi, father of the Nephites, held the Priesthood, for, while yet in the wilderness, he and his family offered sacrifice and burnt offerings, priestly ordinances of the Church before the coming of Christ. (1 Nephi 5:9) Nephi, the son of Lehi, also held the Priesthood, probably conferred by his father. Nephi in turn ordained two of his brothers, Jacob and Joseph, to the Priesthood. "They should be priests and teachers over the land of my people." (2 Nephi 5:26) The elder and younger Alma (Alma 5:3), several of the latter's sons, and Nephi, the son of Helaman, together with many others, some of whom are not mentioned by name, held the Priesthood even to the coming of Christ. (2 Nephi 18:2; 25:4; Alma 30:20, 23; 46:38) At no time, it would seem, were the Nephites without the Priesthood.

It would appear that not every man held the Priesthood, yet it must have been rather widely distributed. Mosiah records that there was "one priest to every fifty of their number." (Mosiah 18:18) Every Church unit was presided over by the Priesthood. (Mosiah 25:21)

The nature of the Nephite Priesthood is gathered from various statements made by Book of Mormon characters. Jacob, the brother of Nephi, declared that he had been "called of God, and ordained after the manner of his holy order." (2 Nephi 6:2) Alma, the younger, says, "I am called . . . according to the holy order of God, which is in Christ Jesus" (Alma 5:44), and he later states that he confined himself wholly to the High Priesthood of "the holy order of God." (Alma 49:30) This holy order was "after the order of his Son." (Alma 13:2; Helaman 8:18) The "holy order of God," especially when coupled with the order of the Son of God, has always been held to refer to the Melchizedek or High Priesthood. (D. & C. 77:11; 84:19)

Alma was a high priest. (Alma 8:23) His sons were ordained high priests, and also many others. (Alma 46:6; Helaman 3:25) Since there were many Nephite high priests, this office in the Priesthood could not refer to the one high priest, of the order of Aaron, required to stand at the head of the Lesser Priesthood. It is clear that Alma cited in his famous sermon (Alma 13) the story of earlier high priests of the Melchizedek order, to explain and to emphasize his own calling. The existence of numerous high priests is thus another evidence that the Higher Priesthood was among the Nephites.

Under the authority of the Priesthood, the Nephites performed baptisms from the days of the first Nephi. (Mosiah 18:13-16; Alma 5:3; 15:13; 48:19) Now, baptism is by itself an incomplete ordinance. Its full value comes when it is followed by the reception of the gift of the Holy Ghost. Numerous references in the Book of Mormon indicate that the Holy Ghost was received by those who had been baptized. For example: "The gate by which ye should enter is repentance and baptism by water; and then cometh a remission of your sins by fire and by the Holy Ghost." (2 Nephi 31:17) "He that is baptized . . . him will the Father give the Holy Ghost . . . baptism of fire and of the Holy Ghost." (2 Nephi 31:12, 14) Alma likewise says that he had labored "without ceasing" to bring souls unto repentance "that they might also be born of God, and be filled with the Holy Ghost." (Alma 36:24)

The ordinance of baptism could be administered by holders of the Lesser Priesthood (priests), but the conferring of the Holy Ghost requires the authority of the Higher Priesthood. Again the conclusion seems warranted that the Nephites had the Higher Priesthood.

President Brigham H. Roberts came to the same conclusion in his comprehensive study of the Book of Mormon. He says:

> Lehi held the Priesthood, . . . the higher priesthood, which was after the order of Melchizedek, and was a prophet and minister of righteousness. This, Lehi conferred upon his son, Nephi; and Nephi, shortly after his separation from his elder brothers on the land of promise, consecrated his two younger brothers, Jacob and Joseph, to be priests and teachers unto his people. (Roberts, *New Witnesses for God*, Vol. 2, p. 219)

Undoubtedly, various offices in the Priesthood were recognized by the Nephites. Teachers, priests, and high priests are specifically mentioned in the Book of Mormon. The terms teachers and priests probably refer to offices in the Lesser Priesthood; and the term high priest to an office in the Higher Priesthood. The Priesthood organization of the Nephites may not have been just as it is today, but it was such as to meet the needs of the people of that day. The Priesthood itself was, of course, the same.

5. WHO IS ELIAS AND WHAT IS HIS MISSION?

At the dedication of the Kirtland Temple in April, 1836, several ancient prophets appeared and delivered their keys of authority to Joseph Smith and Oliver Cowdery. Among these worthies was Elias, who "committed the dispensation of the gospel of Abraham, saying that in us and our seed all generations after us should be blessed." (D. & C. 110:12; see also, Matthew 17:1-13) From this reference to "the *dispensation* of the gospel of Abraham," it has been concluded that Elias was a prophet who lived near the time of the patriarch, Abraham. Really, nothing more definite is known about the person Elias and his activity on earth. It is very evident that he was a personage of importance, for he held the "keys" of authority in a mission of vital importance in carrying out on earth the plan of salvation.

More is known about the nature of the mission of Elias. In a revelation to the Prophet, in August, 1830, it is stated that the Lord has committed to Elias "the keys of bringing to pass the *restoration* of all things spoken by the mouth of all the holy prophets since the world began, concerning the last days." (D. & C. 27:6) In the same revelation it is stated that the angel who visited Zacharias, the father of John the Baptist, promised "that he should have a son, and his name should be John, and he should be filled with the spirit of Elias." (D. & C. 26:7; see also, Luke 1:17) Now, it has been made clear from a later revelation that the mission of John was "to prepare them [the Jews and others] for the coming of the Lord." (D. & C. 84:28; see also, Luke 1:5-17; John 1:19-28) It is concluded from this and other passages (D. & C. 77:9, 14) that the mission and spirit of the prophet Elias are to do the necessary preparatory work whenever the gospel dispensation or period is about to be opened. This is in full accord with the teachings of the Prophet Joseph Smith that "The spirit of Elias is to prepare the way for a greater revelation of God, which is the Priesthood of Elias, or the Priesthood that Aaron was ordained unto. And when God sends a man into the world to prepare for a greater work, holding the keys of the power of Elias, it was called the doctrine of

Elias. . . ." (*Teachings of the Prophet Joseph Smith*, pp. 335, 336)

This understanding of the mission and spirit of Elias has led many writers, ancient and modern, to speak of any person charged with preparatory work, one who goes before, as an Elias. Thus, John the Baptist was an Elias in his work as a forerunner of the Christ. Similarly, each personage, from Moroni to those appearing in the Kirtland Temple, who introduced the present, last dispensation of the gospel, may be spoken of as an Elias. Elias, then, is often used as a title, as the titles of bishop, prophet, or president are used, betokening a special position, mission, service, power, or authority. With this in mind, many otherwise obscure scriptural passages may be understood. (D. & C. 77:9, 14; Revelation 7:2, 3; 10:1-11)

The names Elijah and Elias are but variations of one original name. Therefore, in many languages these names are translated alike, as Elias. This has tended to confuse many gospel students who do not use English Bibles as to the personality of Elias. Indeed, Elias and Elijah have been made to appear as one person. Yet it should not be so, for many different men in various historical periods may have borne the same name. For example, the Baptist and the Revelator were both named John.

We do know that Elias was a mighty man of God charged in his day with a most important mission. We know also that any man who may be called to prepare the way for the consummation of the Lord's purposes is engaged in the mission of Elias, and therefore may be called an Elias.

It should be said that some students believe that Elias who appeared in the Kirtland Temple was Noah, the patriarch. Modern revelation informs us that Elias visited Zacharias to inform him that he should have a son known later as John the Baptist. (D. & C. 27:7) The Bible says that it was the angel Gabriel who visited Zacharias. (Luke 1:19) Joseph Smith said that Gabriel is Noah. These students conclude, therefore, that Elias is another name or title for Noah. This inference may or may not be correct. The name Gabriel may be borne by more than one personage or it may be a title as in the case of Elias. When Elias, the man, lived, and what he did in his life, must for the present remain in the field of conjecture.

6. WHO ARE THE SONS OF LEVI, AND WHAT IS THEIR FUTURE OFFERING IN RIGHTEOUSNESS?

The sons of Levi are the male members of the tribe of Levi, descendants of Levi, the third son of the patriarch, Jacob.

While ancient Israel journeyed in the Sinaitic wilderness, they showed themselves unworthy to hold the higher or Melchizedek Priesthood. Consequently the Lord took this Priesthood from them, but allowed the lesser Priesthood to remain. (D. & C. 84:23-37)

This lesser Priesthood that remained was confined to the male members of the tribe of Levi; therefore, it is often spoken of as the Levitical Priesthood. Aaron, of the tribe of Levi, and his sons, were called to the office of priest, that is to the presidency of this Priesthood; therefore, it is also called the Aaronic Priesthood. The organization of the lesser Priesthood under the Mosaic dispensation must have been much like that of this day. Aaron and his sons served in offices similar to the priests and were so specifically designated. The other male members of the tribe of Levi served in offices similar to the teachers and deacons of this dispensation of the gospel. This seems to be borne out by the words of the Lord to Moses when the Levitical organization was perfected:

> . . . from twenty and five years old and upward they shall go in and wait upon the service of the tabernacle of the congregation:
>
> And from the age of fifty years they shall cease waiting upon the service thereof, and shall serve no more:
>
> But shall minister with their brethren in the tabernacle of the congregation, to keep the charge, and shall do no service. (Numbers 8:24-26)

The presiding priest, called the high priest, probably served as does the presiding bishop of our times. This is the view taken by President John Taylor. (*Items on Priesthood*)

The activities of the lesser Priesthood among ancient Israel were designated to meet the needs and conditions then existing. The law of bloody sacrifice or burnt offerings, in witness of the coming Savior, was in operation from this time until the coming of Jesus, the Christ. The Levites performed the labors and ordinances pertaining to this law. Explicit directions for the duties of the Levites are found in the Books of Moses. In course of time, the ordinances under the Levitical law became largely corrupted and unacceptable to the Lord. Only a few of the Levites held the true authority of the Priesthood. At the coming of the Savior, John the Baptist held the keys of the Aaronic Priesthood, that is, he was the presiding officer of that Priesthood.

On May 15, 1829, this John the Baptist appeared to Joseph Smith and Oliver Cowdery, and conferred upon them the "Priesthood of Aaron," that is, the keys of the lesser Priesthood. In so doing he declared that this Priesthood "shall never be taken again from the earth, until the sons of Levi do offer again an offering unto the Lord in righteousness." (D. & C. 13)

It does not seem probable that this offering will be a burnt offering. The coming of Christ ended the Mosaic law. The earlier sacrifices were in similitude of the coming sacrifice of Jesus, the Christ. After His crucifixion, death, and resurrection, the sacrament was instituted to keep His sacrifice in constant living memory.

It seems more probable that the "offering in righteousness," which will terminate the functions of the sons of Levi under the Levitical Priesthood, will be the full acceptance of the gospel, when their Priesthood will come under the direction of the higher or Melchizedek Priesthood.

This view seems borne out by Latter-day revelation. In the Doctrine and Covenants, section 84, verse 27, it is stated that this Priesthood the Lord caused "to continue with the house of Aaron among the children of Israel *until John.*" This suggests a termination with the coming of Christ. In section 124, verse 39, where the work of the modern temples is summarized, "*memorials* for your sacrifices by the sons of Levi" are mentioned as part of the temple service. No provision has been made in the temples for the ancient type of burnt offerings, and the word memorials would seem to exclude such an interpretation. A more explicit suggestion is found in section 128:

> For he is like a refiner's fire, and like fuller's soap; and he shall sit as a refiner and purifier of silver, and he shall purify the sons of

Levi, and purge them as gold and silver, that they may offer unto the Lord an offering in righteousness. Let us, therefore, as a church and a people, and as Latter-day Saints, offer unto the Lord an offering in righteousness; and let us present in his holy temple, when it is finished, a book containing the records of our dead, which shall be worthy of all acceptation. (D. & C. 128:24)

The "offering in righteousness" is here identified with temple work for the salvation of the dead, which encompasses all the principles of the plan of salvation.

When, therefore, the sons of Levi accept Christ and His gospel, subject themselves to the ordinances of the Church, and become active in gospel requirements, they will offer the offering in righteousness of which has been spoken.

Though the type of sacrifice connected with the Levitical Priesthood is no more, yet the law of sacrifice remains. The Prophet Joseph Smith made it clear that sacrifice is ever a part of the gospel. In the restored Church, this law is in full operation. None can retain the spirit of the gospel unless he gives to the cause of the Lord of himself, of his substance, time and strength. (Joseph Smith, *History of the Church*, 4:207-212)

7. WHO IS THE MAN LIKE UNTO MOSES?

In the early days of the Church, persecution raged against the Saints in Jackson County, Missouri. For the comfort of the people, the Lord gave several revelations. In one He promised, "I will raise up unto my people a man, who shall lead them like as Moses led the children of Israel." (D. & C. 103:16) There have been many conjectures concerning this statement. There have even been misguided men who have declared themselves to be this man "like as Moses."

Yet, the meaning as set forth in the scriptures, is very simple. In modern revelation the President of the Church is frequently compared to Moses. Soon after the organization of the Church, the Lord said, "no one shall be appointed to receive commandments and revelations in this church excepting my servant Joseph Smith, Jun., for he receiveth them even as Moses." (D. & C. 28:2) In one of the great revelations upon Priesthood, this is more specifically expressed: "the duty of the President of the office of the High Priesthood is to preside over the whole church, and to be like unto Moses." (D. & C. 107:91)

The discussion of this question among the Saints, led to the following statement in the *Times and Seasons* (6:922) by John Taylor, then the editor: "The President [of the Church] stands in the Church as Moses did to the children of Israel, according to the revelations."

The man like unto Moses in the Church is the President of the Church.

8. WHICH IS GREATER—PRIESTHOOD OR THE CHURCH?

According to John Taylor, third President of the Church, priesthood "... is the power of God delegated to intelligences in the heavens and to man on earth."[1] This definition has been confirmed by the leaders of the Church. For example, Joseph F. Smith, sixth president of the Church, said that: "It is nothing more nor less than the power of God delegated to man by which man can act in the earth for the salvation of the human family."[2] Under this definition nothing can be greater than priesthood. Nothing can transcend the power of God. All things must be the product of that power.

Of course, man does not possess all of God's power. Enough has been bestowed upon him to perform every work connected with the plan of salvation for the human family. On earth, man needs no more.

However, whenever the Church of Christ exists on earth, all priesthood activity operates within the Church. Only when the Church does not exist on earth, can men hold the priesthood "at large." The moment the Church is organized, all holders of the priesthood can use their priesthood only under the authority and direction of the Church. That is, at no time when the Church is organized can there be on earth two classes of priesthood bearers: those who use their power within the Church; and those who use it outside the Church.

In fact, the Church is a product of priesthood, and can be organized only by those who hold the priesthood. It is the instrument through which priesthood operates. In a true sense, on earth, priesthood and the Church are as one—neither can function without the other.

This was clearly set forth in the beginning of the restored Church of Christ. On May 15, 1829, before the Church was organized, Joseph Smith and Oliver Cowdery were ordained by the resurrected John the Baptist, to the authority of the Aaronic or Lesser Priesthood. Under that authority they were then baptized. A short time later, the resurrected

---

[1]*The Gospel Kingdom,* edited by G. Homer Durham, p. 129.

[2]*Gospel Doctrine,* p. 173 (first to fourth editions); 239 (fifth edition ff.).

apostles, Peter, James, and John, conferred the Melchizedek, or Higher Priesthood, upon the young men. They were now baptized and had been given all necessary priesthood power, all that the Lord has seen fit to confer upon anyone on earth.

But the Church of Christ had not yet been organized. Therefore, about this same time the Lord instructed Joseph and Oliver to organize the Church of Christ. This they were to do under the authority of the priesthood conferred upon them. However, it was made clear that when the Church was organized both of these young men must be baptized into the Church, and ordained elders in the Church. The instructions were explicit.[3]

This was actually accomplished, for on April 6, 1830, the Church was organized. The six organizers, including Joseph Smith and Oliver Cowdery, were baptized into the Church, confirmed members of the Church, received the gift of the Holy Ghost, and ordained to an office in the priesthood.

"I then laid my hands upon Oliver Cowdery, and ordained him an Elder of the 'Church of Jesus Christ of Latter-day Saints'; after which he ordained me also to the office of an Elder of said Church.

". . . We now proceeded to call out and ordain some others of the brethren to different offices of the Priesthood, according as the Spirit manifested unto us."

The baptism and ordinations already received, empowered Joseph and Oliver, under God's command, to organize the Church. But, thenceforth their power and authority could be exercised only within the Church, and under its authority and direction. Thenceforth the priesthood would be conferred only by the Church. No one in mortality could exercise priesthood rights outside the Church.

Thus, without the priesthood there can be no Church; without the Church, there can be no priesthood in full operation on earth. Priesthood and the Church are as one, inseparable. Therefore, the question as to the relative importance of priesthood and the Church has no meaning for mortal man.

There are those, who having been excommunicated from the Church, believe that they yet retain the priesthood which

---

[3]See *Documentary History of the Church,* vol. 1, pp. 60-61.

they received under Church authority. That is folly. Whatever has been received under Church authority is taken from a man when he is cut off from the Church. Only the memory remains to vex his soul.

9. WHAT IS THE OATH AND COVENANT OF THE PRIESTHOOD?

In the fall of 1832, meetings were held in Kirtland, Ohio, to hear the reports of groups of missionaries who had recently returned from the eastern states. These elders were filled with the spirit of their work. They had preached the doctrine of the restored gospel; they had been successful in bringing souls to a knowledge of the truth; their hearts were filled with joy.

Under the influence of the missionary spirit, they had glimpsed the vast meaning of the Lord's plan of salvation for the human family. As their fervent testimonies were borne, many gospel questions were asked. Especially were these ambassadors of truth concerned with the priesthood, under the authority of which they had labored—its history, extent, and power.

The Prophet Joseph Smith inquired of the Lord, and received, on September 22 and 23, one of the great revelations on priesthood, now known as section 84 of the Doctrine and Covenants. While the Prophet called it a revelation on priesthood, it goes beyond the technical limits of the subject, and discusses many related or cognate items. The Lord then, as now, gave more than was asked for.

After discussing the history and offices of the two divisions of the priesthood, the Aaronic and Melchizedek, the revelation continues:

> For whoso is faithful unto the obtaining these two priesthoods of which I have spoken, and the magnifying their calling, are sanctified by the Spirit unto the renewing of their bodies.
>
> They become the sons of Moses and of Aaron and the seed of Abraham, and the church and kingdom, and the elect of God.
>
> And also all they who receive this priesthood receive me, saith the Lord;
>
> For he that receiveth my servants receiveth me;
>
> And he that receiveth me receiveth my Father;
>
> And he that receiveth my Father receiveth my Father's kingdom; therefore all that my Father hath shall be given unto him.
>
> And this is according to the oath and covenant which belongeth to the priesthood.

> Therefore, all those who receive the priesthood, receive this oath and covenant of my Father, which he cannot break, neither can it be moved.[5]

These words clearly refer to the covenant which the Lord makes with all who receive the priesthood worthily, and who attempt to magnify it in their lives. "All that my Father hath shall be given unto him"—the worthy priesthood bearer.

Wilford Woodruff, fourth president of the Church, speaking upon this revelation commented upon the greatness of the promises made to faithful priesthood bearers.

> I often reflect upon the promises made concerning the priesthood, . . . Now, I sometimes ask myself the question, Do we comprehend these things? Do we comprehend that if we abide the laws of the priesthood we shall become heirs of God and joint-heirs with Jesus Christ?—Who in the name of the Lord can apprehend such language as this? Who can comprehend that, by obeying the celestial law, all that our Father has shall be given unto us—exaltations, thrones, principalities, power, dominion—who can comprehend it? Nevertheless it is here stated.[6]

However, a covenant concerns two persons. Both parties must do something to make the covenant effective. That principle is in full operation in the oath and covenant of the priesthood. He who receives the priesthood covenants to magnify his calling in the priesthood. That makes the covenant valid. That is too often forgotten.

The revelation sets this forth clearly. A man who has received the priesthood and then fails to use it is a covenant breaker, subject to punishment.

> But whoso breaketh this covenant after he hath received it, and altogether turneth therefrom, shall not have forgiveness of sins in this world nor in the world to come.[7]

That makes it a most serious offense to dishonor the priesthood by not using it in the building of the Lord's latter-day kingdom.

* * * *

The oath and covenant of the priesthood is between man and God. The Lord promises him great blessings if he magnifies the priesthood he receives. The man in turn, when

---

[5]D. & C. 84:33-40.

[6]G. Homer Durham, *The Discourses of Wilford Woodruff*, pp. 79, 80.

[7]D. & C. 84:41.

he receives the priesthood, promises that he will honor the priesthood received, by magnifying it.

Every ordination to the priesthood implies this covenant between man and God, whether so stated or not. It would be well, if in all priesthood ordinations the oath and covenant of the priesthood were explained. Too many priesthood bearers feel that they have been given something without a corresponding promise by themselves. They forget too often that every ordinance in the gospel is accompanied by a covenant between God and man. We are a covenant people.

10. IN THE EVENT OF THE DEATH OF THE PRESIDENT OF THE CHURCH, WHY DOES THE COUNCIL OF THE TWELVE APOSTLES TAKE OVER THE PRESIDENCY OF THE CHURCH?

The Twelve Apostles "form a quorum, equal in authority and power" to the First Presidency. (D. & C. 107:23, 24)

This doctrine was amplified in a revelation concerning the Twelve Apostles:

> For unto you, the Twelve, and those, the First Presidency, who are appointed with you to be your counselors and your leaders, is the power of this priesthood given, for the last days and for the last time, in the which is the dispensation of the fulness of times.
>
> Which power you hold, in connection with all those who have received a dispensation at any time from the beginning of the creation; For verily I say unto you, the keys of the dispensation, which ye have received, have come down from the fathers, and last of all, being sent down from heaven unto you. (D. & C. 112:30-32)

This authority of the quorum of the Twelve Apostles was frequently referred to by the Prophet Joseph Smith. He said: [I] "next proceeded to explain the duty of the Twelve, and their authority which is next to the present Presidency." (Joseph Smith, *History of the Church* 2:373) Later he said: "The time has come when the Twelve should be called upon to stand in their place next to the First Presidency." (*Times and Seasons* 2:521) He also said to the Twelve Apostles: "Now, if they kill me, you have all the keys, and all the ordinances, and you can confer them upon others, and the hosts of Satan will not be able to tear down the Kingdom as fast as you will be able to build it up; and upon your shoulders will the responsibility of leading this people rest." (*Times and Seasons* 5:651)

The counselors in the presidency lose their presiding authority when the President of the Church dies. In the words of the Prophet: "The Twelve are not subject to any other than the First Presidency, . . . and where I am not, there is no First Presidency over the Twelve." (Joseph Smith *History of the Church* 2:374)

11. WHAT IS THE MEANING OF THE TITLE, "PROPHET, SEER, AND REVELATOR"?

The President of the Church is sustained by the people as "Prophet, Seer, and Revelator, and President of the Church of Jesus Christ of Latter-day Saints." This is in compliance with the revealed word of God. The first revelation received by Joseph Smith after the organization of the Church on April 6, 1830, specifically declares that "there shall be a record kept among you; and in it thou shalt be called a seer, a translator, a prophet, an apostle of Jesus Christ, an elder of the church through the will of God the Father, and the grace of your Lord Jesus Christ." (D. & C. 21:1)

This was reiterated by revelation in 1835: "the President of the office of the High Priesthood is to preside over the whole church, . . . yea, to be a seer, a revelator, a translator, and a prophet, having all the gifts of God which he bestows upon the head of the church." (D. & C. 107:91, 92) and was further restated in 1841: "I give upon you my servant Joseph to be a presiding elder over all my church, to be a translator, a revelator, a seer, and a prophet." (D. & C. 124:125)

In current practice, the word "translator" is omitted, since should records appear needing translation, the President of the Church may at any time be called, through revelation, to the special labor of translation.

The counselors to the President and the Council of the Twelve Apostles and, usually, the Patriarch to the Church, are also sustained as "prophets, seers, and revelators." This conforms to the Priesthood conferred upon them, and to their official calling in the Church. That others than the president may hold these exalted titles also conforms to the revealed word of God. For example, speaking of Hyrum Smith: "I appoint unto him that he may be a prophet, and a seer, and a revelator unto my church." (D. & C. 124:94)

On March 27, 1836, at the dedication of the Kirtland Temple the authorities of the Church were sustained:

> I [Joseph Smith] made a short address, and called upon the several quorums, and all the congregation of Saints, to acknowledge

the Presidency as Prophets and Seers and uphold them by their prayers. . . . I then called upon the quorums and congregation of Saints to acknowledge the Twelve, who were present, as Prophets, Seers, Revelators, and special witnesses to all the nations of the earth holding the keys of the kingdom, to unlock it, or cause it to be done, among them, and uphold them by their prayers. (Joseph Smith, *History of the Church,* 2:417)

When others besides the President of the Church hold the title "prophet, seer, and revelator," it follows that the "power and authority" thus represented are called into action only by appointment from the President of the Church, otherwise there might be a conflict of authority. This is well illustrated in the practice of the Church. For example, a man may be ordained a High Priest, an office in which the right of presidency is inherent, but he presides only when called to do so. It is even so with the exercise of authority under these sacred titles.

The three separate titles in the general title have much the same meaning in popular usage, yet there are differences sufficiently important to justify their use.

A prophet is a teacher. That is the essential meaning of the word. He teaches the body of truth, the gospel, revealed by the Lord to man; and under inspiration explains it to the understanding of the people. He is an expounder of truth. Moreover, he shows that the way to human happiness is through obedience to God's law. He calls to repentance those who wander away from the truth. He becomes a warrior for the consummation of the Lord's purposes with respect to the human family. The purpose of his life is to uphold the Lord's plan of salvation. All this he does by close communion with the Lord, until he is "full of power by the spirit of the Lord." (Micah 3:8; see also D. & C. 20:26; 34:10; 43:16)

The teacher must learn before he can teach. Therefore, in ancient and modern times there have been schools of the prophets, in which the mysteries of the kingdom have been taught to men who would go out to teach the gospel and to fight the battles of the Lord. These "prophets" need not be called to an office; they go out as teachers of truth, always and everywhere.

In the course of time the word "prophet" has come to mean, perhaps chiefly, a man who receives revelations, and directions from the Lord. The principal business of a prophet has mistakenly been thought to foretell coming events, to utter prophecies, which is only one of the several prophetic functions.

In the sense that a prophet is a man who receives revelations from the Lord, the titles "seer and revelator" merely amplify the larger and inclusive meaning of the title "prophet." Clearly, however, there is much wisdom in the specific statement of the functions of the prophet as seer and revelator, as is done in the conferences of the Church.

A prophet also receives revelations from the Lord. These may be explanations of truths alreadv received, or new truths not formerly possessed by man. Such revelations are always confined to the official position held. The lower will not receive revelations for the higher office.

A seer is one who sees with spiritual eyes. He perceives the meaning of that which seems obscure to others; therefore he is an interpreter and clarifier of eternal truth. He foresees the future from the past and the present. This he does by the power of the Lord operating through him directly, or indirectly with the aid of divine instruments such as the Urim and Thummim. In short, he is one who sees, who walks in the Lord's light with open eyes. (Book of Mormon, Mosiah 8:15-17)

A revelator makes known, with the Lord's help, something before unknown. It may be new or forgotten truth, or a new or forgotten application of known truth to man's need. Always, the revelator deals with truth, certain truth (D. & C. 100:11) and always it comes with the divine stamp of approval. Revelation may be received in various ways, but it always presupposes that the revelator has so lived and conducted himself as to be in tune or harmony with the divine spirit of revelation, the spirit of truth, and therefore capable of receiving divine messages.

In summary: A prophet is a teacher of known truth; a seer is a perceiver of hidden truth, a revelator is a bearer of new truth. In the widest sense, the one most commonly used, the title, prophet, includes the other titles and makes of the prophet, a teacher, perceiver, and bearer of truth.

One who bears the title of prophet, and they who sustain him as such, are first of all believers in God, and in a divine plan of salvation for the human family; and, secondly, they commit themselves to the task of bringing to pass the purposes of the Almighty. They believe that the children of men are capable of receiving and obeying truth. Were it not so, the title "prophet, seer, and revelator" would be empty, hollow words. As it is, they are clarion calls of the Church of Christ to a world walking in the dim shadows of misunderstanding.

12. WHO IS PRESIDENT OF THE "TWELVE"?

The members of the Council of the Twelve are of equal priesthood authority. Yet when they meet in their deliberations one is called to act as chairman or President.

Since these men are of equal priesthood authority, it might be thought that any one of them might be called to the presidential office. Under the practice of the Church, based upon the latter-day revelations of the Lord, this is not done. Instead, the senior member of the council, that is, the one who has held the apostleship longest, is appointed and sustained as the President of the Council of the Twelve Apostles.

The members of the first apostolic quorum in this day, all called at the same time, were arranged according to their ages. Elder Thomas B. Marsh became the senior member and President of the Council, but apostatized and was excommunicated from the Church.[8] That left Brigham Young the ranking Apostle.

The position of Brigham Young as President of the Council of Twelve was confirmed by the Lord in a revelation given January 19, 1841.[9] This was little more than three years before the martyrdom of Joseph Smith. During these years Joseph was moved upon by the Lord to set up securely the order of organization within the Church. The presidency of the Twelve was not forgotten.

In this revelation the main priesthood officers of the Church are presented to the Church for their acceptance. After presenting the Patriarch, and the President with his two counselors, the President of the Council of Twelve is presented, in the following words: "I give unto you my servant Brigham Young to be a president over the twelve traveling council."[10] The names of the members of the Council are later given, thus preventing any misunderstanding.

Since that time there has been no deviation from the rule that the senior member should preside over the Council. In the troublesome days following the death of the Prophet,

-----

[8]*D.H.C.*, II:248.
[9]D. & C. 124.
[10]D. & C. 124:127.

Brigham Young became the President of the Council, which, until a new President was chosen, presided over the Church. When finally the Lord moved upon the Council to reorganize the First Presidency, Brigham Young, then President of the Council of Twelve, was called to be President of the Church.[11]

This order of succession to the presidency of the Council of Twelve, and to the presidency of the Church has been followed, and will continue to be the rule of the Church until the Lord speaks and commands another procedure.

When Brigham Young became President of the Church, Elder Orson Hyde, a member of the original Quorum of Twelve Apostles, was sustained as President of the Council of Twelve.[12] He was so sustained for many years. However, one fact had been overlooked. In October 1838, Orson Hyde, then just recovering from a serious illness, had yielded to the importunities of Thomas B. Marsh to sign a vicious paper against Joseph Smith. Brother Hyde was promptly cut off from the Church, and of course lost his apostleship.[13] The charges against the Prophet were, however, shown to be unfounded. Brother Hyde repented and was restored to his position as an Apostle on June 27, 1839.[14] This incident made Brother Hyde a junior rather than a senior member of the Council. In matters of seniority, in case of an excommunication, the length of service dates from the time of re-entry, should they occur, into the Quorum. When this matter was considered by the First Presidency and the Council of the Twelve, John Taylor assumed the presidency of the Council.[15]

President Heber J. Grant succeeded President Joseph F. Smith as President of the Church in 1918. In the Council of Twelve at that time the next in order of seniority was Anthon H. Lund, who was serving as a counselor in the presidency of the Church. An Apostle does not surrender his rights in the Quorum of Apostles by being called to serve in the First Presidency. To preserve President Lund's rights in priesthood succession, he was sustained as President of the Twelve, though retaining his place in the First Presidency. Elder Rudger Clawson, the next ranking member of the Council,

[11] *D.H.C.* VII:621-623.

[12] *Journal History,* 6 April 1848.

[13] *D.H.C.* III:168 and *The Gospel Kingdom,* p. 188.

[14] *Ibid.,* III:379.

[15] *The Gospel Kingdom,* (John Taylor), pp. 182-194, G. Homer Durham, Ed.

was appointed acting president, and so served until President Lund's death when Elder Clawson became the President of the Council.

So runs the story of the presidency of the Twelve. The principle followed in the past will no doubt be followed in the future, except as the Lord may speak and command changes. It is well for Latter-day Saints to understand these matters as they pertain to the Quorum of the Twelve upon which lies the responsibility of maintaining the presidential leadership of the Church.

13. HOW IS A PRESIDENT OF THE CHURCH CHOSEN?

After the martyrdom of Joseph Smith, there were several contenders for the position of President or "guardian" of the Church. With the sustaining vote of the people, the Council of Twelve Apostles took over the leadership of the Church. Since that day, at the demise of the President, the Twelve have become the presiding body.

That the Council of the Twelve actually hold the necessary "authority and power" was frequently set forth in the days of the Prophet Joseph Smith and his successors. For example, in a revelation concerning the Council of the Twelve, given in 1837, the following statement is made:

"For unto you, the Twelve, and those, the First Presidency, who are appointed with you to be your counselors and your leaders, is the power of this priesthood given, for the last days and for the last time, in the which is the dispensation of the fulness of times." (D. & C. 112:30)

On several occasions this vital relationship between the Presidency and the Twelve was referred to by the Prophet. He said, "[I] . . . next proceeded to explain the duty of the Twelve, and their authority, which is next to the Presidency." (*D. H. C.*, 2:373) Shortly before his death the Prophet said, "The time has come when the Twelve should be called upon to stand in their place next to the First Presidency." (*Times and Seasons*, 2:521) To the Twelve he said, "Now, if they kill me, you have got all the keys, and all the ordinances and you can confer them upon others, and the hosts of Satan will not be able to tear down the kingdom, as fast as you will be able to build it up; and on your shoulders will the responsibility of leading this people rest." (*Ibid.*, 5:651)

However, the Lord has revealed the order of the government of the Church. "Three Presiding High Priests . . . form a quorum of the Presidency of the Church." (D. & C. 107:22; see also 102:10; 124:125, 126.) In conformity with the revealed will of God, Joseph Smith Jr., was sustained January 25, 1832, as President of the Church, and on March 18, 1833, Sidney Rigdon and Frederick G. Williams were set apart as counselors to the Prophet. The Church is never fully organized if any of the quorums set up by the Lord is missing.

It would not be proper, therefore, for the Twelve to continue indefinitely to preside over the Church. Under the spirit of revelation they should proceed to appoint another President of the Church, who should select his counselors. These actions then should be acknowledged "by the voice of the church" (*Ibid.*, 102:9, 10)

The revelations do not say directly who shall be chosen President of the Church. When the First Presidency was organized three years after the death of the Prophet, on December 27, 1847, the senior apostle and president of the Council of the Twelve, Brigham Young, was appointed. Since his day, whenever the First Presidency has been disorganized by death, the president of the Twelve has succeeded to the Presidency. (Before a U. S. Senate investigating committee, in the Smoot case, President Joseph F. Smith testified as follows: "It has been the custom, since the death of Joseph Smith, that the president of the Twelve succeed to the Presidency of the Church. . . . It is just simply a custom."

This is a wise procedure. It places at the head of the Church the apostle who has been longest in service. He is known well to the people and trusted by them. He himself knows the procedure of Church affairs. He is no novice to be trained for the position. He can call to his assistance, in addition to his counselors, any helpers from among the priesthood of the Church. It eliminates the shadow of politics from the operations of the Council.

Should there be any deviation from the practices of the past, it would come by revelation to the President of the Twelve, who by virtue of his presidency, holds the keys of authority committed to this quorum of the priesthood. However, President Woodruff declared that in his opinion, the President of the council would never be set aside for someone else in appointing a president of the Church. (Cowley, *Wilford Woodruff*, p. 561.)

Moreover, it has been found that a long interval of presidency by the Twelve is not for the best interests of the Church. Therefore, since the days of President John Taylor, the selection has been made within a few days after the death of the President.

On Tuesday, May 15, 1945, the day after President Grant died, the Twelve assembled as the presiding authority of the Church, to arrange for the funeral, and to consider other matters. On the following Monday, the quorum met again, fasting and praying, and moved upon by the spirit of revelation, called Elder George Albert Smith to the position of First Elder, Prophet, Seer, and Revelator to the Church. This action was, of course, in due time confirmed by the Church.

The Lord has so provided safeguards, that the continuity of his Church cannot be broken. Should all the Twelve disappear, there remain the First Quorum of the Seventy to carry on. Should the members of this quorum vanish from mortal life, the standing high councils of the stakes would remain to carry on. And should they be destroyed, the priesthood would yet remain, and the Lord would call upon a remaining elder to go forth to reorganize the Church according to the divine pattern. Indeed, the restored Church is a marvelous work and a wonder. (D. & C. 107:22-26, 36, 37; *Discourses of Brigham Young*, 1941 edition, page 128.)

VIII. Freedom Versus Organization and the Church

1. ARE THE LATTER-DAY SAINTS A FREE PEOPLE?

The right to choose for himself what he will believe and do is the choicest possession of every intelligent man and woman. The unhindered exercise of this right is freedom.

In Latter-day Saint terminology this is the right of free agency, which is valued above all else, for it insures a membership which thinks and acts for itself and stands upon its own convictions and conclusions. Because of this basic law, the Church is diametrically opposed to tyranny or dictatorships of any form or under any name, that enslave the minds and actions of men. The Church seeks truth, and more truth, and believes that truth makes men free. And the Lord in these latter days has declared, ". . . Hear my voice and follow me, and you shall be a free people . . ." (D. & C. 38:22.)

Nevertheless, freedom operates under many conditions or limitations beyond the power of any one person. There are laws of nature, society, and God, which must always be taken into account in the exercise of free agency. Under the right of choice a person may oppose them or obey them. It is not possible to abrogate them; nor can they be ignored with safety.

A person may choose to jump from the mountain precipice to the jagged rocks below; or seize with naked hands the wires charged with high tension electric power; or cast himself into a living fire. The result is certain death. Or, he may decide to obey the laws of nature, and use them if he can. So he builds a parachute, to descend safely from the precipice; with insulated hands he makes the current do work for him; and he applies heat to confined water so that he may ride across the continent luxuriously in steam-driven trains. True freedom, in the midst of the multiplicity of natural forces, comes from conformity to law. Thereby, man becomes also the master of nature.

This principle is in equal operation in society. A person among his fellows, may think as he pleases; but in his actions he is limited. His inalienable right to free agency does not permit him to interfere with the same right of another individual. Even Robinson Crusoe had to consider his man Friday in all his actions. Therefore, a sound society sets up rules and regulations by which the right of freedom may be available to all people. To live happily in society these laws must be obeyed. If they are not the best laws, they may be improved; but while they do exist, they must be obeyed. Freedom in society waits only upon those who obey the laws of society.

The Church, though essentially an institution for freedom, exists under many laws that govern the right of choice. These are the commandments of God to his children on earth. The best laws enacted by and for society are based upon divine law, such, for example, as the Ten Commandments. The very value of the Church to man comes from these laws based upon the will of our Heavenly Father, which may limit our right of choice, but which are for our good, if we choose to obey them.

A person must exercise his right of choice when he enters the Church. The new convert is not baptized until he is well acquainted with the doctrine and practice of the Church. After he has been taught, he asks with open eyes for admission to Church membership. Children are likewise taught the meaning of the ordinance, before they are baptized at eight years of age.

This means that the candidate for baptism accepts of his own free will and choice all that the Church has to offer, and all that it requires. He accepts the organization, code of doctrine, and manner of living within the Church. As by the free exercise of his agency he seeks baptism, so by that agency he becomes subject to the order of life within the Church. The requirements of the Church are not in any sense infringements upon his right of choice. He has made his choice. The principles of truth upon which the Church rests must henceforth determine his actions and conduct in life.

In minor matters of Church regulations, when questions arise in his mind, he compares them with the basic truths he accepted in the waters of baptism, and judges them accordingly. He soon finds that every so-called Church requirement is for his good. For example, among other things, obedience to the Word of Wisdom yields health and spiritual power; the payment of tithing makes man master of selfish impulses, and a benefactor to others; and attendance at meetings feeds his spiritual nature. Every requirement, if obeyed, lifts man into higher realms of joy; helps him approach the likeness of God.

Political differences show the freedom of action of the Latter-day Saints. Political issues usually touch matters which are not of fundamental importance. Whether Smith or Jones shall be mayor; whether a road shall be built south or north, are not ordinarily questions of principle. Church members act freely in deciding upon such matters. Likewise, they choose, without interference, from time to time, their political party affiliations, as party platforms change. Should larger political problems arise, such as involve fundamental Church doctrine or practice, they would be solved simply by comparing them with the essential doctrines of the gospel. Latter-day Saint people are free, politically.

Another evidence of the freedom of Latter-day Saints is the manner in which all Church Authorities are sustained, whether general, stake, or ward. It is a law of the Church that all nominations for Church positions, or releases, must be made by the officers of the priesthood; but the men and women thus nominated must be confirmed by the people. Without such confirmation the nominees cannot act, and other choices must be made, as has occasionally happened. Therefore, at the conferences of the Church or Church divisions, officers are presented for the sustaining vote of the congregations; not only when the names are first proposed, but at regular, frequent intervals thereafter, to insure that the Church continues to be led by worthy men and women.

This is more than an ordinary vote. It is a sustaining vote, which means that we not only accept the people as our leaders, but also that we support them with our good will, help, and prayers. Every person may vote freely, for or against a name; and should do so according to his convictions. The voting is not a perfunctory act, but one of great importance.

However, if a member votes against a nominee or officer, it must be for some good reason. If for acts unworthy of a Latter-day Saint, charges should be filed against him in the courts of the Church by those who know of his errors; if the charges are substantiated, and no reconciliation is effected, the person may be removed from office. If the contrary vote is merely a distrust of the person's ability to perform the duties of the office, or because of personal dislike, nothing further need be done. The new officer will probably grow in fitness, if he has the good will, faith, and prayers of the people. Moreover, the history of the Church shows that under the power of the Lord, weak men are made strong, and strong men stronger, to the joy of all. Any personal dislike should, of course, be overcome. Learning to love our neighbor is a sure path to happiness. Meanwhile, the Latter-day Saints know and trust their leaders so well that they are nearly always willing to accept their nominations, and to give those nominated a chance to succeed in the office, which is not for life. The unanimous support of our Church officers is really an indication of the united feeling of the people to carry forward the latter-day work of the Lord.

That the Latter-day Saints are a free people is further emphasized by the treatment given those who fail to keep the promises implied in their baptism. They are not cast out, nor held in ill repute. Apostasy and immorality are the usual causes that lead to excommunication. The purpose of the Church is to save souls. They who are weak should be helped into strength, and they who are straying, into the correct path of life.

Those who prate about lack of freedom among Latter-day Saints, either do not understand the Church and its organization, or are trying to cover up their own weaknesses.

The feeling of the people of the Church is summed up in the words of a vigorous thinker, and faithful Latter-day Saint: If we were not a free people, I would not be a member of the Church.

2. IS THERE COERCION IN THE CHURCH?

Free agency is held by the Church to be the first of man's rights. Every human being should be free to act for himself. This doctrine is repeatedly stated in the revelations of God to man. "I . . . have given unto the children of men to be agents unto themselves." (D. & C. 104:17.) "For the power is in them, wherein they are agents unto themselves." (D. & C. 58:28.)

Brigham Young declared that:

> All rational beings have a volition of their own. . . . The volition of the creature is free. This is a law of their existence. (*Discourses of Brigham Young,* 1941 edition, p. 62)

Coercion, which is in direct opposition to free agency, must not be applied in any form. Under whatever name it may be practised, it is of the evil one. President Joseph F. Smith said:

> The freedom of the Latter-day Saints has never been curtailed . . . rather it has been enlarged (*Gospel Doctrine,* 1939 edition, p. 47)

There are, however, strict limitations placed upon the divinely established freedom of man. The man who jumps from the housetop will fall to the ground. Free agency does not cancel out the law of gravity. It merely determines whether the man shall make the jump or remain on the roof or descend in some other manner. That is the greatness of free agency. It gives power to conform to external law and thereby to benefit himself, or to oppose it and injure himself. This power, in the end, makes man the master of the universe about him.

The gospel consists of a series of immutable laws. Church membership cannot be obtained or retained without faith, repentance, baptism, and the gift of the Holy Ghost. That is not a violation of man's right of free agency. It is the recognition of eternal principles and ordinances. He decides for himself whether on these conditions he desires affiliation with the Church. Once he has decided, he must conform to that which he has accepted, or else be prepared to lose his Church membership. Free agency is primarily a matter of decision—how a man shall act in the midst of universal law.

Further, the free agent must always remember that all men have the same right of free agency. Therefore, there must be no trespassing upon the freedom of others. There must be no attempt to force even a needed gift upon another. It is better that one live in darkness than to be forced into light. There is ample place among men for teaching but none for compelling others to accept what is taught. Every person is under obligation to respect the free agency of every other individual. Had that principle been observed throughout the years, the world would have been spared its bloody wars and dark miseries.

The application of these principles to daily affairs sometimes leads to misunderstandings. Certain Church members may feel that a Church official is invading their personal liberties when he gives counsel. For example, the card player may say that the advice by successive Church Presidents against this form of amusement is an invasion of his right to act for himself. Advice on other matters of conduct by the constituted leadership of the Church may be questioned by those who are affected by the advice.

The first answer to such person is that all advice is given for the good of the individual concerned, and that it is wise to follow those who have had experience and are unselfishly giving help to others. Properly analyzed, counsel and Church regulations are for the benefit of the people. The Church which exists for the welfare of man, would be derelict to its divinely imposed obligations did it not exercise its responsibility as a guardian against all evil and for all good.

The second answer is that under the law of free agency no one is obliged to obey or disobey the counsel given. Man is always free to act for himself. But, to members of the Church, this answer may be misleading. They are under the necessity of acknowledging that consistency requires them to conform to counsel given and regulations set up.

The members of the Church are free men and women. That may be said safely. But their joy in the gospel depends greatly upon their faith in the inspiration guiding the Church. If that faith grows dim or vanishes, the way of life must be traveled alone, in darkness. That leaves man helpless. Conformity to authorized Church counsel and regulation, on the other hand, lights the path and gives man joy in the whole journey. Those who do so, soon grow in faith and understanding. And, it is really easy to choose to follow Church leadership, for nothing is required by the Church that does not in the end benefit humanity.

Members of the Church glory in their freedom to think and act for themselves. Converts to the Church have dared to break away from inherited beliefs. They who are born into the Church have upon their own volition accepted the gospel as their guide in life. Both classes have acted for themselves.

The spirit of man must not be fettered. Let a man believe as he chooses. That is gospel doctrine.

Naturally, therefore, Latter-day Saints look with horror upon the days of the inquisition, when men were tortured and burned at the stake for their beliefs; and with equal repugnance upon the similar persecutions and executions under Protestant rule in the early days of the Reformation. Such things were not of God.

Matters of belief are between the man and his God. Should a member of the Church repudiate the principles of the gospel, or teach false doctrine to the people, the Church of course will discipline him; but the utmost punishment will be excommunication from the Church. Then, under his own flag, he may carry on as he chooses.

But, if a member conforms to the principles, rules, and regulations of the Church, all founded in truth and in love of mankind, he will find great joy. There is no other way to taste the sweetness of the work.

3. WHAT IS ORTHODOXY?

The word orthodoxy is not applicable to Church doctrine or practice. Therefore it is seldom used within Church circles. Latter-day Saints should be careful in speaking about themselves or others as being orthodox or unorthodox in the Church. It is not an accurate statement of their position.

Commonly, an orthodox member of any organization—scientific, social, or religious—is one who accepts the fundamental principles of the organization. One who does not do so, is sometimes called unorthodox, but this is not correct. Since he rejects the foundation on which the organization rests, he really does not belong to the group.

Of course, when the foundations, not necessarily rooted in truth, are made by the group, differences in opinion may properly arise, and the contending parties may with some propriety be called orthodox or unorthodox. Likewise, though the foundation be accepted, some may hold that it should be applied in one way, others in another. He who differs with the regulations of the organization often likes to call himself unorthodox, when really he is out of harmony with the group, playing the part of the "lone wolf." Those of the Church who call themselves unorthodox generally use the word to cover the fact that they are out of harmony with the established and accepted regulations of the Church.

However, when the foundation rests on truth, there can be little contention. One cannot quarrel with truth. Two and two make four; there is light by day and there is darkness by night. This rose is red to the eye; that one is yellow. Such facts must be accepted; there is neither orthodoxy nor unorthodoxy about them.

For example, Christians who do not believe in the divine mission of Jesus Christ, and his resurrection after the crucifixion—basic facts of Christianity—are not Christians at all. They should not claim the name. But if their differences hinge on opinions concerning the very nature of Jesus, or on the exact manner of his resurrection, neither fully understood – they cannot justly be called unorthodox. They may only need to be taught that the universe is filled with things we do not fully know. At the worst, they may be spoken of as foolish people who seek to unravel mysteries yet closed to the human mind.

It is so in the Church. A person who does not believe that Joseph Smith saw and heard God the Father, and his son Jesus Christ, or that he received revelations for the Church, or that he translated the Book of Mormon from engraved plates delivered to him by a heavenly being, is not a Latter-day Saint, and has no claim upon the name. There should be no question about these truths in the minds of Latter-day Saints. But differences of opinion about the application of a doctrine in daily life do not necessarily mean that people are unorthodox. Differences of opinion in the use of the truth may often lead to helpful discussions of life within the Church.

The important matter is that Latter-day Saints must accept all the fundamentals of the Church. They cannot choose to believe a certain doctrine of the Church; they must accept them all. They cannot select the Church requirements they will obey; they must conform to all. They who do not do so are not unorthodox, they are weak in the faith. Usually they do not know enough, or their wills for righteousness are flabby. It is useless for them to try to escape by calling themselves unorthodox. Neither can they say that their rights as free agents have been violated, for the acceptance of truth is one of the limitations under which free agency operates.

There are, of course, many persons, sometimes among those born in the Church, who are honestly seeking to win for themselves testimonies of the truth of the restored gospel, for people are not born with a testimony. Such seekers for truth are treading the road at one time followed by every believer that Joseph Smith was a prophet of God. Their course is praiseworthy. They are not unorthodox. Happily, the gospel lends itself to searching and testing; it never fails the seeker if correct methods are followed.

To summarize: They who accept basic doctrines of the Church are not orthodox; they are believers. They who deny the truth of the fundamentals of the restored gospel are not unorthodox members of the Church; they are unbelievers. They who have not yet found the truth, but are earnestly seeking it, are on the way and will find truth.

The word orthodox is really foreign to the language of Latter-day Saints. No one should call himself unorthodox.

4. WHY DOES NOT THE CHURCH CONFINE ITSELF TO SPIRITUAL MATTERS?

The Church exists for the welfare of its members. It holds to the doctrine that "men are that they might have joy." Therefore, whatever affects human welfare, temporally or spiritually, on earth or in heaven, is accepted as the concern of the Church.

This doctrine leads the Church into problems of man's physical, mental, moral, economic, social, and political well-being, into his every need. It strives to bring about conditions that will promote general, rounded, complete welfare. It cannot look with favor upon one-sidedness in life—one part of man's nature satisfied, another unsatisfied. It does not hesitate, because of individual prejudices or the danger of making enemies, to speak frankly and fully about any and every phase of human life. To cower in some one corner of human need is held in contempt by the Church; and certainly such a church should be held in contempt.

The history of Mormonism can best be understood in the light of this doctrine. The attempts at the United Order in Kirtland and Missouri, the founding of wilderness universities in Nauvoo and Salt Lake City, the formulation of city planning recognizable everywhere in Mormon settlements, the trek across the desert to the Great Salt Lake Valley, the cooperative enterprises in the building of the intermountain West, the present L. D. S. Welfare program, and innumerable other events and enterprises are but evidences of the conception that the Church must care for the whole man, not merely for a part of him.

In the revelations to the Prophet Joseph Smith, this matter is made very clear. Man is engaged in an eternal journey. Life on earth is but an episode in everlasting life. Therefore, all things that touch this eternal traveler belong to the plan under which he is moving forward. The distinction between things spiritual and temporal vanishes; they become merged, as the palm and back of the hand, as the warp and woof of the cloth. Man's physical concerns acquire a spiritual value; and his spiritual activities have temporal counterparts. "Wherefore, verily I say unto you that all things unto me are spiritual, and not at any time have I given unto you a law which was temporal . . . for my commandments are spiritual; they are not natural nor temporal, neither carnal nor sensual" (D. & C. 29:34, 35). This makes the Word of Wisdom, tithing, prayer, or temple work, princpiles alike of spiritual essence. In that sense, the Church never departs from spiritual teachings.

By this doctrine, Church leaders feel themselves free and under obligation to discourse on any and every need of the day and of man, no matter under what man-given name it appears. They would be poor leaders if silence was enjoined upon them within any field of human interest. Indeed, the very life of the Church is involved in this free discussion of man's welfare.

However, let no misconceptions arise. The Church holds itself aloof from propagandists or parties. In politics, for example, it is neither Republican, Democratic nor "mugwump." It tests and measures every man-made policy by the eternal, unchanging principles of the gospel. If a proposed policy is in harmony with these principles, it is approved by the Church, if in opposition to gospel principles it is disapproved. The ax hews at untruth no matter where the chips may fall. Whether Democrats wail or Republicans weep is of no consequence. The Church is not in politics, but up to the shoulders in the fight for truth, which is the battle for humanity's welfare.

If the teachings of the Church be examined, whether of today or yesterday, and they are published far and wide, it will be found that they rest upon the principles of the gospel. That makes it safe to give and to accept them. The laws of the gospel root in truth. Just as, under the law of gravity, one who jumps from the house-roof will fall to his destruction, so the breaking of the laws of the gospel will bring inevitable punishment.

Though all this be so, the principle of free agency remains. The Church may teach, but each member has the right to accept or reject, in his life, the truth propounded. There is no more basic law of conduct in the gospel. The Lord has formulated the plan of salvation; he offers His help, but each individual must act for himself in winning the salvation offered. Measurably, with the aid of the Lord, each one of us "works out his own salvation"; and we must each face the consequences of our disobedience to law.

The Church cannot refrain from teaching eternal truth, both in doctrine and in the practice of the doctrine; but it has no right nor does it attempt, to secure obedience by exercising compulsion upon its members. The severest punishment meted out to violators of the order of the Church is excommunication. But every such person, through the judicial provisions of the Church, has a full and free hearing. Moreover, any officer of the Church, from the highest to the least, found in default, may be brought before the tribunals of the Church. Fair justice, and the untrammeled will of man are dear to the heart of every Latter-day Saint.

In no sense can the Church be called autocratic. No one, from the President down, can dictate to the Church. All must be done in harmony with gospel principles, and by common consent. Even new revelations from the Lord are presented to the people for acceptance as part of the doctrine of the Church. It is a Church of full freedom. However, the Church is the watchman on the tower for the people. It is its duty to preserve the gospel in its purity, to teach it with full courage, to secure gospel activity among Church members, to strengthen the weak, to care for the common welfare, and necessarily to cast out such iniquity as may have crept in among the membership.

Without the use of autocratic methods, but with the fearless, and unhesitating voice of truth, it will continue, as in the past, to labor for the whole welfare of men, "that they might have joy."

5. WHY IS IT UNDESIRABLE TO JOIN SECRET SOCIETIES?

The Church ever operates in full light. There is no secrecy about its doctrine, aim, or work. It is open to all men who will conform to its requirements. Access to the temples, where the most sacred ordinances are performed, may be had by every member of the Church who lives the honorable life expected of faithful Latter-day Saints. No promise is exacted of any Church member except to live as nearly as may be in conformity with the teachings of the Lord Jesus Christ. The activities of the Church, in all departments, are sacred, not secret.

This point of view makes it difficult for Latter-day Saints to look with favor upon secret, oath-bound societies. The words of the Prophet Joseph Smith are sufficient answer to the question: (Note especially the last sentence.)

> And again, I would further suggest the impropriety of the organization of bands or companies, by covenant or oaths, by penalties or secrecies; but let the time past of our experience and sufferings by the wickedness of Doctor Avard suffice and let our covenant be that of the Everlasting Covenant, as is contained in the Holy Writ and the things that God hath revealed unto us. *Pure friendship always becomes weakened that very moment you undertake to make it stronger by penal oaths and secrecy.* (*Teachings of the Prophet Joseph Smith,* p. 146)

Many secret organizations may be actuated by high ideals. None, however, can transcend the ideals of the gospel of Jesus Christ. Therefore, from the point of view of encouraging people to walk uprightly they would seem unnecessary. Besides, they are likely to take time that should be given to Church activities. Sometimes they cause loss of interest in Church duties, for no one can serve two masters with equal interest.

Let it be remembered also that the authorized organizations of the Church for social and fraternal purposes, coupled with our professional and business organizations, will not only serve our needs, but will consume all the time that we can spare in these busy days. Divided allegiance is always unsatisfactory and often dangerous.

6. WHY AND HOW SHOULD TITHING BE PAID?

Tithing means the voluntary giving of one-tenth of one's income, increase, or interest, for the furtherance of the Lord's work on earth. It is an ancient, divine law, which has been practised in every dispensation of the gospel. In nearly every land, Christian or pagan, it has been recognized and practised in some form.

The law of tithing has been reaffirmed by the Lord in our day. (D. & C., section 119) It is a binding commandment upon the Church.

Like all divine commandments, the law of tithing is for the benefit of those who practise it. Great rewards follow the honest observance of this requirement.

First, the tithepayer builds up loyalty to the Church. He becomes closely identified with the Latter-day movement. He is henceforth a party to the many activities of the Church. Temples, schools, missionary work, and all Church programs, the care of the poor, the widow, and the fatherless, are built and fostered by him in association with other tithepayers. He cooperates with the Lord in achieving his mighty purposes. He stands definitely for a great cause. He dares to sacrifice for beliefs that have for their objective the welfare of all men. Courage and power come to every man who sacrifices for a noble cause. He becomes a bigger man. The world is in sad need of men who believe and have the courage to give of their substance and of themselves for their founded convictions.

Second, it trains the human will for more than material gains. The love of money and the material goods it can buy is one of the most powerful motives within man. When this love overpowers other normal desires, money indeed becomes "the root of all evil." Men must learn the relative values of things of earth and of spirit. To part with our earthly belongings seems to us to be a sacrifice—but sacrifice always begets blessings. The first lesson in the art of happiness is to do without. Whoever lifts his affections above earthly things expands in spirit and begins to grow. Latter-day Saints are a happy people because they grow and progress. They must be able to control and subordinate the love of earthly things if they are to rise to greatness. Otherwise they become dangerous to society and destructive of their better selves. The regular payment of tithing creates unselfishness and lifts a man above the dross of earth. His capacity to do well is enlarged. His vision is freed from the blur of material things. He gains a truer perspective of life. Others recognize in him the subtle quality of greatness; the product of self-forgetfulness. He gains a new and larger freedom. Peace waits upon him. His will is disciplined for righteousness.

Third, the tithepayer is brought into closer communion with the Lord. The offering is an acknowledgment that the earth is the Lord's, and men are but stewards of that which they possess. The Lord is the giver of all good things—seed time and harvest. Payment of tithing is an admission by the tithepayer that his income came from the Lord. The return of the tithe is to say, "As evidence that this gift is from Thee, I return herewith one-tenth."

This faith of every true Latter-day Saint establishes a nearness between God and man. Every payment of tithing builds a living faith. It becomes a testimony of the reality of the Living God, and his relationship to the children of men. To witness so of the Lord and his goodness gives increased spiritual power. Every tithepayer increases in faith and receives the attendant peace and joy. Prayer becomes easier. Doubt retreats; faith advances. Certainty and courage buoy up the soul. The spiritual sense is sharpened; the eternal voice is heard more clearly. Man becomes more like his Father in heaven.

Fourth, the faithful tithepayer has a claim upon the needed blessings of life. Rewards, spiritual and temporal, flow abundantly from obedience to the law. The blessings may not always come as he may wish, but they come and are for man's good. They may be of a material or spiritual nature, as the Lord may design; but they will carry with them always the higher joys of life. Yet it may be safely said that whoever can lay aside the love of earthly things has the gifts of earth at his feet.

The blessings of the Church are necessarily withheld from non-tithepayers. The Lord has so stated. They "shall not be found, neither the names of the fathers, nor the names of the children written in the book of the law of God." (D. & C. 85:5)

In the last days there are also great upheavals. Destruction and death stalk the highways of earth. There is danger all about. But, the tithepayer has claim upon protection. "Verily it is a day of sacrifice, and a day for the tithing of my people; for he that is tithed shall not be burned. . . . For after today cometh the burning." (D. & C. 64:23, 24) The Lord in his mercy opens the windows of heaven upon his faithful children and repays a thousandfold according to their needs.

The blessings promised the tithepayer are great.

Fifth, the tithepayer senses the gladness of heart that comes from obeying the Lord's commandments. By obedience to the laws of heaven he secures harmony with the unseen world. He moves through the tasks of the day, looking the world in the face. He knows his path and destiny. He has the full assurance that all is well. This, the greatest effect of tithepaying, glorifies life in the midst of the world's tribulations. Only when a person's whole being is turned to the Lord, by free and full acceptance of divine law, does he hold full communion with heavenly things.

Such are some of the benefits the tithepayer receives from the payment of tithing.

* * * *

Every member of the Church who has an income, or earns money or its equivalent, should observe the law of tithing. The President of the Church is under the same obligation as the humblest member. Every boy and girl should be taught to give one-tenth of their income to the Lord. It should be as a joyous privilege, an expression of grateful confidence in the Lord, to contribute for the maintenance of the Church, the promulgation of the gospel, and the welfare of the needy.

Tithing means one-tenth. Those who give less do not really pay tithing; they are lesser contributors to the Latter-day cause of the Lord. Tithing means one-tenth of a person's income, interest, or increase. The merchant should pay tithing upon the net income of his business, the farmer upon the net income of his farming operations; the wage earner or salaried man upon the wage or salary earned by him. Out of the remaining nine-tenths he pays his current expenses, taxes, savings, etc. To deduct living costs, taxes, and similar expenses from the income and pay tithing upon the remainder does not conform to the Lord's commandment. Under such a system most people would show nothing on which to pay tithing. There is really no place for quibbling on this point. Tithing should be given upon the basis of our full earned income. If the nature of a business requires special interpretation, the tithepayer should consult the father of his ward, the bishop.

When tithing has been paid, there should be no question about its use. They who are sustained as leaders of the Church return all offerings to the people for various purposes. The tithing of the people make it possible for the Church to carry out the duties entrusted to it by the Lord in the development of the plan of salvation. By divine revelation the tithes of the people are administered by the Presidency of the Church, assisted by the Council of the Twelve and the Presiding Bishopric. These men exercise prayerful care in the use of tithing. It is disbursed with scrupulous care, for it is sacred. No moneys in all the world are more honestly administered.

The quibbler about the use of the revenues of the Church is usually a part or non-tithepayer. The faith that leads to such voluntary contribution includes faith in the other principles of the gospel; including trust in the chosen and sustained servants of the Lord.

Tithing should be paid only to the authorized agents of the Church—the Presiding Bishopric, bishops of wards. presidents of branches and mission presidents. Technically, it should be paid in kind. That is, the farmer would give of his crops and herds, the professional man of his cash income. However, inconveniences of transportation, storing, and disposition, sometimes causing losses, make it permissible and often desirable to pay all tithing in cash.

Tithing is a lesser law. The greater and more perfect law is the law of consecration, also known as the Order of Enoch or the United Order. The Latter-day Saints have not yet attained to a degree of perfection enabling them to live under this more comprehensive law. Until that time comes the Lord requires obedience to the law of tithing—an equitable law under which the widow's mite counts for as much as the rich man's thousands. When all the members of the Church are full and honest tithepayers, we may begin to look for the establishment of the law of consecration. Then the Lord may re-establish the higher law.

It is the invariable testimony of thousands that obedience to this law of tithing brings unalloyed happiness, the power to solve the problems of life, a nearness to God. All should covenant individually with the Lord who has given us life and all we have, that we will obey all his laws, including the law of revenue. Let us trust the Lord. He will not fail us.

7. WHAT TITHES AND OFFERINGS WERE REQUIRED OF ANCIENT ISRAEL?

The practice of giving tithes and offerings was generally understood and observed among ancient Israel. In fact, the principle was so well known that it was taken for granted. The casual manner in which the Hebrew historians refer to it is evidence that it was of common knowledge.

Adam and those who came immediately after him were taught the necessity of making offerings and sacrifices to the Lord. It is probable, however, that the early patriarchs lived under the law of consecration. It is known that Enoch and his people accepted this higher law, successfully, and others may have done so. (Moses 7:18; *Discourses of Brigham Young*, p. 178)

The first mention of tithing in the Bible is in connection with the giving of tithes by Abraham to Melchizedek, a high priest, authorized to receive offerings. (Gen. 14:20; Heb. 7:2, 6) Abraham appears to have understood clearly the existence and necessity of the law. His grandson, Jacob, confirmed the family's adherence to the law after his meeting with the heavenly messenger, for he declared:

> Of all that thou shalt give me I will surely give the tenth unto thee. (Gen. 28:22)

Tithing was made a definite part of the Mosaic law:

> And all the tithe of the land, whether of the seed of the land, or of the fruit of the tree, is the Lord's: it is holy unto the Lord . . . and concerning the tithe of the herd, or of the flock, even of whatever passeth under the rod, the tenth shall be holy unto the Lord. (Lev. 27:30, 32)

Israel ever after lived by the law of Moses, and consequently tithing was a standing law for the people, one that never was abrogated.

Offerings and sacrifices to the Lord and the dedication of property to sacred purposes is mentioned frequently in the Old Testament history of Israel, from Joshua, through the times of Judges, during the reigns of the kings, and throughout the stirring times after the captivity, even to the coming of the Savior. The general terms, offerings or gifts to the

Lord are ordinarily used, but tithes are mentioned specifically. The prophets Amos, Nehemiah, and Malachi, made direct reference to tithing in their discussions of the divine claim for offerings. (Amos 4:4; Nehemiah 10:37, 38; 12:44; 13:5, 12; Malachi 3:8, 10). The Talmud, the spoken and traditional law of the Jews, likewise makes frequent and often detailed mention of tithing as an established law of Israel. There can be no doubt about the knowledge and partial observance of the law of tithing among the descendants of Jacob.

However, several tithes were enjoined upon the people under the law of Moses. The first already quoted, was the tenth of the produce of the land and the livestock, to be set apart for holy purposes by giving it to the Levites, the priestly tribe. The commandment for a second tithe, given in a passage in the Book of Deuteronomy, began as follows:

> Thou shalt truly tithe all the increase of thy seed, that the field bringeth forth year by year. And thou shalt eat before the Lord thy God, in the place which he shall choose to place his name there, the tithe of thy corn, of thy wine, and of thine oil, and the firstlings of thy herds and of thy flocks; that thou mayest learn to fear the Lord thy God always. (Deut. 14:22-23)

From the context, it would appear that this tenth was to be used by the man and his family to enable them to visit the holy sanctuaries and to take part properly in the sacred celebrations of Israel, several of which occur annually under the law of Moses. That is, it was to be used to permit the people to engage in holy ordinances by which they might keep the Lord in remembrance, as indicated by the following passage:

> And thither ye shall bring your . . . tithes. . . . And there ye shall eat before the Lord your God, and ye shall rejoice in all that ye put your hand unto, ye and your households. (Deut. 12:6-7)

A third tithe was imposed upon ancient Israel, one that came every third year, and which was to be used for local purposes for the relief of human distress. (Deut. 14:28, 29) The existence and acceptance of these three tithes is recognized by competent writers of early days. For example, Josephus declares:

> Besides those two tithes, which I have already said you are to pay every year, the one for the Levites, the other for the festivals;

you are to bring every third year a third tithe, to be distributed to those that want; to women also that are widows, and to children that are orpans. (*Antiquities of the Jews,* Book IV, p. 132)

In addition to these tithes, the people were required, under the law of Moses, to make a variety of offerings; corners of the fields should be left standing, gleanings and forgotten sheaves in the field be available, all for the purpose, and estimated to amount to about one-sixtieth of the crop (Lev. 19:9, 10; 23:22; Deut. 24:19-21); the first fruits, estimated to be about one-fortieth of the harvest, should be dedicated to the Lord; and several other smaller but important offerings should be made. (Neh. 10:32-39; II Chron. 31:3-10; Deut. 12:17; 18:3, 4)

In short, ancient Israel were expected to use for sacred purposes, such as the maintenance of the priesthood, holy festivals, and care of the poor, between one-fourth and one-third of their increase. And throughout the generations, many complied with these requirements and were blessed.

In view of these historical facts, the requirements made of modern Israel do not seem so large.

Those who had authority to receive the Lord's tenth clearly specified:

> Behold, I have given the children of Levi all the tenth in Israel for an inheritance, for their service which they serve, even the service of the tabernacle of the congregation. (Num. 18:21)

This refers to the selection of the tribe of Levi to perform the priestly service for the hosts of Israel. The importance of the principle of tithing is emphasized by the injunction that the Levites themselves were to give a tenth of that which they received to the priests. (Num. 18:26; *Antiquities of the Jews,* Book IV, p. 119) None were exempt from the law.

Under the perfect law of the gospel all worthy men hold the priesthood, first the Aaronic, including the Levitical, and then the Melchizedek Priesthood. But the rebellion of the children of Israel in the wilderness caused the Lord to take away from them the high priesthood, and to change the remaining organization as outlined in the Pentateuch. Thus it came about that the Lord's tithe was to be given to the Levites.

By divine revelation the tithes of the people are to be

expended for the benefit of the Church by a council consisting of the First Presidency, the Council of the Twelve, and the Presiding Bishopric, or through their agents. (D. & C., section 120) Tithing is disbursed with scrupulous care—it is sacred. At the general conference the President of the Church makes a report of expenditures made from the tithing of the people.

8. DOES THE PAYMENT OF TITHING CAUSE ECONOMIC DISTRESS?

"No," would be the unanimous and emphatic answer of those who have obeyed the law of tithing. Indeed, the question is usually asked by non-tithe payers who seek to find excuses for not obeying the law.

When mortal man places one-tenth of his income in the treasury of the Lord, he acknowledges by that act that all his earthly income is a gift from the Lord, the real Owner and Master of Earth. The giving of tithing becomes then an evidence of the man's faith in God and of the man's conquest of his selfish self. This is the essence of the law of tithing.

The law of tithing is on a par, in every respect, with every other commandment of the Lord. Obedience to His commandments is required by the Lord. "For this cause have I sent you—that you might be obedient." (D. & C. 58:6) In fact, disobedience is an offense to the Lord. "In nothing doth man offend God, or against none is his wrath kindled, save those who confess not his hand in all things, and obey not his commandments." (D. & C. 59:21)

The great purpose of life is to develop such conquest over self that obedience may be willingly, easily, and gladly yielded to every commandment issuing from the mouth of the Lord. Commandments then become means by which a man's spiritual condition may be determined. Every person may be, in a sense, the judge of his own spiritual progress, for he knows how readily he yields obedience to the laws of the Lord. The commandments of first value are those which demand most unselfish action; that lead, if obeyed, to the greatest self-conquest.

Tithing is a law of special value for this purpose. Man naturally is slow to part with his worldly goods. Too often spiritual wealth is overshadowed by material possessions. If he can so master himself as to part with a tenth of his earthly income, he has won victory over one of the most stubborn phases of his nature.

While self-conquest may be the chief result of man's obedience to law, other blessings follow. Man gives little; the Lord gives much in return even here on earth. Those who are obedient to law will gain knowledge and intelligence. They may escape the scourges and afflictions of the world (D. & C. 97:25-28); health, endurance, wisdom, and hidden treasures of knowledge shall be theirs. (D. & C. 89:18-21) The joys and blessings of heaven shall be tasted by them on earth. (D. & C. 105:18)

Obedience to the law of tithing is certain to bring blessings in return, even of a temporal character. Yet, it must ever be remembered that the blessings of life come according to the Lord's will. Material property may not be the blessing we most need. If we can trust the Lord enough to pay Him a tenth of our increase, we must trust Him to bless us according to our needs. Material, earthly property does not have the same value before God as before man. Love of property is often nothing more than covetousness, which is a deadly sin. "What is property unto me? saith the Lord." (D. & C. 117:4) Let man do his best to provide for himself and his family, gather property around him, pay his tithing, obey all other laws of God, and accept, with joy, such blessings as the Lord may vouchsafe him.

Now, after all this has been said, it is interesting to note that the very great majority of tithe payers, perhaps all, succeed in finding sufficient for their temporal welfare. The group of tithe payers within the Church are not only more spiritually active, but generally they are more prosperous than the non-tithe paying group. Tithing is not a factor that works against economic prosperity. In most cases material as well as spiritual blessings follow obedience to the law of tithing.

This view is confirmed by an investigation by a non-Mormon agency. A government bank, having loaned very large sums to Utah farmers, mostly Latter-day Saints, and noting an abnormally high percentage of delinquency, wondered if the practice of tithe paying were reducing the ability of the farmers to make proper repayments. The assistance of the Utah State Agricultural College was secured in carrying on the investigation. The Church gave full cooperation.

The first study was made in Utah County, Utah. Four hundred and eighty-five names were submitted by a bank and college. Of these, seventy-one could not be found on the records of the Church. Of the remaining four hundred and fourteen persons, seventy-eight had no indebtedness, two hundred and twenty-nine had loans, but were non-delinquent, and one hundred and seven were delinquent.

The percentage of tithe payers was about the same in the three groups, but the proportion of full tithe payers among the delinquent group was only a little more than half of the full tithe payers in the non-delinquent and no-debt classes. The total amount paid in tithing per person in the delinquent group was only about three-fourths of that paid by the non-delinquent and no-debt groups. Examined from every angle, the investigation showed that tithing had no depressing economic influence, but rather that the qualities in a man that led him to pay tithing, also enabled him to win more success in his economic life.

It should be added that two of the four hundred and eighty-five farmers listed kept three missionaries in the field, and these two men were in the non-delinquent group and paid a full tithing. Neither tithing nor missionary costs seemed to have a depressing effect upon the economic welfare of the farmers. The gift of amassing money beyond ordinary needs is much like any other special gift such as in music, art, education, or other human activities.

Another, smaller investigation was conducted by the same agencies in Cache County, Utah. In the section studied one hundred ninety farmers were owing money to the bank. Thirty-three of them were delinquent, and these had farms of equal size and productive power with the non-delinquent farmers. The Church records showed that of these thirty-three delinquents, eighteen paid no tithing, eight paid part tithing, and seven paid a full tithing. The investigator calculated that in one of the prosperous villages in the Cache County study about 11 percent of the farmers are delinquent in their bank payments, and these 11 percent pay 2 percent of the tithing in the village. It seemed clear therefore that in this as in the Utah County area, tithing is a very unimportant factor in the delinquency problem. Here also it seems evident that the man who pays tithing has power to do the things that bring reasonable economic prosperity.

As far as available experience can guide us, the answer to the question at the head of this writing is, "No." The payment of tithing does not cause economic distress. A host of testimonies might be secured of the joy in life that follows obedience to this important law of the Lord.

IX. Marriage and the Family

1. WHY MARRY IN THE TEMPLE?

Marriage, the most important event between birth and death, is a determining condition of life's happiness. Therefore, it should be entered into with the greatest of care. A companion for life should be one who lives righteously, to whom abundant love may be given, and who can be respected in his or her daily walk and talk. Likewise, the marriage covenant should be of such a nature as to help create, build, and maintain daily happiness. As the successive days are, so all of life will be. Wealth, power, and fame are beggared in comparison with the joy that comes from a happy family life.

The Church offers the privilege of marriage in the temple as the foremost means of establishing and maintaining happiness in the households of its members. It is a privilege beyond compare, which every prospective bride and groom should seek and use. The conditions are such that every person may fit himself to receive this privilege, so earnestly coveted by true Latter-day Saints.

Here are nine brief answers to the question, "Why Marry in the Temple?"

1. *It is the Lord's desire and will.* The temple is by divine decree the place where marriages should if possible be performed. Marriage is of such crucial importance in life that it should begin with full obedience to God's law. Love is the foundation of marriage, but love itself is a product of law and lives by law. True love is law-abiding, for the highest satisfactions come to a law-abiding life.

Moreover, true love of man for woman always includes love of God from whom all good things issue. The proof of our love of God is obedience to His law. Besides, life is so full of problems that the married couple should from the first seek the constant favor of the Lord. A sense of security and comfort comes to all who are wedded within the temple. They have obeyed the law. They have pleased the Lord. As law-abiding citizens in the kingdom of God, they have a special claim upon divine aid, blessings, and protection. Conformity to the practices of the Church always builds happiness in life. Marriage should begin right—by obedience to law.

2. *It is in harmony with the sacred nature of the marriage covenant.* Temple marriages are also more in harmony with the nature and importance of the occasion. They are performed in an attractive sealing room, especially dedicated for the purpose. The ceremony itself is simple, beautiful, and profound. Relatively few witnesses are present. Quiet and order prevail. There are no external trappings to confuse the mind. Full attention may be given to the sacred covenants to be made, and the blessings to follow, covering the vast period of eternal existence. The attention is focused upon the meaning of the marriage ceremony, and not upon distracting outside features which characterize a wedding in an elaborate social setting. Such concentration of the soul upon the covenants entered into and the blessings promised, becomes a joyful, happy memory incomparably sweeter than that of the usual rush and show of a wedding outside temple walls. Lovely in its simple beauty and deep import is a temple wedding.

There is ample opportunity after the ceremony in the temple for a reception, simple or elaborate, at which friends may gather to congratulate the couple and to wish them happiness.

3. *It tends to insure marital happiness.* Experience has shown that temple marriages are generally the happiest. There are relatively fewer divorces among couples who have been sealed over the altars of the temple. This is shown by dependable statistics. Today's views of marriage are notably loose; yet no person with a decent outlook on life will enter the marriage state as an experiment. Life's happiness is made or marred by marriage. Divorce does not return the individuals to their former condition. Scars remain. Hasty weddings and the easy divorces that follow menace individual and public welfare. When the integrity of the family, the unit of society, vanishes, and family relationships are held in disrespect, society is headed for disaster. The deliberation that precedes a temple marriage, the solemnity that accompanies it, and the power that seals and blesses it, form a bulwark against many evils of the day. The temple marriage hedges about, and keeps inviolate, the happiness that of right belongs to the married state.

4. *It permits the association of husband and wife for*

time and for all eternity. The essential difference between temple and all other marriages is of the greatest consequence. In the temple, and only there, the bridal couple are wedded for time and eternity. The contract is endless. Here and hereafter, on earth and beyond, they may travel together in loving companionship. This precious gift conforms to the Latter-day Saint belief that existence in the life after this may be active, useful, progressive. Love, content to end with death, is perishable, poor, and helpless. Marriage that lasts only during earth life is a sad one, for the love established between man and woman, as they live together and rear their family, should not die, but live and grow richer with the eternal years. True love hopes and prays for an endless continuation of association with the loved one. To those who are sealed to each other for all existence, love is ever warm, more hopeful, believing, courageous, and fearless. Such people live the richer, more joyful life. To them happiness and the making of it have no end. Dismal, dreary, full of fear, is the outlook upon love that ends with death. The youth of the Church dare not forego the gift of everlasting marriage.

5. *It provides the eternal possession of children and family relationship.* There is yet an added blessing. Children born under the temple covenant belong to their parents for all time and eternity. That is, the family relationships on earth are continued, forever, here and hereafter. The family, continued from earth into the next world, becomes a unit in everlasting life. In the long eternities we shall not be lonely wanderers, but side by side, with our loved ones who have gone before and those who shall follow, we shall travel the endless journey. What mother does not value this promise! What father does not feel his heart warm towards the eternal possession of his family! What heartbreakings might have been avoided if humanity had been true to the truth, and had surrendered to the sealing power of the Priesthood of God. Temple marriage becomes a promise of unending joy.

6. *It acts as a restraint against evil.* The powers of darkness are ever active to push mankind into evil paths. Often, we are tempted to do foolish things. In the family little things may lead to discord. To create unhappiness is the aim of the adversary of righteousness. Here appears one of

the foremost blessings of the temple marriage. Those who have been sealed in the temple have their eyes fixed upon eternity. They dare not forfeit the promised blessings. The family is to them an everlasting possession. They remember the covenants which make possible this eternal association. The temple marriage, with all that it means, becomes a restraining force in the presence of temptation. All family acts are more likely to be shaped in anticipation of an undying relationship. Under the influence of the memory of the temple ceremony, family differences are swallowed up in peace; hate is transmuted into love; fear, into courage; and evil is rebuked and cast out. Peace is the world's great need. From the temples of the Lord, and from everything done within them, issues the spirit of truth which is the foundation of peace.

7. *It furnishes the opportunity for endless progression.* Modern revelation sets forth the high destiny of those who are sealed for everlasting companionship. They will be given opportunity for a greater use of their powers. That means progress. They will attain more readily to their place in the presence of the Lord; they will increase more rapidly in every divine power; they will approach more nearly to the likeness of God; they will more completely realize their divine destiny. And this progress is not delayed until life after death. It begins here, today, for those who yield obedience to the law. Life is tasteless without progress. Eternal marriage, with all that it means, provides for unending advancement. "Eternal increase" is the gift to all who enter into the eternal marriage covenant, as made in the temples of the Lord.

8. *It places the family under the protection of the power of the Priesthood.* They who have won a temple marriage have been sealed for time and eternity by the power of the Holy Priesthood. This is the supreme power committed to man's keeping. That power issues from the unseen world. It gives life and light to the world. Human life with its cares and worries is transfigured into a radiant experience and adventure when it clings to this divine power and is blessed by it. To walk under divine authority, to possess it, to be a part of it, is to walk with heads erect, with grateful hearts, before our fellow men and our Father in heaven. The men and women who have come with this power out of the Lord's holy house will be hedged about by divine protection and

walk more safely among the perplexities of earth. They will be indeed the ultimate conquerors of earth, for they come with the infinite power of God to solve the problems of earth. Spiritual power accompanies all who marry in the temple, if they thenceforth keep their sacred covenants.

9. *It provides a God-like destiny for human beings.* "If a man marry a wife by my word, which is my law, and by the new and everlasting covenant, and it is sealed unto them by the Holy Spirit of promise, by him who is anointed, unto whom I have appointed this power and the keys of this priesthood; and it shall be said unto them—Ye shall come forth in the first resurrection; and if it be after the first resurrection, in the next resurrection; and shall inherit thrones, kingdoms, principalities, and powers, dominions, all heights and depths . . .

"Then shall they be gods, because they have no end; therefore they shall be from everlasting to everlasting, because they continue; then shall they be above all, because all things are subject unto them. Then shall they be gods, because they have all power, and the angels are subject unto them." (D. & C. 132:19, 20; see also *The Improvement Era*, 17:1064; 30:1098; 34:704; 39:214; 41:136, 220, 268, 330; 43:586)

2. WHY NOT MARRY OUTSIDE OF THE CHURCH?

There are good people in every church, and among those who claim no church affiliation. But, good people, kind, honest, charitable people, may be in error concerning the meaning of life. That has always been the view and position of Latter-day Saints. The groom of one faith and the bride of another may be equally virtuous. It is their differing beliefs or convictions relative to the truths of existence that make the success of their marriage questionable or more difficult to attain.

Love is the foundation of every truly happy marriage. The more genuine the love, the greater the joy of association between husband and wife. A loveless marriage, or one in which love diminishes with the years, always ends in grief.

The beginning of love is usually physical attraction. There are gifts of body, of face and form, of eyes and voice, that awaken desire for acquaintanceship and possession. That is nature's way, respected by all sensible people.

Above physical charm, love is begotten by qualities, often subtle, of mind and spirit. The beautiful face may hide an empty mind; the sweet voice may utter coarse words; the lovely form may be ill-mannered; the woman of radiant beauty and the man of kingly form may be intolerable bores on nearer acquaintanceship; or, the person who looks attractive may really have no faults, may excel us in knowledge and courtesy, yet he is not of our kind, his ways are not ours. Under either condition, love wilts in its first stage. "Falling in love" is always from within, rather than from without. That is, physical attractiveness must be reinforced with mental and spiritual harmony if true love is to be born and have long life—from the Latter-day Saint point of view, to last throughout the eternities. The man and his wife, to make love secure, must have much the same outlook on the major issues of life; they must grow in the same direction. If one is an infidel and the other a believer in God, the resulting disagreement of spirit will tend to drive the two apart despite physical attractions. The association of husband and wife is so close and intimate that every difference becomes evident and important.

This is especially true in matters pertaining to religious faith. Religion, under its wide definition, is the philosophy of life, by which we regulate our conduct. As we believe, so we act. The past, the present, and the future, all that we are and shall be, are involved in our religion. We cannot by any means be in full sympathy with any person who, in this most profound of man's concerns, is not in sincere harmony with us. Under circumstances of differing faiths, love rises only to its partial height. The fullness of love fails us. Drabness enters where only sunlight should be found.

A common result of such a marriage is an attempt at compromise. Then, neither one lives religion properly. Both become lukewarm in their duties, unless, indeed, one through superior power of will or dominance, compels the other to follow his way. In either case, an inner disintegration follows; the sensitive plant called love withers and often dies. The surpassing joy of love comes only to those who are in harmony of belief and mutual understanding.

Husband and wife of different faiths, however fine they may be in character, and earnest in their attempts to rise above their differences, become acutely aware of their situation when children come into the household. In what faith shall they be reared? Sunday after Sunday, and oftener, that question arises. When illness enters the home, the Latter-day Saint wife longs to call in the elders to administer to the sick, but hesitates because there is no unity of faith in the household; and the Latter-day Saint husband hesitates to exercise his Priesthood for the same reason. The children, themselves, grow up cognizant of a family strain, crowding their happiness, often compelling them to take sides for one parent as against another. The differences persist through more than one generation, often affecting great-grandchildren. Time and again, spoken or unspoken, under the many vicissitudes of life, the lack of common spiritual understanding becomes a torment to husband and wife and also to the children. Inward happiness of individual and family, so necessary to full joy, is stifled.

Another mighty objection to "mixed" marriages rises before Latter-day Saints. Only members of the Church may be married in the temple of the Lord, and be sealed to each other for time and eternity. Marriage outside of the temple removes one of the sweetest promises of true love—its eternal continuation. No promised gift feeds love so fully or helps so much to face the storms of life. To forfeit that privilege may mean eternal regret. True, the unbelieving wife or husband does at times join the Church and may then receive all the blessings of the Church. But, such cases are relatively rare. It is a remote chance.

Human experience and safe counsel are clearly against "mixed" marriages. The countless cases on record are full evidence that more joy is realized, more usefulness attained, when persons of the same faith marry. Members of the Church, to conserve their own happiness, should marry within the Church. Usually, more deliberation, the avoidance of haste, will prevent many a contemplated marriage with someone outside of the Church. Such delay, with patience, will be well repaid in life's happiness. Certainly, any Latter-day Saint considering marriage outside of the Church should seriously count the cost, one that continues through life.

We are regretfully mindful of the marriages within the Church which are unhappy. That probably, under the limitations of human weaknesses, cannot be avoided. Whether in or out of the Church, we are free agents, and to a certain extent, moulders and makers of our own lives. The fact remains, however, that the proportion of happy marriages is higher among those of the same faith, and highest among those married in the temple.

Let there be no misunderstanding. The excellent people of differing faiths who have married, and who earnestly, sincerely are seeking to make their unions happy, are entitled to our highest respect. For them our hope is that they may come to a unity of faith—faith in the restored gospel of the Lord Jesus Christ. Yet, such couples are probably the first to admit, perhaps only inwardly, that the contentions made in answer to the question at the head of this chapter, are sound and worthy of serious consideration by all who look forward to matrimony.

Youth of Israel! Marry within the Church!

3. WHAT IS THE PLACE OF WOMAN IN THE CHURCH?

The place of woman in the Church is to walk beside the man, not in front of him nor behind him.

In the Church there is full equality between man and woman. The gospel, which is the only concern of the Church, was devised by the Lord for men and women alike. Every person on earth, man or woman, earned the right in the pre-existent life to come here; and must earn the right, by righteous actions, to live hereafter where "God and Christ dwell." The privileges and requirements of the gospel are fundamentally alike for men and women. The Lord loves His daughters as well as He loves His sons.

This doctrine of equality is confirmed in the ordinances of the Church, which are alike for man and woman. Faith, repentance, baptism are the same for all. The rewards, such as the gift of the Holy Ghost, and the temple ordinances, are alike. The highest attainable glory cannot be won by man or woman alone. Only those who are united, as husband and wife, by the sealing power, can attain exaltation in the celestial glory in the hereafter. "Neither is the man without the woman, neither the woman without the man, in the Lord." (1 Corinthians 11:11) And provision will be made for the righteous who live unmarried to receive the sealing blessing in the hereafter, through vicarious work performed in our temples.

This makes individuals of men and women—individuals with the right of free agency, with the power of individual decision, with individual opportunity for everlasting joy, whose own actions throughout the eternities, with the loving aid of the Father, will determine individual achievement. There can be no question in the Church of man's rights versus woman's rights. They have the same and equal rights.

This equality has been respected in the history of the Church. Equal suffrage within the Church has always been recognized. Church members, men and women, have always been asked to sustain by vote, the uplifted hand, the persons nominated to fill the various offices of the church

(D. & C. 20:65; 26:2; 107:22; *Teachings of the Prophet Joseph Smith,* p. 75; Joseph F. Smith, *Gospel Doctrine,* pp. 196, 197). Equal suffrage in civic life has likewise been defended by the Church. "Now, sisters, I want you to vote also, because women are the characters that rule the ballot box." (*Discourses of Brigham Young,* p. 563) The right to vote for national, state, and local officials was granted women in the early days of the territory of Utah, when Church members were in control of territorial activities. In fact, it was in Utah, in 1870, that women first exercised full political franchise in the United States. Brigham Young saw no objection to a woman's holding public office if compatible with her other duties.

The right of woman to develop her native gifts through education has been held before the Church from its organization. Women have, indeed, been urged to train for the various life pursuits of society. The fine arts, music, painting, literature, teaching, business, science, mining, medicine, civil government, and law were mentioned by Brigham Young as suitable studies for women. (*Discourses of Brigham Young,* chapter 22) President Joseph F. Smith spoke similarly: "It is very important to the welfare, usefulness, happiness, and comfort of our daughters (in view of certain circumstances) that they learn some branch of industry that could be turned to practical account in the way of making a living, should circumstances require it." (Joseph F. Smith, *Gospel Doctrine,* p. 440) President Smith also declared his belief that "spiritually, morally, religiously, and in faith" woman is as strong as man. (*Ibid.*)

However, the Church has never ignored, as many political and social theorists have done, the natural differences between men and women. These differences in function determine in a rational society the major duties of man and woman. The design of nature is that man and woman together shall form the unit of society, known as the family; shall beget and rear children to carry on the race; and shall find in family life not only their greatest joy, but also their chief incentive to useful activity. It is recognized that whenever this purpose is ignored, the frustrated functions lead to defeat in life.

Therefore, the Church has taught and urged that man and woman accept their respective responsibilities as man and woman, husband and wife, father and mother. This really is another evidence of equality, since, in conforming to natural law, greater freedom and power are won by both. For the woman, it means that she, at least during a large part of her life, devotes herself chiefly to the duties of home; for the man, that he devote himself chiefly to the providing of the means of support of the home. Naturally, this does not prohibit outside interest for leisure or free time. The importance of such functional division of labor is set forth powerfully by President Heber J. Grant: "The mother in the family far more than the father is the one who instils in the hearts of the children a testimony, and love of the gospel—and wherever you find a woman who is devoted to this work, almost without exception you will find that her children are devoted to it. She shapes their lives more than the father, because he is away much more." (Heber J. Grant, *Gospel Standards,* pp. 150, 151)

In harmony with this view, the Church has always favored a system of education to fit man and woman for their respective spheres of activity—that is, a practical education. Home-making, today a well-established applied science and art, is looked upon as the wise education for woman. Speaking on this subject, President Brigham Young said: "It is more necessary that they [women] should know themselves and the duties that will be required of them when they are wives and mothers." (*Journal of Discourses,* 10: 370). This does not imply a narrowed education, for in the words of President Joseph F. Smith, the Church says to woman, "Seek to be educated in the highest meaning of the term; get the most possible service out of your time, your body and brains, and let all your efforts be directed into honorable channels, that no effort be wasted, and no labor result in loss or evil." (Joseph F. Smith, *Gospel Doctrine,* p. 439) In brief, the major education for life's duties may be supplemented by training for the development of special activities or endowment.

This recognition of natural function appears in the organization of the Church. By divine fiat, the Priesthood is conferred on the men. This means that organization must prevail in the family, the ultimate unit of the Church. The husband, the Priesthood bearer, presides over the family; the Priesthood conferred upon him is intended for the blessing of the whole family. Every member shares in the gift bestowed, but under a proper organization. No man who understands the gospel believes that he is greater than his wife, or more beloved of the Lord, because he holds the Priesthood, but rather that he is under the responsibility of speaking and acting for the family in official matters. It is a protection to the woman who, because of her motherhood, is under a large physical and spiritual obligation. Motherhood is an eternal part of Priesthood. It is a wise provision that the man, who is the freer to move about both at home and abroad, should be called to the family presidency and be under the responsibility of holding the Priesthood. This does not limit equality among men and women. Citizens in a free land are not unequal because some hold office and others do not.

Meanwhile, within the Church are organizations for the benefit of women. These are presided over by women. These have the same general objective as the Priesthood organizations—the fitting of the individual more fully for gospel living. The Prophet Joseph Smith said when he formed the Relief Society, "I will organize the sisters under the Priesthood and after the pattern of the Priesthood." President Grant has declared, "Without the wonderful work of the women I realize that the Church would have been a failure. . . . It is our sisters who carry the burden of the work. . . . They are leaders in all things that make for spiritual uplift." (Heber J. Grant, *Gospel Standards,* pp. 150, 151)

The program of the National Women's Relief Society, which is really international, illustrates the comprehensiveness of woman's place in the Church. "The Ladies' Relief Society is not only to relieve the poor, but to save souls," was the Porphet's message to the sisters. (Joseph Smith, *History of the Church,* 5:25) To save souls opens the whole field of human activity and development: Relief of poverty, relief of illness; relief of doubt, relief of ignorance—relief of all that hinders the joy and progress of woman. What a magnificent commission! The activities of the Society correspond to this charge. For example, in the program for the weekly meetings provision is made for the study of theology, homemaking, social science, and practical work. The men in their Priesthood organizations have no wider program. The

Young Women's Mutual Improvement Associations have a similar, widely-conceived program. No limitations, except those inherent in the gospel plan, restrict the labors of these organizations for women.

"What is the place of woman in the Church?" To walk by the side of the man, not before him nor behind him.

4. SHOULD BIRTH CONTROL BE PRACTICED?

This is an insistent subject. It raises at least three vital questions: Why should married people want to practice birth control? What is the effect on those who practice it? Are large families desirable?

Ill health may make birth control necessary. A weakened body or actual disease may justify protection of the mother and the unborn child against any further physiological burden. However, for those of sound health, who conform to the laws of nature, child bearing promotes physical well-being. As a rule, women who have large families are healthy throughout life.

A more frequent cause of birth control is real or fancied economic pressure. Under modern conditions requiring the services of an obstetric physician and hospital care, the husband and wife of moderate means hesitate to incur this added draft upon their resources. And, often they delay the coming of children because they prefer first to pay for and enjoy the house or piano or automobile or refrigerator or radio-phonograph, or other desirable but not indispensable things. Married students sometimes feel that if they have children they must forego or greatly delay the completion of their educations. In one form or another the economic excuse is a common one.

Others practice birth control because they feel that the care of having children consumes their time and strength, and therefore interferes with social or professional ambitions. They want to be free to "live life as they choose." To this class belong those who absurdly declare that they look for quality instead of quantity and therefore limit the size of their families.

The having of children and the rearing of a family entail expense, especially while the children are young. That goes without saying. Yet, the economic excuse for birth control is seldom convincing. A way is usually found to meet family costs, if the desire for children is stronger than for the new piano, let us say. Sacrifices for a time on the part of the parents and on the part of the older children if there be any, will usually provide the necessary means. The economic excuse roots, in the majority of cases, in selfishness. Yet, it should be said that society, which benefits from its citizens, should make provisions by which the expense incident to motherhood would be within the reach of the poorest.

Those who practice birth control to further their personal ambitions are of course motivated wholly by selfishness. They might well be asked why they married.

Birth control when necessary should be accomplished in nature's way, which does not injure the man or the woman. A careful recognition of the fertile and sterile periods of woman would prove effective in the great majority of cases. Recent knowledge of woman's physiology reveals "the natural method for controlling birth." This method "violates no principle of nature."

Birth control as generally understood implies the use of physical or chemical means to prevent conception. A large number of these devices, known as contraceptives, are on the market. None of them is certain to accomplish the purpose desired. Besides, any contraceptive is unnatural and interferes in one way or another with the physiological processes of life. All of them are in varying degrees injurious to those who use them, especially to women. That may be safely contended. The ill effects may not be felt at once, but in time will overtake the parents to their detriment.

Moreover, since birth control roots in a species of selfishness, the spiritual life of the user of contraceptives is also weakened. Women seem to become more masculine in thought and action; men more callous and reserved; both husband and wife become more careless of each other, and increasingly indifferent to the higher duties and joys of living.

The quality versus quantity contention is a fallacy. The only child in a family is to be pitied. He does not learn the art of living harmoniously with other people. Within the home he is either in opposition to his parents or dominated by them. Outside of the home he sulks if he can not selfishly run the show, or he stands apart from the crowd in uneasy self-consciousness. The shaping and polishing of character which go on in a loving household of many children he receives less effectively from less friendly strangers. He misses many of the joys and pleasures of childhood which are possible only in a family of several children. He often becomes inordinately selfish if all gifts and consideration of father and mother are centered in him. The effect of a lone childhood is felt throughout life. The unspoken, unrealized longings for family intimacies are frequently reflected in foiled attempts to make up for the lost experience of childhood and youth. As the years creep on, he misses more and more the intimate understanding and affectionate sympathy which accompany blood relationships. The only child is likely to remain lonely throughout the journey of life. The same might be said measurably of two children several years apart.

Large families are the most genuinely happy. That is the verdict of human experience. In such a family circle there is steady development and joyful living for parents and children. The Psalmist spoke wisely when he said: "Happy is the man that hath his quiver full of them." (Psalm 127:5)

A home with several children of varying ages approximates the social situations to be met in later life. There the possibilities of life may be experienced in miniature form. Under the loving protection of father and mother, in games and contests, in the exchange of wits, in sacrifices for one another, in mutual rejoicings and sorrows, in discussions of family affairs and daily happenings, the business of living in a world of many men is taught. The home with a family of children becomes a laboratory for learning the importance of truth, virtue, and honesty, industry, and the ethical and religious bases of conduct. And, since love for one another tempers and directs all that is done, the children will enter the world's citizenship better fitted to help build an increasingly improving world. In the training of good citizens or happy human beings, there is no substitute for the home with a large family.

The benefits of a home with several children is not confined to the children. Parents are perhaps equally benefited. Parents who have children show their willingness to accept obligations of good citizenship. They have faith in the future. They dare to continue the race. They are not ashamed to perpetuate themselves. Thereby they win strength to perform other duties of life. Besides, in the rearing of children there is real development of father and mother, a development which can be won in no other way. There is also a supreme satisfaction in presenting men and women, sons and daughters, to the coming age, to carry on the work of the world.

Every parent lives on in his descendants. Above all, is the joy of family life. Father, mother and children, perhaps grandchildren, at the table, or at play, in family councils, share in divine satisfactions. It has been so ordained that the family comes nearest to the heavenly pattern in organization and joys. And, these joys continue into old age. Loneliness is banished. The childless couple miss much in life; and as the years move on the sense of loss becomes keener. The finest, most important, and happiest institution on earth is the family, composed of father, mother and children.

The future of the state and of the race depends upon the willingness of its citizens to beget and rear children without artificial interference. During the last centuries mankind has learned much. The comforts and blessings in every modest home surpass those of the emperors of old. Who shall inherit these gifts and the others in process of making? —Our children, of course, if we have any, and if they are numerous enough to claim consideration. It is a cruel fact, to which we must give heed, that those most highly prepared to enjoy and advance our civilization have a decreasing birthrate; while those of less training, or perhaps inferior gifts, continue fruitful. Many a college class of picked men and women half a century after graduation have fewer children than the original number of the class. It takes more than two children to keep the population from decreasing. The worldwide view is the same. The birthrate of the more advanced nations is falling rapidly; while that of the more backward peoples is large and increasing.

In the last twenty-five years, the birthrate of the United States has fallen from twenty-five to seventeen per thousand of population. In 1941, in the United States the births did not quite equal the deaths; while in Japan the births exceeded the deaths by one-half. *Time* (Sept. 14, 1942) reports that Great Britain has a million and half fewer babies, and a million and a half more pet dogs than at the time of the Boer War. If there is no change, they whom we are inclined to call semi-civilized or barbarians will take over the earth. The survival of our civilization may yet depend on an increasing birthrate in the nations which have made that civilization possible.

Latter-day Saints take literally the command of the Lord to the first couple: "Multiply, and replenish the earth." (Genesis 1:28) That is the purpose of marriage and means more than one or two children. We understand that hosts of waiting spirits desire to come on earth through our lineage. We know that the family is the unit of heavenly society; and that the greatest gift of God is to give His children the opportunity of continuing family relationships throughout the eternities. Are they who will not obey the law on earth worthy of this great reward in the hereafter? Gospel doctrine should make every Latter-day Saint married couple eager for the privilege and obligations of parenthood. And they should have the faith and trust that the Lord will provide the means for obeying His law.

5. WHY SHOULD FAMILY PRAYERS BE HELD?

Man's needs are many. He has little, if any, power of himself to supply them. Therefore, he turns to God for the necessary help. This he can properly do, for the Lord, who has placed man on earth with limited powers, has declared Himself ready to assist His children. He has given them the privilege to address Divinity, with the assurance of being heard. Indeed, He has requested them to approach Him in prayer for guidance in solving life's problems.

Prayer is really the beginning of wisdom. By prayer, communion between man and God is established and maintained. It brings man and his Maker into close association. Earnest, sincere prayer places man in tune with heaven and with the Beings who dwell therein. The knowledge and power thus gained from the unseen world are very real. Brigham Young said:

> If we draw near to him, he will draw near to us; if we seek him early we shall find him; if we apply our minds faithfully and diligently day by day, to know and understand the mind and will of God, it is as easy as, yes, I will say easier than, it is to know the minds of each other, for to know and understand ourselves and our own being is to know and understand God and his being. (*Discourses of Brigham Young*, p. 65)

Prayer may be offered concerning all religious activities. The Lord is concerned with every phase of human welfare, material or spiritual. In the words of the Prophet Joseph Smith:

> We would say to the brethren, seek to know God in your closets, call upon him in the fields. Follow the directions of the Book of Mormon, and pray over, and for your families, your cattle, your flocks, your herds, your corn, and all things that you possess; ask the blessing of God upon all your labors, and everything that you engage in. (*Teachings of the Prophet Joseph Smith*, p. 247)

Such prayers may be offered at any time, on bended knees in the closet or family circle, or when walking, driving, or working, in public or in private. One should do all that he does in the spirit of prayer.

The sacred importance of prayer demands, however, that certain periods of prayer be set aside regularly, daily, when all distracting elements are absent. When the set time comes, prayers should be offered. They are more important than the trivial duties that often take us away from the altar of prayer.

Prayer should be direct and simple as if spoken to our earthly father. Routine forms of prayer should be avoided. The words spoken are less important than the humble faith in which they are uttered. "Prayer is the soul's sincere desire, uttered or unexpressed." It is the spirit of prayer that gives life to our desires. The direct simplicity of the Lord's prayer should be kept in mind.

While we should feel free to open our hearts to the Lord, yet the things sought in prayer should be necessary to our welfare, as explained by President Joseph F. Smith:

> My brethren and sisters, let us remember and call upon God and implore his blessings and his favor upon us. Let us do it, nevertheless, in wisdom and in righteousness, and when we pray we should call upon him in a consistent and reasonable way. We should not ask the Lord for that which is unnecessary or which would not be beneficial to us. We should ask for that which we need, and we should ask in faith, "nothing wavering, for he that wavereth," as the apostle said, "is like the wave of the sea, driven by the wind and tossed. For let not that man think that he shall receive anything of the Lord." But when we ask of God for blessings let us ask in the faith of the gospel, in that faith that he has promised to give to those who believe in him and obey his commandments. (Joseph F. Smith, *Gospel Doctrine*, p. 273)

Every prayer is heard, and every sincere prayer is answered. They who pray should be content to await the answer at the time and in the manner comporting with God's wisdom. He knows what is for our good and bestows His blessings accordingly. The testimony of untold millions that their prayers have been heard is a convincing testimony that God hears and answers prayer.

A prayer is not complete unless gratitude for blessings received is expressed. It is by the power of the Lord that we "live and move and have our being." This should be frankly stated gratefully as we pray to our Father in heaven.

Private prayer has been enjoined upon us, but we are also commanded to pray as families and in public meetings. A united prayer, one in which many join, comes with greater strength and power before the Lord. "In union there is strength."

The family is the ultimate unit of the organized Church. It represents the patriarchal order, which is the order of heaven. All members of this unit should be conscious of the family needs, and should regularly and unitedly petition the Lord for His blessings. Unless this is done, family ties are weakened, and the blessings of the Lord may be withheld. A happier understanding prevails among families who pray together. Therefore, every effort should me made to engage the family regularly in prayer.

Family prayers also become a training school for the younger members of the family. They acquire the habit of prayer, which usually remains with them throughout life. They are taught how to pray as they listen to their elders. They are given practice in vocal prayer, before others, as they are asked to take their turn in prayer. Children who have been brought up under the influence of family prayer, remain stauncher in their faith, live more conscientious lives, and look back gratefully upon the family prayers of their childhoods. Parents who do not have family prayers make sad mistakes.

It is not wise for one member of the family to be voice in prayer constantly. It is better for all members of the family to take their turns in praying. The short prayer of the lisping child is transmuted by heavenly forces into a petition of power, dealing with all the needs of the family. It is selfish for any one member of the family to deprive others of the privilege of participating in family prayer.

Regularity is necessary to make family prayers effective. There should be at least one daily family prayer; two are better. When labor and other conditions permit, there should be a morning and an evening prayer. In many families, terms of employment are such that all the family cannot gather at a morning hour. In practically every home, however, all members of the family are present at the evening meal. That may then be the best time for prayer. All kneel around the table or elsewhere and supplicate the Lord for help and guidance before the meal begins.

6. WHICH COMES FIRST—CHURCH OR HOME?

The Church is composed of homes. Church and home cannot be separated. Neither one comes first. They are one.

Therefore, a home not properly cared for weakens the Church; one cared for strengthens the Church. The condition of the Church as a whole is but as a reflection of the homes of the people.

The question, however, is asked sincerely by persons who, voluntarily or under call, would divide their time, wisely, between the official work of the Church, the assemblage of homes, and the work required in the home.

Fathers, mothers, and children who earnestly strive to make a happy home are really doing Church work—the most important, because it is the most basic work in the Church.

Mothers are especially important in building happy homes and an acceptable Church. They are called divinely to rear children toward maturity, in the spirit and practice of the gospel. Great men have always given tributes to their mothers. Mothers are the makers of men.

Note these words from President Brigham Young: "When I reflect upon duties and responsibilities devolving upon our mothers and sisters, and the influence they wield, I look upon them as the mainspring and soul of our being here."[1]

This of course does not absolve the father from parental duties. A mother who does not have the cooperation of her husband faces a difficult task in her home. Cooperation of mother and father is indispensable for full home success. The father must do his part, support the mother, and add to her attempts to make of the children Latter-day Saints, and worthy citizens of Church and state.

In the home lies the beginning of wisdom in making the Church acceptable to the Lord. The Church, organized from the homes and for the people in them, has its special obligations and responsibilities. It must help provide means by which the homes may function most completely. It must be as arms for the fathers and mothers of the many homes.

-----

[1]*Discourses of Brigham Young*, p. 199.

Through its various organizations, priesthood and auxiliary, and by its publications, the Church must teach its members the principles of the gospel. It must carry the gospel message to the world. It must open the doors of salvation to the dead. Every member of the Church must learn to understand the principles involved in these activities, and must devote some time to one or more of these activities.

However, this work should not be done at the sacrifice of the home; it should rather stimulate home activities. At times fathers and especially mothers give themselves so assiduously to the task of business or of home, that they eliminate all outside activities. They become slaves to a daily routine, when they should be its masters. This is not wise. The mother, as every member of her household, needs change from the daily routine of required tasks. Some time should be found by everyone for relaxation or recreation. The Church activities offer the best outlet for required change. Some mothers, and others, sensing the need of change forget the opportunities the Church offers, and try to find most of their release from routine duties in recreation away from both home and Church. This is equally undesirable. It is unwise.

Latter-day Saints should remember that the Church is so organized that all normal desires may find expression in its program. By entering heartily into this program, love for the Church is not only maintained, but also increased. Moreover, only homes that are active in the affairs of the Church are really happy. The Church is ours—as homes and individuals. We should ever seek to build the Church by our individual efforts.

Most members of the Church are at one time or another called to serve as teacher or officer in some Church organization. This is of necessity so in a Church without a paid ministry, in which the required work is done voluntarily by the members. Naturally the most willing or most capable are likely to be called most frequently to such service.

Sometimes, especially in smaller wards or stakes, the same person may be called to fill several offices at the same time. This is not in full harmony with the spirit of the Church, which provides that one of the functions of the Church is to help develop the innate powers of all of its members. There are usually a sufficient number of members to fill offices, if they are but trusted. The weak become strong under the labors to which they may be called. Presiding officers everywhere should distribute the work to be done among the members. It is often remarkable how well a backward person does work when given the opportunity.

It is when a person, especially a mother, is called to several offices, that the question at the head of this writing appears. No one refuses, or should refuse, a Church call. Every member of the Church, however heavy the duties of home or business may be, could no doubt be active in one Church activity. Should another call come, the person so called has the right to lay before the presiding officer the conditions of his life. Then, the one who has the right to call will determine whether the person called may be honorably released from service.

By such a procedure there will be no interference with home duties; no person be over-worked in the sacred cause of home and Church; all who are able will have the blessed opportunity to serve in building the kingdom of God on earth.

Every member of the Church should divide his time wisely between Church and home. He should be careful not to neglect either. Both are parts of the Lord's great plan of salvation for his children.

7. WHAT IS THE MEANING OF PATRIARCHAL BLESSINGS?

In the history of the Prophet Joseph Smith the following occurs:

> An evangelist is a patriarch, even the oldest man of the blood of Joseph or of the seed of Abraham. Wherever the Church of Christ is established on the earth, there should be a patriarch for the benefit of the posterity of the Saints, as it was with Jacob in giving his patriarchal blessing unto his sons, etc. (*Teachings of the Prophet Joseph Smith,* p. 151)

Every father, having children born to him under the covenant, is to them as a patriarch, and he has the right to bless his posterity in the authority of the Priesthood which he holds. The patriarchs of old commonly blessed their children, as, for example, Isaac (Genesis, chapter 27), Jacob (Genesis, chapter 49), Lehi (Book of Mormon, 2 Nephi, chapters 2, 3, 4), and John Taylor (*Times and Seasons,* Vol. 6: 921, 922).

There are many members of the Church whose fathers or nearest male relatives are not in the Church, or unfitted or unwilling to bless their children. For them special provision must be made. Moreover, the Church is a family, composed of many families. The ordained patriarchs speak also for the larger Church family. They act therefore both in behalf of the fathers of families and of the patriarchal head of the Church.

So important are these official patriarchal blessings that they should always be reduced to writing and preserved. Every blessing is entered upon the record of the patriarch, and ultimately deposited with the Church historian. The person blessed receives a copy of the blessing for his use and comfort.

Patriarchs are specially called and ordained to the work. Their authority is derived from the president of the Church, in whom the ultimate power of giving such blessings on earth is vested. Their jurisdiction is limited. With the exception of the patriarch to the Church, each is appointed to serve in a limited geographical area, usually a stake of Zion.

All Church members may claim the patriarchal blessings flowing from their membership in the assemblage of families within the Church, which can be pronounced only by men who represent the group as a whole. Therefore, patriarchs, ordained to the office, are made available in all the stakes of Zion, so that all faithful members may receive the blessings to which they are entitled.

In giving a blessing the patriarch may declare our lineage—that is, that we are of Israel, therefore of the family of Abraham, and of a specific tribe of Jacob. In the great majority of cases, Latter-day Saints are of the tribe of Ephraim, the tribe to which has been committed the leadership of the Latter-day work. Whether this lineage is of blood or adoption does not matter. (Pearl of Great Price, Abraham, 2:10) This is very important, for it is through the lineage of Abraham alone that the mighty blessings of the Lord for His children on earth are to be consummated. (Genesis 12:2, 3; Pearl of Great Price, Abraham, 2:11)

Then, the patriarch, looking into the future, enumerates the blessings and promises, some special, others general, to which the person of the proper lineage, who receives the blessings, is entitled; and through his authority seals them upon him, so that they may be his forever through faithfulness. The obligations resting upon those who receive such promises are often stated. These blessings are parts of the larger promise made by the Lord to Abraham and his seed. They vary somewhat from person to person, for each has his specific assignment or calling in the gospel plan; but in essence they deal with the gifts, responsibilities, powers, and ultimate destiny of those who have received and obeyed the gospel, and thereby have become members of the great family represented by the Church.

Usually, blessings are added as the spirit may indicate, to meet our special requirements in life, for our comfort, success, and strength. Our special needs may be pointed out; special gifts may be promised us; we may be blessed to overcome our weaknesses, to resist temptation, or to develop our powers, so that we may the more surely achieve the promised blessings. Since all men differ, their blessings may differ; but a patriarchal blessing always confers promises upon us, becomes a warning against failure in life, and a means of guidance in attaining the blessings of the Lord. It may be made of daily help in all the affairs of life.

These blessings are possibilities predicated upon faithful devotion to the cause of truth. They must be earned. Otherwise they are but empty words. Indeed, they rise to their highest value when used as ideals, specific possibilities, toward which we may strive throughout life. To look upon a patriarch as a fortune-teller is an offense to the Priesthood; the patriarch only indicates the gifts the Lord would give us, if we labor for them. He helps us by pointing out the divine goal which we may enjoy if we pay the price.

Such a blessing, given in the spirit of a father's love, and sealed upon us in the authority of the Priesthood, becomes a power in our lives; a comfort to our days. It is a message which if read and honored aright, will become an anchor in stormy days, our encouragement in cloudy days. It states our certain destination here and hereafter, if we live by the law; and as life goes on, it strengthens our faith and leads us into truth. (Joseph F. Smith, *Gospel Doctrine,* p. 226)

It should always be kept in mind that the realization of the promises made may come in this or the future life. Men have stumbled at times because promised blessings have not occurred in this life. They have failed to remember that, in the gospel, life with all its activities continues forever and that the labors of earth may be continued in heaven. Besides, the Giver of the blessings, the Lord, reserves the right to have them become active in our lives, as suits His divine purpose. We and our blessings are in the hands of the Lord. But, there is the general testimony that when the gospel law has been obeyed, the promised blessings have been realized.

Those who seek patriarchal blessings should ask for them with faith in the reality of the power of the Priesthood. They should seek them with an earnest, prayerful desire to become, through the blessings, more completely happy in their lives, and more perfectly serviceable in the work of the Lord. And they should, of course, be qualified to receive their blessings by conformity in their lives to the requirements of the gospel. The unclean or disobedient person should cleanse himself, and learn obedience before going to the patriarch. Only under such conditions can a person expect to learn of the will of the Lord.

The patriarchal blessing should be read and reread. It should be made useful in life. This should be done with faith in spiritual blessings.

It is a gift of the Lord. The purpose of asking for the blessing must be remembered. It must be read with intelligent consideration of its meaning. Attention should be fixed upon the one great meaning of the blessing rather than upon particular statements. There must be no quibbling about the time or place when the promises should be fulfilled or about the man who gave it. As the blessing was given through the inspiration of the Lord, so its meaning will be made clear by the same power; and its fulfilment will be in His hands. Above all, it must ever be remembered that every blessing is conditioned upon our faithfulness. Let us examine our lives from time to time to learn whether we are so living as to be worthy of the blessings promised. It is certain that our patriarchal blessing, if we give it proper respect, may be a source of divine help in life's journey.

It may be added that the sacred patriarchal blessings are personal in their nature. They should not be talked about or shown about; they should be read frequently and pondered upon for our personal good. It is for that reason that each person receives a copy of his blessing.

Necessarily, since patriarchs are but men, they are subject to human frailties. Their manner of speech and thinking is reflected in their blessings. Different men express the same idea in different words. The Lord does not dictate blessings to them word for word. Likewise, portions of the blessing may be emphasized by the nature or desire of the patriarch. Nevertheless, if the patriarch lives worthily, he is sustained by the power and authority of his calling, and will pronounce blessings intended for us. And we, if we live worthily, will comprehend the blessings and find deep comfort in them.

A patriarchal blessing is also a constant reminder of the patriarchal form of organization and government, emphasizing the importance of the family, which prevailed in the early days of the world. The father, holding the holy Priesthood, was then the legislator, judge, and governor of his family, each father presiding over his own family; and the oldest, over the group of families of common descent. Thus, every family as it increased became a tribe, kingdom, or nation, under the presidency of the living father of them all. It is the ideal form of government, wherever the Priesthood prevails, and it appears to be the form of organization in the world to come.

In summary: a patriarchal blessing (1) is for those who are of the chosen people, the family of obedient children, through whom the Lord is working out His earthly purposes; (2) it promises the members of the family certain blessings which are in store for them, on earth and in heaven, which are sealed upon them on conditions of obedience to the law of the Lord; (3) it confers power upon us, if we will use it, to win the fulfilment of these promises, as we journey through life; and (4) special blessings are made available to us to meet our daily needs.

All Latter-day Saints should seek their blessings under the hands of the patriarch; and should use them in their lives.

8. WHY ARE BUILDINGS DEDICATED?

The practice of dedicating buildings is as old as the Church, and older. Solomon's temple was dedicated amidst elaborate ceremonies. Soon after the Church in this dispensation was organized, a temple was built in Kirtland, Ohio. On March 27, 1836, it was dedicated. All the other temples of the Church have been dedicated in a public and solemn manner. Meetinghouses of the Latter-day Saints, when fully paid for, are also always dedicated. Many of the most glorious manifestations of the Church have occurred in connection with the dedications of temples and meetinghouses.

This practice is not confined to temples and meetinghouses. The practice of the Church is to dedicate any building intended for a good purpose. For example, in 1852, a few years after entering Salt Lake Valley, the pioneers built a social hall to provide a place for the recreation of the people. This building was formally dedicated just before its opening. In 1862 when the Salt Lake Theatre had been completed, President Daniel H. Wells, counselor to President Brigham Young, dedicated the building.

It has been a common practice also among Latter-day Saints to dedicate the homes in which they live. When a home has been secured and paid for, a dedication is frequently held. This practice carries with it the same ideals, hopes, and aspirations embodied in a dedication of more public places.

The Latter-day Saints do not claim to be the originators of the practice of dedicating buildings, but are very sincere and earnest followers of it. Throughout the world, the practice of dedicating public places is very common. Churches, hospitals, libraries, and cathedrals are dedicated amidst much pomp and splendor.

The central event in dedicating ceremonies among the Latter-day Saints is the prayer of dedication. Those of past dedications are as inspiring today as when they were given. The prayer given when Solomon's temple was dedicated has comforted hosts of people.[2] Joseph Smith's prayer when the Kirtland Temple was dedicated is published as section

-----

[2]I Kings, chapter 8; II Chronicles, chapter 6.

109 in the Doctrine and Covenants. The prayers offered at the dedication of the various temples show the prophetic power which guides this Church.[3] The noble prayer at the dedication of the Salt Lake Theatre might profitably be read by all who offer dramatic recreation.[4] They are models which might well be followed by all who are called upon to dedicate buildings.

The dedicatory prayers, as reported, fall into several parts, instructive, enlightening, and inspiring.

First, there is in such prayers an expression of gratitude to the Lord for the possession of the building, an acknowledgment that without his help man cannot succeed in any endeavor. Then follows, usually, a promise that the house will be used to help advance the gospel cause in this day. That is, that in all activities within the building the Spirit of the Lord shall rule and direct. Only things will be done in the house which are in harmony with the principles and laws laid down by the Lord for the guidance of his children.

Blessings are also asked upon all who have helped in the construction of the building, and those who participate in the dedicatory service. Special blessings are asked for all who may use the building so that help from heaven may be received by them in all their labors and in every moment of need.

The prayer also asks that the building may be protected from all harm of an external nature, and from the designs of wicked men, that it may be kept whole and intact for the purposes for which it was erected.

A prayer of dedication surrenders the building to the Lord for the establishment of his great cause. That is, the building and the people in it commit themselves to the great Latter-day purposes of the Lord.

As the Spirit may dictate, any prayer and supplication may be a part of the dedicatory prayer. It is really a simple approach to the Lord in thanksgiving, praise, promise, and prayer.

Some people ask why homes are dedicated. The prayers

-----

[3]Nauvoo Temple, *Journal History,* 1846. April 30, p. 1; St. George, *Journal History,* April 6, 1877; Logan, *Millennial Star,* 46:386; Manti, ibid., 50:385; Salt Lake, *Contributor,* 14:292; Hawaiian, *The Improvement Era* 23:281; Alberta, *ibid.,* 26:1075; Arizona, *Liahona,* 25:245; Idaho Falls, *The Improvement Era,* 48:562.

[4]*Daniel H. Wells,* Byrant S. Hinckley, p. 323.

themselves furnish the answer. The very things that appear most regularly in dedicatory prayers are those that we need in our homes, in our daily lives. We thank the Lord for our homes. We ask that they, with those who dwell in them, may be under the overshadowing hand of the Lord. We ask the Lord to assist us in our daily labor. We promise him to devote our homes and our labors therein to the advancement of the cause of the Lord—the salvation of humankind. Then we may expect help from above; then we may expect to have peace and happiness in our homes.

Out of the homes issues the spirit of the people. As the homes are conducted, so the Church in a large measure will be. We have good reason, therefore, to dedicate our homes and all our possessions to the mighty purpose of the restoration of the gospel. Dedicated homes are the best abiding places of peace and happiness.

Wilford Woodruff speaking on this subject said:

"The Lord has blessed . . . the earth for our use; and we ought to dedicate our families, our fields, our crops, our herds to God."[5]

-----

[5]*Discourses of Wilford Woodruff*, p. 174.

X. Joseph Smith

1. IS THE "HISTORY OF JOSEPH SMITH" TRUSTWORTHY?

The Church of Jesus Christ of Latter-day Saints was commanded on the day of its organization (April 6, 1830) to keep an accurate record of its history. This has been done faithfully to this day. So complete and minute is this record that no existing organization can surpass it.

Frequent moves, stirring events, and ceaseless persecution characterized the early years of the Church. This made necessary changes in recorders and scribes. Undoubtedly, now and then an event may have escaped the historian, or the record may have been lost. Nevertheless, every effort was made to preserve Church annals of all kinds, even to casual memoranda, correspondence, newspaper accounts of Church affairs, and even payments of postage on letters. (*History of the Church* 2:325) Besides, Joseph Smith's own journal was kept very regularly.

Early in 1838, the Prophet set about to present the historical events of the Church in connected form. On April 27, 1838, he writes, "This day I chiefly spent in writing a history of the Church from the earliest period of its existence, up to this date." (*Ibid.*, 3:25) The following Monday, April 30, 1838, he says, "The First Presidency were engaged in writing the Church history." (*Ibid.*, 3:26) The "history" so written was under the Prophet's supervision, with the help of his counselors and clerks. This work was continued until the Prophet's death.

In 1842 the Church newspaper, *The Times and Seasons,* under the editorship of John Taylor, began the publication of the work, under the title, "History of Joseph Smith." Its publication there ran from June 1842, to May 1845. Later, the *Millennial Star* republished the series beginning April 1852, and ending May 1863. At length, beginning in 1904 the work was published in modern book form, forming the first six volumes of the projected full history of the Church.

In these successive printings, conflicts of dates were rectified, errors corrected, and later-discovered materials added. The 1904 edition is well annotated. So well has the work been done, and so carefully has the truth been respected, that writers and speakers for and against Mormonism have used it fully as a sound historical document.

The "history" is really a compilation. It is the journal of the Prophet, interlaced with available, original documents including the revelations to the Prophet. His own comments generally serve to tie the documents together in historical form. The wealth of original documents makes the volumes of double interest and importance.

In some respects this history is a prime evidence of the truth of Mormonism. It recounts intimate family accounts, and sometimes apparently trifling Church matters. It sets forth boldly the documents of the day, and the faith and opinions of the author. The Prophet and the Church stand in this history free of historical interpretations and other external trappings. There are no arguments for its case. There are no attempts to "cover over" any event. Here are the naked facts; let every man draw his own conclusions. This challenge to all readers becomes a splendid record of a people who did not fear the truth.

Three kinds of historical occurrences are presented:

First, events among Church members, and between the Church and the outside world. There were many such. Each one is documented, often with the Prophet's comments. Eternal human nature springs up on almost every page. There has been no refutation of such reported historical facts. Friend and foe have been obliged to accept them as they stand.

Second, spiritual experiences in the life of the Prophet which were witnessed in part or in full by others. The coming forth of the Book of Mormon is recited in full. His connection with the men who saw the plates is recounted. The visions in the Kirtland Temple were had by the Prophet and Oliver Cowdery. The vision of graded salvation, known as Section 76 in the Doctrine and Covenants, was shared with Sidney Rigdon. Again, these stories of spiritual experiences, witnessed by others, are told without argument. The plain telling is enough. Let every man read and judge, seems to be the Prophet's message.

Third, spiritual manifestations witnessed only by the Prophet. These are also very simply told. At times, under the influence of the divine message, the language rises to great beauty. But, there is no argument for their reality. They must speak for themselves. Seekers after truth, who test them properly will accept them. That is the implied message of the compilation.

These "unwitnessed" revelations have been chosen by enemies of the Church to be targets of attack. However, such critics have failed to take into account that the unquestioned truth of the record in the matters experienced by many persons is an evidence for the truth of the whole record, including the personal, private experiences of the Prophet.

Therefore, the foiled critics have often resorted to the cheap and unscientific method of declaring the Prophet to be a mendacious deceiver, who invented his revelations, which they dare not explore. Desperately, they have thrown dust in the eyes of their readers, to obscure plain truth.

To call witnesses liars is an easy way to write history, but it is not in harmony with the accepted canons of historical writing. Yet, such breaches of historical study and writing make the foundation of anti-Mormon books, of which there are many.

The *History of Joseph Smith*, published by the Church, as to events and dates, may be accepted as an unusually accurate historical document. It will increase in importance with the years, and become more and more a proof of the sincerity of the founders of the Church in this dispensation.

2. WHEN DID JOSEPH SMITH HAVE THE FIRST VISION?

In the history of Joseph Smith written by himself is an account of his first vision. He tells that it was received in the spring of 1820, when he was between fourteen and fifteen years of age. A religious revival in his neighborhood led him to wonder which of the contending sects was right before God. (See also Oliver Cowdery Letters No. 3) In his perplexity he retired to a quiet grove and appealed to God in prayer. In answer he had a vision of God, the Father, and God, the Son. These heavenly personages informed him that all the churches had strayed from the full truth, and that the true Church was soon to be re-established. (*History of the Church* I, 2-6)

Because the earliest available written or printed account of this vision is dated 1838 and 1839, some enemies of the Church have cast doubt upon the authenticity of the date claimed for the vision. They have suggested that the vision was invented by the Prophet in 1838, when he set about to write the formal history of the Church. This not only implies that Joseph Smith lied, but also that the facts of history to be acceptable must be written and circulated at the time of their occurrence. This is a preposterous claim, made only by enemies of the Church to mislead those who are unacquainted with Mormon history.

Whether the story of the first vision existed in written form in the early days of the Church is not known. Many manuscripts of that time have been lost. In some cases, secretaries deliberately carried Church records away from Church possession. But, even were they all available, minutes of meetings as they are usually kept might seldom mention the first vision, for familiar and repeated things are often not recorded because they are taken for granted. Certainly, the people in Joseph Smith's neighborhood would pay little attention to the claim of a fourteen-year-old boy that he had had a visitation from God.

It must be remembered that the Book of Mormon, printed in 1830, became at once the storm center of the claims of Joseph Smith. All other issues were forgotten when friend or foe held the printed Nephite record in his hands. The coming forth of this volume, with the establishment of the Church soon following, presented claims of superlative importance. These events declared that heavenly visitations may occur now as in the past, that translations of unknown languages may be made by the "gift and power of God," that the authoritative priesthood of God had been conferred on men by resurrected beings, and that the true Church of Christ was re-established. The book with its accompanying claims overshadowed then as now other equally weighty matters, such as the first vision. The Book of Mormon was a tangible thing which could be argued about. The vision of a boy, whether true or false, could not be attacked in the same way. Nevertheless, it is evident that the first vision was known to the people and on their lips, before the Prophet began the writing of his history. Moreover, it was always understood in the Church that the vision was received in 1820, before the revelations concerning the Book of Mormon, which are dated beyond question from 1823 to 1827. Indeed, unfriendly non-Mormon writers have contributed to the evidence for this view.

The first vision is not mentioned in many non-Mormon books dealing with the time of Joseph Smith. The writers plunge at once into the Book of Mormon controversy. A few have mildly suggested or have had the temerity to distort history by ignoring the facts and to insist that the story of the first vision was invented by the Prophet many years later than 1820. (G. B. Arbaugh, *Revelation Among the Mormons*, pp. 34, 35, 238; W. A. Linn, *History of the Mormons*, p. 30; Fawn M. Brodie, *No Man Knows My History*, pp. 21-25) All other non-Mormon or anti-Mormon writers accept the first vision and the time of its occurrence, as one of the early claims of the Prophet.

In later books, after the days of the Prophet, the visions of Joseph Smith, the first vision, the visitations of Moroni, and later visions, are all jumbled together, so that no distinction can be made among them. In fact, testimony of any consequence must come from the lips of those who lived in the early days of Mormonism, when the Prophet was alive.

Pomeroy Tucker, the proprietor and editor of the Wayne *Sentinel*, on the press of which the Book of Mormon was first printed, knew most of the persons and events connected with the early days of the Church. He was deeply prejudiced against the claims of Joseph Smith, and looked upon them as hoaxes.

Nevertheless, he had reason to know the succession of events, even if he did not believe their authenticity. Upon the basis of contemporaneous knowledge, he held that the first claim of Joseph Smith to have had a vision came before the manifestations relative to the Book of Mormon occurred. He writes:

> About this time (he places the date about 1823) Smith had a remarkable vision. He pretended that, while engaged in secret prayer, alone in the wilderness, an "angel of the Lord" appeared to him, with the glad tidings that "all his sins had been forgiven him," and proclaiming further that "all the religious denominations were believing in false doctrines and consequently that none of them were accepted of God as his Church and Kingdom," and also that he had received a "promise that the true doctrine and the fulness of the gospel should at some future time be revealed to him." *Following this* soon came another angel . . . "that the American Indians were a remnant of the Israelites, . . . that . . . their writings were safely deposited . . . and that . . . he would be the chosen prophet to translate them."

Despite the errors in detail, this statement repeats in essence, the first vision as told by the Prophet himself, and sets the time of its occurrence before the coming forth of the Book of Mormon.

J. B. Turner, a non-Mormon, was one of the earliest writers on Mormonism. His book was published in 1842, written, no doubt, before he could have had access to Joseph's own printed story, also published in 1842. He mentions the first vision. His version, though containing errors of date, corroborates the Prophet's story. He writes:

> In the year 1823, when our prophet was about seventeen years of age, his mind became, for the first time, deeply excited on the subject of religion by Mr. Lane, a devoted and talented elder of the Methodist Church, under whose preaching there was a "great awakening," and numbers, among whom was our prophet and several members of his family, were "profoundly added to the Kingdom of the Lord."
>
> After the revival ceased, the usual strife for proselytes between the several sects commenced, this resulted, so far as the Smiths are concerned, in bringing the mother, one sister, and two brothers into the Presbyterian church; but leaving Joseph as he states, in disgust

with all the sects, and almost in despair of ever coming to the knowledge of the truth amid so many contradictory and conflicting claims. He resorted to prayer for a "full manifestation of divine approbation" and "for the assurance that he was accepted of him." This occurred sometime in the winter of 1823.

On the memorable evening of the 21*st of September following* . . . a form stood before him . . . (who) proceeded to inform Smith that . . . the Lord had chosen him to bring forth and translate the Book of Mormon.

This early author thus confirms the claims of Joseph Smith that the first vision antedated the promise of the Book of Mormon.

The quotations made by these two writers are not from the Prophet's story. Apparently they had not read it. If they had other sources of information, it would add to the evidence that the first vision was known among the people in the early years of the Church. However, both writers agree that the first vision antedated the revelations received by the Prophet concerning the Nephite record.

B. Pixley, after visiting the Saints in Missouri, writes under date of October 12, 1832, that

. . . their creed appears to have undergone but little change . . . The Mormons still prefer to talk with angels, visit the third heaven, and converse with Christ face to face.

The Missouri Intelligencer, under August 10, 1833, speaking of a meeting held in Independence the previous month, says:

Of all their pretended revelations from heaven . . . their personal intercourse with God and his angels . . . converse with God and his angels . . . may be better imagined than described.

Others of the same period speak of the claim that Joseph Smith conversed with God, which, no doubt, had reference to the first vision.

A correspondent of the *Episcopal Recorder* describes the visit of Martin Harris in 1827 who told of a supernatural experience of Joseph Smith, followed later by another divine communication directing him to find the plates. The story is wildly distorted, but the elements of the first vision are clearly evident: Joseph was alone in the woods; a dazzling illumination occurred; an evil power first overcame him; he was overcome by the succeeding vision of God, and a *later vision* concerning the plates of the Book of Mormon. (The correspondent was J. A. Clark, D.D., and his story appeared as a series of letters in the *Recorder* in 1840, reproduced in the *Weekly Visitor,* 1841, pp. 61-64, and in his book *Gleanings by the Way,* New York, 1842, 222-8)

J. H. Kennedy who much later professed to write an unbiased book on the Mormons, accepts without question Joseph Smith's own story as to time and date. (J. H. Kennedy, *Early Days of Mormonism,* pp. 23, 24) So, as has been said, do most of the writers who discuss the first vision. (For example, T. B. H. Stenhouse, *Rocky Mountain Saints,* p. 15; I. W. Riley, *The Founder of Mormonism,* p. 66; Ellen Dickenson, *New Light on Mormonism,* p. 33; Doris H. Bays, *Doctrines and Dogmas of Mormonism,* p. 19; E. Meyer, *Ursprung and Gerschichte der Mormonen,* pp. 16, 17) In fact, proof of the occurrence of the vision in Joseph Smith's early years, if needed, could be established wholly from non-Mormon sources.

Mormon writers and speakers who lived in the days of Joseph Smith believed without exception that the first vision occurred in the early life of the boy, before the Book of Mormon visitations. His mother accepted her son's own story in full, and added more about his early spiritual experiences. (Lucy M. Smith, *Joseph Smith the Prophet,* pp. 73-77, [1902 ed.] pp. 69-74, [1945 ed.]) Elder Edward Stevenson wrote:

> In . . . 1834 in the midst of many large congregations, the Prophet testified with great power concerning the visit of the Father and the Son. (Edward Stevenson, *Reminiscences of Joseph, the Prophet,* p. 4)

Joseph Smith himself relates how in 1835, he told one Erastus Holmes of his "first vision which was when I was about fourteen years old." (*History of the Church,* II, 312) His brother William in his old age described the circumstances of his first vision as told by his prophet brother. (*Deseret News,* January 20, 1894)

Orson Pratt, who lived for some time in the Prophet's home issued a pamphlet in 1839, in which the first vision is described, and it is there placed in 1820. (Orson Pratt, *Remarkable Visions,* pp. 4, 5) Later in life, Orson Pratt said, "I have often heard him (the Prophet) relate it." (*Journal of Discourses* 7:220-221; 11:65-66; 12:302; 14:150-141; 15:-180-182. See also N. B. Lundwall, *Masterful Discourses and Writings of Orson Pratt*, pp. 235-236) Brigham Young who often spoke about the Prophet and his early experiences, said on one occasion:

> The Lord called Joseph Smith, called upon him at fourteen years of age, gave him visions, and led him along, guided and directed him in his obscurity, until he brought forth the plates and translated them. (*Journal of Discourses,* 8:354; see also 12:6)

Heber C. Kimball, Wilford Woodruff, John Taylor, George A. Smith, and numerous others who lived in the days of the Prophet, have spoken of the first vision as a fact accomplished in 1820, and before the Prophet saw the Book of Mormon plates, according to Joseph Smith's own story. (Heber C. Kimball, *Journal of Discourses* 6:29; John Taylor, *The Gospel Kingdom,* p. 121; Wilford Woodruff, *Leaves from My Journal,* first edition, p. 86; George A. Smith, *Journal of Discourses* 12:334; 13:78; 11:1-2)

These men were among the early converts to Mormonism. They were hardheaded men, who wanted to be certain about things. Brigham Young took two long years to study Joseph Smith and his message before he was baptized into the Church in 1831. If these men had heard for the first time in 1838 of the Prophet's first vision, Joseph Smith would have had to do some explaining. They were not the men to follow a deceiver.

All acceptable evidence within and beyond the Church confirms the Prophet's story that his first vision occurred when he was between fourteen and fifteen years of age in the year 1820 and before the Book of Mormon revelations occurred.

3. DID JOSEPH SMITH INTRODUCE PLURAL MARRIAGE?

Moral purity is required of all Latter-day Saints. Men must be as clean as women, and both must be free from any violation of the moral law. That is the basis of all marriages performed under the authority of the Church of Jesus Christ of Latter-day Saints.

The Church solemnizes two kinds of marriages. First, those that unite husband or wife for the duration of mortal life. These marriages end with death. Second, those that continue the family relationship after death, in the hereafter. This is often known as eternal or celestial marriage.

Faithful members of the Church seek to enjoy both of these kinds of marriages. They wish to be wedded for time and eternity, that is, to continue their associations forever. To be able to do this is one of the happiest privileges of Church membership. Such marriages, usually called sealings, must be performed in the temples, whenever they exist.

Several approaches to eternal marriage may be made: Two living person may be sealed to each other for time and eternity. A living man may be sealed for eternity to a dead woman; or a living woman to a dead man. Two dead persons may be sealed to each other. It is also possible, though the Church does not now permit it, to seal two living people for eternity only, with no association on earth.

Further, under a divine command to the Prophet Joseph Smith, it was possible for one man to be sealed to more than one woman for time and for eternity. Thus came plural marriage among the Latter-day Saints. By another divine command, to Wilford Woodruff, a successor to Joseph Smith, this order of marriage was withdrawn in 1890. Since that time the Church has not sanctioned plural marriages. Anyone who enters into them now is married unlawfully, and is excommunicated from the Church.

That Joseph Smith actually was the person who introduced plural marriage into the Church and that he practised it himself are amply proved by existing facts.

1. The revelation known as section one hundred thirty-two in the Doctrine and Covenants, which contains the

doctrine of celestial marriage and also the practice of plural marriage, was dictated to his scribe, William Clayton, by Joseph Smith on July 12, 1843, a year before the martyrdom of the Prophet. It had been received by the Prophet some years before, and taught to many, but was not reduced to writing until 1843. William Clayton lived as an honorable citizen, of the highest character, until December 4, 1879, thirty-six years after the revelation was written. He never wavered in his simple declaration that the revelation as now found in the Doctrine and Covenants was dictated to him, sentence by sentence. He adds that "after the whole was written, Joseph asked me to read it through, slowly and carefully, which I did, and he pronounced it correct." (Andrew Jenson, *Historical Record,* Volume VI, pp. 225, 226)

On the day the revelation was written, or the day after, Joseph C. Kingsbury was asked to make a copy of it. This copy was carefully compared with the original by Bishop Newell K. Whitney, and preserved by him. Elder Kingsbury, of unblemished character and reputation, lived fifty-five years after this event (dying October 5, 1898), and always bore solemn testimony to the written origin of the revelation in 1843, through the lips of the Prophet. In further corroboration of the claim that the revelation came from the lips of the Prophet, are the statements of numerous men and women, then living, who either saw the revelation or heard it read. In fact, the document was read to the high council in Nauvoo.

2. A number of men, who in their lives showed themselves honest, have testified that they actually performed the ceremonies that united Joseph Smith to plural wives. Among these were Joseph B. Noble, Hyrum Smith, James Adams, Newell K. Whitney, Willard Richards, and others. Several of these men lived long after the Prophet's death and always declared that they officiated in marrying the Prophet to a plural wife, giving place, date, and the witnesses present.

3. Many of the women who were thus sealed to Joseph Smith lived long after his death. They declared that they lived with the Prophet as husband and wives. These women were of unblemished character, gentle and lovely in their lives, who spoke with loving respect of their martyr husband. They substantiated in detail the statements of those who performed the ceremonies.

4. Many of the elders in Nauvoo entered into plural marriage, under the authority of Joseph Smith who was yet living, as certified to by the men and their wives. Among these were Willam Clayton, Orson Hyde, Hyrum Smith, John Smith, Erastus Snow, Lyman Wight, James J. Strang, Gladden Bishop, William Smith, Heber C. Kimball, and Brigham Young. These men and their wives who survived the Prophet, made affidavits of their marriages in Joseph's day in answer to the charge by enemies of the Church that plural marriage was not instituted nor practised, neither authorized by the Prophet. These men and women were good citizens, so well-known over such long periods of time that their concordant declarations cannot be gainsaid.

5. The Nauvoo Temple records, which are in the possession of the Church, likewise furnish evidence that Joseph Smith practised plural marriage. Before the completion of the temple, marriage sealings were usually performed in rooms in the home of the Prophet. When the temple was dedicated in 1846 for such ceremonies, the plural marriages of Joseph were given temple sanction, and where the marriages were for time only, they were often made to continue through eternity.

This was done within a year and a half of the assassination of the Prophet. Many received plural wives in the Nauvoo Temple. It is utterly improbable, if not impossible, that such a new doctrine could have been conceived and carried out by the men who succeeded the Prophet. There would have been a serious resentment among those who entered the temple, if the teachings of the Prophet had been violated. Such criticism would have overflowed to the outside.

6. After the death of the Prophet, women applied for the privilege of being sealed to him for eternity. They felt no doubt that in the eternal ages they would then share the companionship of the Prophet. They wanted to enjoy eternity with the man whom they revered as one chosen of God to open the last dispensation of the gospel on earth. To these requests, assent was often given. Such action by women who lived in the days of the Prophet implies a belief in plural marriage. These women, who were not in any sense earthly wives of the Prophet, have been counted by uninformed or antagonistic writers as wives of the Prophet.

Women no longer living, whether in Joseph's day or

later, have also been sealed to the Prophet for eternity. The request for such unions has usually come from relatives or friends who would have their loved one share eternity with the Prophet, rather than with anyone else. Unscrupulous and unreliable writers have even added such marriages to the list of Joseph's wives.

7. Another kind of celestial marriage seems to have been practised in the early days of plural marriage. It has not been practised since Nauvoo days, for it is under Church prohibition. Zealous women, married or unmarried, loving the cause of the restored gospel, considered their condition in the hereafter. Some of them asked that they might be sealed to the Prophet for eternity. They were not to be his wives on earth, in mortality, but only after death in the eternities. This came often to be spoken of as celestial marriage. Such marriages led to misunderstandings by those not of the Church, and unfamiliar with its doctrines. To them marriage meant only association on earth. Therefore any ceremony uniting a married woman, for example, to Joseph Smith for eternity seemed adulterous to such people. Yet, in any day, in our day, there may be women who prefer to spend eternity with another than their husband on earth.

Such cases, if any, and they must have been few in number, gave enemies of the Church occasion to fan the flaming hatred against the Latter-day Saints. The full truth was not told. Enemies made the most of the untruth. They found it difficult to believe that the Church rests on truth and virtue.

The literature and existing documents dealing with plural marriage in Nauvoo in the day of Joseph Smith are very numerous. Hundreds of affidavits on the subject are in the Church Historian's office in Salt Lake City. Most of the books and newspaper and magazine articles on the subject are found there also. (For a fairly condensed but complete discussion consult Andrew Jenson, *Historical Record,* Vol. VI, pp. 219-236; Joseph Fielding Smith, *Blood Atonement and the Origin of Plural Marriage*, pp. 67-94; *Woman's Exponent,* Vol. XIII and XIV; *The Deseret News,* especially in 1886)

The careful study of all available information leads to but one conclusion. Joseph Smith received the revelation in question, and practised plural marriage. The issue is not one of doctrine but of history. No honest student can declare the host of witnesses, hundreds of them, from Nauvoo days, Mormon and non-Mormon of various residence, pursuits and temperaments to have united in lying about the matter. The evidence is confirmed by those who place the introduction of plural marriage on others, for they seek feeble, unworthy shelter in the statement that Joseph Smith did practise plural marriage, but later repented of it. (*The Saints Herald,* Vol. I, pp. 9, 26, 27) That is throwing dust in the eyes of seekers after truth. The case is clear. Authentic history says that plural marriage originated with Joseph Smith the Prophet. And so it did. The apparent denials by Church leaders in Nauvoo days that the Church practised plural marriage were correct. At that time, the Church members as a whole had not heard the revelation, nor had they been given an opportunity to accept it. But many of the leaders knew of it and were polygamists.

The chaotic conditions of the years immediately following the Prophet's death, delayed the formal presentation of the revelation. Soon after the Church was established in the Great Salt Lake region, at the conference in 1852, the doctrine of celestial and plural marriage was accepted by the Church as a whole. During the intervening years, however, it was taught and practised.

4. DID JOSEPH SMITH PLAN THE WESTWARD MIGRATION OF THE CHURCH?

In 1847 the Pioneer company entered the Great Salt Lake Valley. They were the forerunners of the tens of thousands who in orderly procession toiled across plain and desert in search of a haven of peace. Their story of suffering, sacrifice, and eventual success will live while the generations of men endure. It is fitting that 1947 is dedicated to the memory of these intrepid men and women, the founders of the intermountain empire of North America.

The westward movement of the Latter-day Saints was not desired by them. Instead it was thrust upon them. They came west because they were obliged to do so. They would have preferred to enjoy their comfortable homes in beautiful Nauvoo and elsewhere. They were driven out and forced to seek another place of settlement. It was with heavy hearts that they trudged through the winter in Iowa and built temporary homes in Nebraska. Had it not been for the courage born of faith in their destiny, they would have scattered over the country, and the opening of the west would have been delayed by many years.

The trail of the Church from New York, Ohio, and Missouri had been littered with persecutions from enemies, who stooped to every evil and inhuman device to prevent the progress of the Church. At length the persecuted people found a peaceful haven, as they thought, in Illinois. But among neighboring villages, outdistanced by the city of Nauvoo, hate was being fanned into a destructive flame.

That these conditions would ultimately compel another removal of the people became clear to the mind of the Prophet Joseph, the sustained leader of the Church. He began to look around for a place to which his people could move and remain relatively unmolested from unfriendly neighbors. The far west, then being opened on the Pacific Coast, was almost naturally the place to which the Prophet's mind would be directed. None had as yet suggested settlement in the valleys of the Rocky Mountains or on the surrounding interior deserts. That seemed to be a place where the Saints could live undisturbed at least for a while. The spirit of revelation confirmed this view.

The Prophet then set about to prepare the people for this coming event. Under date of August 6, 1842, he wrote in his journal:

"Passed over the river to Montrose, Iowa. . . . I prophesied that the Saints would continue to suffer much affliction and would be driven to the Rocky Mountains, many would apostatize, others would be put to death by our persecutors or lose their lives in consequence of exposure or disease, and some of you will live to go and assist in making settlements and build cities and see the Saints become a mighty people in the midst of the Rocky Mountains." (*History of the Church,* V:85)

Anson Call, who was present on that occasion and wrote his recollection of it, says that the Prophet, after uttering this prophecy, began a vivid description of the western country, much as it really is. The Prophet also said that Anson Call, Shadrach Roundy, and others who were present would assist in this building of cities among the Rocky Mountains. He then charged all present to be faithful, so that the priesthood would prevail over all enemies. (*Ibid.,* V:85, 86; Tullidge, Edward, *History of Northern Utah and Southern Idaho,* Biographical Supplement, pp. 271-273; Whitney, Orson F., *History of Utah,* Vol. IV, p. 143)

More than a year and a half later, on Tuesday, February 20, 1844, the proposed westward movement began to take shape. The Prophet writes:

"I instructed the Twelve Apostles to send out a delegation and investigate the locations of California and Oregon, and hunt out a good location, where we can remove to after the temple is completed, and where we can build a city in a day, and have a government of our own, get up into the mountains, where the devil cannot dig us out, and live in a healthful climate, where we can live as old as we have a mind to." (*History of the Church,* VI:222)

Prompt action was taken to obey these instructions, as shown by the following entry:

"At a meeting of the Twelve, at the mayor's office, Nauvoo, February 21, 1844, seven o'clock p.m., Brigham Young,

Parley P. Pratt, Orson Pratt, Wilford Woodruff, John Taylor, George A. Smith, Willard Richards and four others being present, called by previous notice, by instruction of President Joseph Smith on the 20th instant, for the purpose of selecting a company to explore Oregon and California, and select a site for a new city for the Saints.

"Jonathan Dunham, Phineas H. Young, David D. Yearsley, and David Fullmer, volunteered to go; and Alphonso Young, James Emmett, George D. Watt, and Daniel Spencer were requested to go.

"Voted the above persons to be notified to meet with the council on Friday evening next, at the assembly room.

"Willard Richards, Clerk."

(*Ibid.*, VI:223)

Two days later on the 23rd of February, the Prophet met with the Twelve concerning the expedition.

"I told them I wanted an exploration of all that mountain country . . . 'Send twenty-five men: let them preach the gospel wherever they go. Let that man go that can raise $500, a good horse and mule, a double-barrel gun, one-barrel rifle, and the other smooth bore, a saddle and bridle, a pair of revolving pistols, bowie-knife, and a good sabre. Appoint a leader, and let them beat up for volunteers. I want every man that goes to be a king and a priest. When he gets on the mountains he may want to talk with his God; when with the savage nations have power to govern, etc. If we don't get volunteers, wait till after the election.'" (*Ibid.*, VI:-224. [The national election would be held the following November.])

There was no lack of volunteers. Within a week over twenty men had volunteered. (*Ibid.*, VI:223-227) The proposed expedition was widely known. In a letter written to James Arlington Bennett, March 4, 1844, Willard Richards, under the Prophet's instruction says, "We are now fitting out a noble company to explore Oregon and California." (*Ibid.*, VI:232) On March 11, the Prophet spoke to the Council about the desirability of securing "a resting place in the mountains, or some uninhabited region, where we can enjoy the liberty of conscience guaranteed to us by the Constitution of our country." (*Ibid.*, VI:261) Anticipating this westward movement, the Prophet also wrote and sent to Congress, "An Ordinance for the Protection of the Citizens of the United States Emigrating to the Territories, and for the Extension of the Principles of Universal Liberty." (*Ibid.*, VI:275) This document, which Congress ignored, was clearly designed to protect the migration of the whole people after a suitable location had been found.

During this time, while the expedition was being formed, the persecutions of the people reached an unprecedented height. At last, the life of the Prophet was seriously endangered. For his own safety, he left Nauvoo, and as would appear from the records, intended to go westward himself, to explore the country. He was recalled to Nauvoo before the journey had begun, and, on June 27, he and his brother Hyrum were foully assassinated.

There can be no question about Joseph Smith's intention to move the Latter-day Saints to some favorable spot among the Rocky Mountains. (See also B. H. Roberts, *Succession in the Presidency of the Church*, Second Edition, pp. 113-117)

After the martyrdom, the Twelve, with Brigham Young at the head, took over the leadership of the Church. The death of Joseph Smith had not stilled persecution. An exodus from Nauvoo was inevitable. Several places of refuge were presented, as Texas and Vancouver Island, but in accordance with Joseph's prophecy, the then unknown west among the Rocky Mountains was chosen, and the memorable westward migration began.

Brigham Young in all that he did, repeatedly admitted the leadership of Joseph Smith, even in the journey to the Great Salt Lake Valley. For example, this on March 16, 1856:

"The Prophet Joseph has been referred to, and his prophecy that this people would leave Nauvoo and be planted in the midst of the Rocky Mountains. We see it fulfilled . . . it was declared to the people long before we left Nauvoo." (*Journal of Discourses*, III:257, 258. See also IV: 203; VIII: 356)

That the famous trek from Nauvoo to Salt Lake Valley was a fulfillment of prophecy, does not detract from the glorious achievement of Brigham Young and his fellow pioneers. That he repeatedly admitted it, publicly and privately, and gave the Prophet proper credit, rather enhances the greatness of the foremost pioneer. President Young's loyalty to the Prophet was always unsullied. To him, the Prophet was the great restorer of the Lord's eternal truth. His own magnificent work in carrying out the prophecy, subduing the desert, and finding peace for his people, made him one of the world's really great men.

5. WHICH PROPHET IS THE GREATEST?

A prophet as here designated is a man endowed with priesthood authority who is called by the Lord to leadership in the unfolding of the plan of salvation. The prophets have been, in their day and age, the leaders of the Lord's work.

Such men of the past have been Abraham, Moses, Samuel, Isaiah, Jeremiah, Lehi, and others. Such men of the present dispensation have been Joseph Smith and his successors in office.

Each age has its own peculiar problems. Each dispensation carries forward into new situations the Lord's plan for human welfare. Additional revelation from the Lord is needed to meet the problems of a progressive unfolding plan. Such new truths, emanating from divinity, come only through the prophet of the day.

Joseph Smith was commissioned to restore the doctrine, organization, and authority of the Church to a generation which had lost these fundamentals of the Church of Christ. Joseph Smith's successors have been engaged in carrying forward the restoration, in proclaiming its truth to all the world, and in building securely the Church of Christ, through which the Lord will soon accomplish his purposes relative to the last days.

All these men were teachers and defenders of the gospel. In addition, each had his special work to do. Each has left behind a message for succeeding generations.

Above all, so prophetic history reveals, each prophet was called to serve the needs of his own generation. Therein lay his power to advance the unchanging cause of the Lord. In accomplishing this, in admonishing the people to gospel obedience, three major helps and procedures were at his command.

First. The prophet of any age draws upon the records of the past. The keeping of records has ever been enjoined by the Lord upon his people. Each prophet, from the days of the early patriarchs, down the years, has left behind a precious body of teaching and practice, of continuous value. Some have recorded in their messages direct revelations from the Lord. These records are the foundation of all safe gospel teaching. Many have been collected in the volume known as the Holy Bible. Others are found in the Book of Mormon, Doctrine and Covenants, and the Pearl of Great Price. These four books together form the most precious library on earth.

The prophet, of any time, must of necessity draw upon these treasures of the past, in clarifying his own views and in teaching the people.

Second. The great governing principles of truth are unchanging. But, the conditions brought about by human activity are forever changing. From sailboat to steamboat to airship; from horse power to steam power; from grease-soaked wicklight to electric lighting; from the rushing human agent to the telegraph, telephone, and radio—and a multitude of others—we span changes that in the past seemed impossible. And undoubtedly the future holds developments that today are equally inconceivable.

Such changes affect human thinking. New social and economic problems arise. Even the spiritual outlook is invaded. Then, it becomes the duty of the prophet to teach how the eternal laws of the gospel may be applied amidst constant change, for the benefit and blessing of humanity. The prophet does not discard new ways for old ones, if truth is preserved. He is not a reactionary, but ever a progressive, holding, however, the new and the old to gospel law. He gives life to that which is new as it blossoms upon the ruins of the old, by the constant application to it of principles of truth.

This adherence to and use of the principles of the gospel in an age of changing conditions has characterized the lives of the prophets. It has often been their main responsibility.

Third. The prophet is but a man. He draws heavily upon the past. He seeks inspiration from the Lord for his daily work. There comes at times the need for new knowledge from heaven. Then, if it be the proper time, the Lord speaks. New revelation is given. Pressing problems are solved by a knowledge beyond that of man.

The prophet is never wholly dependent upon the past. He may always draw upon the fount of truth and wisdom. All the prophets have done this.

* * * * *

Which then of all these prophets is the greatest? Since all have done equally well the work assigned to them, they are equally great. By the same token, the last ordained elder and the veteran apostle are equal before the Lord, if they do their assigned work equally well. That is the test of heaven.

But, which prophet is the most important to us? That is the more incisive question.

The most important prophet in any age is the living prophet. The prophets who have gone before have left to us their precious teachings which will be used for the instruction and comfort of mankind. But, it is the living prophet who helps us by his teachings, example, and direction to meet and to solve the problems of today, our day. To follow the living prophet, the interpreter of the past, is the essence of wisdom. The very strength of the Church lies in the doctrine of continuous revelation through a living prophet.

In that sense, the living prophet is the greatest prophet.

6. WHAT IS THE "INSPIRED TRANSLATION" OF THE BIBLE?

Joseph Smith, the Prophet, and those associated with him, had been brought up on the teachings of the Holy Bible. It was assumed that the English Bible had been translated correctly and completely from the original manuscripts.

The teachings of the Book of Mormon with other new revelations from the Lord, convinced the Prophet that there were errors, unauthorized additions, and incomplete statements in the sacred volume of the Old and New Testaments.

Such errors seemed to the Prophet, a devoted lover of the truth, out of keeping with the sacred nature of the Bible. Therefore, very soon after the organization of the Church, after placing the matter before the Lord, he began the "inspired translation" of the holy scriptures. In June 1830, less than three months after the Church was organized, he had had revealed to him the "visions of Moses." In December, 1830, Sidney Rigdon, who had just joined the Church, was called to act in this work as scribe to the Prophet.

The two brethren labored on the task with all possible regularity until July 21, 1833, when with divine permission the "translation and review" of the Old and New Testaments was sealed until a suitable time of publication, which unfortunately, in the troubled life of the Prophet never came.

After the death of the Prophet, Brigham Young sent Willard Richards to Emma Smith, to secure the translation which was partly in manuscript, and partly in marginal notes in the family Bible. She refused to surrender the material then, but at last in 1866 she gave the material to the committee of publications of the Reorganized Church by whom the material was later published.

However, at the request of the Prophet, Dr. John M. Bernhisel had made a copy, both of the manuscript, and of the marginal page changes. This copy is now in the library of the Historian's Office in Salt Lake City.

It is not really correct to say that the Prophet translated the Bible. Rather, he corrected errors in the Bible, and under revelation added long statements. Nor is it really certain that the work was finally finished. Had he gone over the Bible again he probably would have made additional corrections. He seems to have given special attention to certain portions of the Bible.

But, as it stands, he performed a vast work. Drs. Sidney B. Sperry and Merrill Y. Van Wagoner state that 12,650 words were added in Genesis, and that 693 verses were changed in the other books of the Old Testament. In the New Testament, these authors say that 1,453 verses were changed. In the four gospels alone, 1,036 verses were altered. Certainly the Prophet used great effort to restore the original meaning of the Bible.

Out of this mass of material only a few examples can be shown here.[1]

The above mentioned work on the Book of Genesis appears as the Book of Moses in the Pearl of Great Price. It adds much information to the somewhat meager account in the Bible.

Numerous slight but important changes were made.

Exodus 32:14 says: "And the Lord repented of the evil which he thought to do unto the people." The inspired version reads: And the Lord said unto Moses, If they will repent of the evil which they have done, I will spare them and turn away my fierce wrath. . . .

Exodus 7:3 says: "And I will harden Pharaoh's heart, and multiply my signs and wonders in the land of Egypt." The inspired version reads, "And Pharaoh will harden his heart, as I said unto thee; and thou shalt multiply my signs and wonders, in the land of Egypt."

I Samuel 16:14 says: "But the Spirit of the Lord departed from Saul, and an evil spirit from the Lord troubled him." The inspired version reads, "But the Spirit of the Lord departed from Saul, and an evil spirit which was not of the Lord troubled him."

There is no need to comment upon the rational improvement in the above verses.

John 4:2 says: "Though Jesus himself baptized not, but his disciples." The inspired version reads: "Though he, him-

---

[1]For further study see Sperry and Van Wagoner, "The Inspired Revision of the Bible." THE IMPROVEMENT ERA, Vol. 43, pp. 206, 270, 336, 408, 472, 536; April to September, 1940; also R. Etzenhouser, *The Three Bibles.*

self baptized not so many as his disciples." So ends a long controversy.

Melchizedek, for whom the higher, Holy Priesthood is named, is a mystical figure in the Bible. He is spoken of as a king of righteousness, King of Salem, priest of the most high God.[2] The Apostle Paul speaks of Christ as a priest after the order of Melchizedek.[3] Little more. The inspired version however makes him a more human being. It says:

"And now, Melchisedek [Melchizedek] was a priest of this order; therefore he obtained peace in Salem, and was called the Prince of peace.

"And his people wrought righteousness, and obtained heaven, and sought for the city of Enoch which God had before taken, separating it from the earth, having reserved it unto the latter days, or the end of the world;

"And hath said, and sworn with an oath, that the heavens and the earth should come together; and the sons of God should be tried so as by fire.

"And this Melchisedek, having thus established righteousness, was called the king of heaven by his people, or, in other words, the King of peace.

"And he lifted up his voice, and he blessed Abram, being the high priest, and the keeper of the storehouse of God;

"Him whom God had appointed to receive tithes for the poor.

"Wherefore, Abram paid unto him tithes of all that he had, of all the riches which he possessed, which God had given him more than that which he had need.

"And it came to pass, that God blessed Abram, and gave unto him riches, and honor, and lands for an everlasting possession; according to the covenant which he had made, and according to the blessing wherewith Melchisedek had blessed him." (Holy Scriptures Inspired Version, Genesis 14:33-40)

The incomprehensible statement that Melchisedek was "Without father, without mother, without descent, having neither beginning of days, nor end of life, but made like unto the Son of God; abideth a priest continually."[4] is made plain and reasonable in the inspired version. "For this Mel-

[2]Genesis 14:18-20; Hebrews 7:1-6.
[3]Psalm 110:4; Hebrews 5:6, 10; 6:20; 7:7-21.
[4]Hebrews 7:3.

chisedec was ordained a priest after the order of the Son of God, which order was without father, without mother, without descent, having neither beginning of days nor end of life. And all those who are ordained unto this priesthood are made like unto the Son of God, abiding a priest continually."[5]

Such comparisons might be multiplied. All would show the great service the Prophet Joseph Smith rendered in correcting Biblical errors, and to make the statements of the Holy Scriptures more understandable to the human mind. The "inspired translation" is one of the mighty evidences of the prophetic power of Joseph Smith.

---

[5]Holy Scriptures, Hebrews 7:3.

7. WHY DID JOSEPH SMITH BECOME A MASON?

Nauvoo, the city beautiful, was founded by the Latter-day Saints in 1839, nearly ten years after the Church had been organized. The decade had been one of unreasoning persecution of the members of the Church. The forces of evil seemed to be combined against the restoration of the simple gospel of Jesus Christ.

The Prophet, to save his life, was obliged to flee from Kirtland, Ohio, headquarters of the Church where a lovely temple and many progressive enterprises had been built. The Saints as a body were expelled from Missouri, under an "exterminating" order by the governor of the state, despite several successful settlements by the Church within the state. In seeking a city of refuge, Nauvoo, then a squalid village called Commerce, was founded.

The settlement in Nauvoo was effected in the hope that the people might now live in peace to worship the God of heaven in their own way.[6] There they built well, for soon Nauvoo was the most populous and thriving city in Illinois. But soon after their arrival there, neighbors began to question the doctrines of the Church, notably revelation. The prosperity of the industrious Saints also incited jealousy on the part of those who would not pay the price of toil for success, or who were speculating in lands and other properties. Persecution began to rise there as in other places. Political differences and hopes also entered into the picture.

The Saints knew well enough the sufferings from mob persecution. Joseph Smith, the leader, looked for means to quell the rising tide of opposition.

Many of the Saints were Masons, such as Joseph's brother Hyrum, Heber C. Kimball, Elijah Fordham, Newel K. Whitney, James Adams, and John C. Bennett. These members called attention to the spirit of brotherhood and brotherly love which are the foundations of Masonic fraternity and which characterize Masonic activities:—as, for example, from this writer,

-----

[6] *Journal of Discourses* 19:60.

On the rolls of Masonry, those lodges will stand highest in which not some few, but each and every member cheerfully gives of his time and labors to make the others happier, not some of the time, but all of the time.[7]

This ideal agreed well with the high ideals of the Prophet. Moreover, it was conceded that many of the prominent and influential men of the state were Masons who could be friends when needed. Association with such a fraternity might help to lessen the mob persecutions to which the Church had been subjected in Ohio and Missouri, so reasoned the Prophet's advisors.

The people of the Church needed friends. The work in Nauvoo would be hindered if opposition to the Church were allowed to grow. The Prophet and his brethren and sisters of the Church had suffered much without cause. They wanted peace. Perhaps Masonry would help. So, in the light of history, ran the thoughts of the people.

With the acquiescence of the Prophet, members of the Church already Masons petitioned the Grand Master of Illinois for permission to set up a lodge in Nauvoo. In answer they were granted permission, in October, 1841, to hold lodge meetings; but it was March 15, 1842, before authority was given to set up a lodge in Nauvoo and to induct new members. Joseph Smith became a member. At the time of the lodge organization, Joseph Smith received some of the degrees in Masonry. He was never an active Mason. His other work consumed his time and energy. His history shows that he was extremely busy at this time with a multitude of Church problems. Lodge matters would have to be left in other hands.

Meanwhile, large numbers of Nauvoo citizens were inducted into the fraternity. Soon the Nauvoo lodge had more members than all the other Illinois lodges together. It became the largest in the state. In this rapid growth, some lodge errors appear to have been made. These however could easily have been corrected.

However, Joseph's Masonic membership did not lessen the persecution. The religious claims of the Mormons were ridiculed; their political power seemed a threat; and their prosperity nettled the less successful neighbors.

[7]Wright, *Indian Masonry*, p. 116, quoted by McGavin, *Mormonism and Masonry*, p. 11.

The attempt to win sufficient friends through Masonry to stop persecution failed. The Masons after all were only a small fraction of the people of the territory surrounding Nauvoo. And no one knows with certainty whether any of them took part in the "Mormon" persecutions. The whole terrible affair leading to the assassination of the Prophet and his brother Hyrum was a local affair within the Nauvoo territory, where lived people of many faiths and allegiances.

8. WHAT WAS THE VOCABULARY OF JOSEPH SMITH?

"It is generally estimated that the total number of different words, exclusive of proper names, in the King James Version is only about 7,000, 5,642 of which are in the Old Testament. Naturally a vocabulary cannot be numbered with mathematical accuracy. . . . This accounts for the fact that estimates of the size of the vocabulary of the English Bible range all the way from 7,000 to 10,000 words."

Joseph Smith's mother wrote that of all her children he was the least inclined to give his time to the reading of books.[8] He was fond of outdoor life and physical games. His history mentions wrestling matches, jumping and ball playing. Children grown to manhood related the story of games with the Prophet.[9]

He grew up used to hard work. His father was chiefly a farmer in the Palmyra days.[10] Joseph had to take his share in the labors of the farm. When their farm labors permitted he sought employment elsewhere. Josiah Stoal employed him to dig for a lost mine,[11] Clark Chase to dig a well.[12] He writes in his journal that he was obliged to earn a scant living by the toil of his hands.[13]

His school education was very meager. He could read, write an imperfect hand, and knew enough arithmetic for his needs. In the words of Orson Pratt who lived in his house and became his great defender,[14] "His advantages for acquiring scientific knowledge were exceedingly small, being limited to a slight acquaintance with two or three of the common branches of learning. He could read without much difficulty and write a very imperfect hand; he had a very limited understanding of the elementary rules of arithmetic. These were his highest and only attainments; while the rest of those branches so universally taught in the common

---

8Lucy Mack Smith, *History of the Prophet Joseph,* 1902, p. 84.
9*Juvenile Instructor*, 27:172.
10Lucy Mack Smith, *Op. cit.*, 1902, p. 24.
11*Ibid.*, 1902, p. 91.
12B. H. Roberts, *Comprehensive History of the Church,* 1:129.
13*History of the Church*, 1902, 1:28.
14Orson Pratt, *Remarkable Visions,* p. 1.

schools throughout the United States were entirely unknown to him." However, he had a fine mind. All who knew him, friend and foe, conceded that his mental ability was high. Under favorable circumstances he would have used educational opportunities to the full. In his later years he sought learning in many fields—languages, law, and others. From his earliest association with the Church, after the translation of the Book of Mormon, he urged education upon the people.

In short, Joseph Smith was not better educated than the average boy of his pioneer period from a family reduced to poverty, inured to toil with little chance for an education. His training came from his observance of nature about him and the people whom he met.

His was a Bible reading family. In those days on the frontier, the Bible was the chief book of the household. Joseph was a Bible reader. That of itself would aid much in the education of the boy. The writings that he left behind him show his fine Bible versatility from Genesis to Revelation. In that sense he grew up a well-educated man, but it would not be suspected that he had a large or technical vocabulary.

Enemies who have read the Book of Mormon have found its contents to be beyond the capacity of a boy with such meager training for writing. Therefore they have set up the theory that some competent person hiding behind Joseph Smith was the real author of the Book of Mormon.[15] Sidney Rigdon, a man of some education, a reader, a student, and an orator was picked by many defeated antagonists, but unsuccessfully, to be the unknown man who really wrote the Book of Mormon.[16]

If a man of superior learning wrote the Book of Mormon, it would be reflected in the extent and character of his vocabulary. If the vocabulary were small and simple, it would be another evidence for the truth of Joseph Smith's claim that he translated the book from engravings on golden plates. Every translator catches the idea in the old language and reports it in the new manner according to the nature of his own speech.

The English language has a multitude of words borrowed from many tongues. So large is this collection that it has

---

[15]E. D. Howe, *Mormonism Unveiled,* 1834, p. 290.
[16]Francis W. Kirkham, *A New Witness for Christ in America,* 1947, p. 299.

been estimated that in ordinary use, in speech and writing, not more than one-tenth or one-twentieth of English words are employed, even by the most learned. Many books and articles on this subject have been published. Recently a competent author declared that with one thousand English words all ordinary ideas could be expressed, and that the common man seldom uses more than five thousand words.[17]

Milton's vocabulary was between seven thousand and eight thousand words.[18] Some double this number. The translators of Homer's *Iliad* and *Odyssey*, linguistic scholars, used about nine thousand words.[19] There are four thousand eight hundred in the New Testament; five thousand six hundred forty-two in the Old Testament. The varying number depends in part on whether inflected forms of words are included. There are those who think that the Bible has twenty thousand words, everything counted; and Shakespeare following with eighteen thousand words. Any translation of any book depends, of course primarily upon the vocabulary of the translator, since a good translation deals with ideas, not with words.

Many studies have been made to discover the number of words used by the average man. Naturally every man uses a number, depending on many factors such as the parental vocabulary, kind and amount of thinking, companions, and reading habits. It is pretty generally agreed, however, that on the average a fairly well-educated man uses about eight thousand words in daily conversation.[20]

Joseph Smith used only between two thousand and three thousand words in his written publications. This smaller number would be expected from a knowledge of his educational opportunities.

An actual count shows (leaving out all inflected forms of words) the following vocabulary for the Book of Mormon:

General Words	2,896
Persons' Names	245
Place Names	166
Total	3,307

---

[17]*Dictionary.*
[18]Mrs. Clark's *Concordance.*
[19]*The Nation,* September 12, 1912.
[20]H. L. Mencken, *The American Language,* p. 4.

XI. Delusions

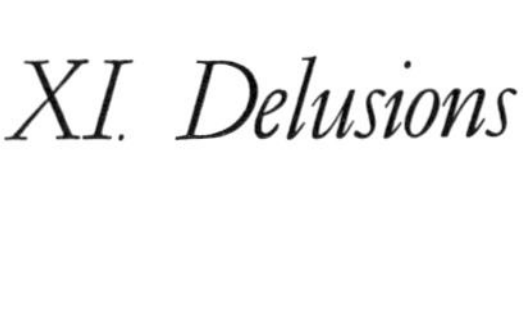

1. WHY IS REINCARNATION A FALSE DOCTRINE?

Reincarnation, often known as metapsychosis, is an ancient doctrine. It dates from the earliest corruption of truth, from the very dawn of human history, when mankind first departed from the simple principles of the gospel. In some form it has existed at all times in all lands. It is an excellent example of the distortion of beautiful, fundamental truths.

Reincarnation, as commonly taught, means that the spirit or "soul" of a human being, after the death of the person, and after intervals of varying duration, returns to earth in another body. This may occur frequently, indeed may be a continuous, unending process.

Usually it is taught that the spirit inhabits from time to time bodies of the same species. That is, the spirit of a man will reappear on earth as a man; a woman as a woman; a human being as a human being. This may not, however, always be the case. Many believers in reincarnation hold that a "soul" which is a man today, may be a woman tomorrow, or vice versa. It is also often taught that the spirit of a man may in the next earthly incarnation, inhabit the body of a lower animal, say a dog or a cat. There is not full agreement among reincarnationists on many of these matters.

Under this doctrine our next-door neighbor may be the reincarnation of a man or a woman who lived centuries ago; our bootblack may be the reincarnation of one of the great philosophers of the past; our school teacher may have been an untutored savage a thousand years ago; our present dog, Sanko, may be nothing else than our dog, Fido, long since dead, in a more recent incarnation. And what is worse, the animating essence, the "soul," of Sanko, may be the former "soul" of a Newton, or a Galileo, or a Plato! Or, the wife who cooks our meals for us, may have been in an earlier reincarnation, the Queen of Sheba. Or, still more to our confusion, a man's wife might have been his husband when he was a woman in an earlier reincarnation.

Three doctrines lie at the foundation of belief in reincarnation. First, the pre-existence of the "soul" of man; second, the indestructibility of the "soul" of man after death; and, third, the possibility of constant development of the pre-existent, eternal "soul." These are all necessary doctrines to the thinking mind. They are supported by divine revelation. But, in the explanations and applications of these truths, the proponents of reincarnation have failed dismally, and have shown how the semblance of truth, becoming untruth, may lead men into vast fields of deception.

The basic doctrine of pre-existence is always presented in an incomplete form. Clearly, if the "soul" of man has occupied from time to time successive and distinct bodies, birth cannot be the beginning of his "soul." There must be existence before each successive embodiment.

But what about the first incarnation?

One group sidestep the question by saying that before the first appearance on earth, God created the "soul." That merely means that after all, the spirit is not really eternal. Since it began on earth, it may end with the earth.

Another group of believers in reincarnation, sensing the inadequacy of this explanation, seek refuge in the doctrine that the "souls" of men began their existence as lower animals, and then they add that "in the lower kingdoms consciousness evolves in the mass, . . . as these group souls slowly develop, . . . they continually divide and subdivide." (Cooper, *Reincarnation,* p. 48.) Finally, by some mysterious process these animals, subdivisions of the mass, acquire a "soul" and become human beings. All of which is merely saying that there is an "ocean of consciousness," out of which God dips individuals.

Contrast these feeble, lame, and incomprehensible explanations with the true doctrine of pre-existence, as taught in the gospel of Jesus Christ. The spirit of man is co-eternal with God. In the eternities before he came on earth he has been a personality, possessing the power to think and learn, to accept or reject the means by which he could ascend or descend, progress or retrograde. He has been himself from the endless beginning through all the waiting eternities.

Reincarnation rests upon an unsound foundation; hence is dangerous, and should be avoided.

The conditions of reincarnation by which the immortal

"soul" may progress are equally unacceptable. "Reincarnation . . . is a plan whereby imperishable conscious beings are supplied with physical bodies appropriate to their stage of growth and through which they can come in contact with the lessons of physical life." (*Ibid.*, p. 17.) This supplying of bodies is repeated endlessly. By this doctrine, the body of man is of little consequence. We take it on, cast it off, and put on another one, much as we do with our old suits of clothing. The "soul" of man is then really confined to this earth, as in a prison. Why this should be so, baffles the mind. His sojourn between incarnations can be of no value to him, since he must return to earth in a mortal body to gain further experience. He is of the earth, earthy. He cannot in reality go beyond the earth or physical experiences. Therefore, an infinity of experiences are beyond his reach. The universe is not his. Such an eternal "soul" demands a vaster area of understanding and action than the earthly life affords. There is no freedom in reincarnation.

Reincarnation fails utterly to comprehend the meaning of the human body.

The gospel of Jesus Christ declares that man, an eternal spirit, acquainted with the spiritual world, came upon the earth when he was fitted and permitted to become acquainted with the material world. To this end he was given a body of material elements. This body belongs to him eternally, to be used by him, in a purified form, in his endless progressive journey among spiritual and material realities. He does not need another. It is a sacred possession, the home of his eternal spirit. With it, composed of celestialized material elements, he may forever explore the universe, in all its aspects, even to the limits of eternity. Without such a body, the immortal spirit would be handicapped in its victorious progress, in the midst of universal elements, toward the likeness of God. Reincarnation has gone far afield to explain that which the Lord has made clear to the human mind.

The doctrine of reincarnation really destroys personality as connected with earth life. The perpetual passage of spirits from body to body on earth, implies that the Lord is using the earth as a playground for a few spirits. As one writer remarks, the soul of the ancient patriarch Seth was probably the spirit of the great prophet Moses. Thus, individuality on the earth is lost. Temporal identification is hopelessly confused. There is no end to the disorder, for the process of reincarnation is unending. That violates the innate desire, even need, of man, for an individual, personal identity on earth as in heaven.

By reincarnation the power of God seems also to be limited. He uses the same, relatively few, spirits over and over again, endlessly, to accomplish whatever may be his purpose. He seems to be short of material and vague in his purpose. This is out of harmony with the gospel, which teaches that there is a host of spirits waiting to take upon themselves mortal bodies, and that the next stage of existence will come when this has been accomplished.

This doctrine of confusion presents no final objective in life. It seems to suggest only living over and over again on earth, much the same experiences, sometimes as a man, sometimes as something else. To what ultimate state does it lead us? Even in human affairs, soldiers who may fight many a battle in various places, come at last to an end—victory or defeat. Reincarnation sets up no understandable objective of existence, except that we are advancing; but how and to what end? It reduces the spirit of man to the position of a treadmill worker in the affairs of the universe. Some say that the end is nirvana, first held to be extinction of existence; now a fusion into a mass of security. That does not help.

This is in clearest opposition to the doctrine of progression, which lies fundamentally in the gospel of the Lord Jesus Christ. The objective of life is to move toward the likeness of God. Man rises continually. Once on earth, he experiences earth life, with its joys and sorrows: then bids it farewell, to enter into another life where he continues with added power, in the advancing program of existence. He outgrows the past throughout eternal existence. Reincarnation moves in a circle; the gospel in an ascending spiral. Existence without a definite objective, but with constant repetitions, is valueless.

Finally, reincarnation is incompatible with the resurrection of the body, through the redeeming service of Jesus Christ. The continuous changing of bodies makes the resurrection and any redeeming act, unnecessary. It places the Christ in the class of fakirs. A Christian cannot believe in reincarnation. That should be, in itself, a sufficient answer to the question at the head of this writing.

References: Rt. Reverend Irving S. Cooper, *Reincarnation, The Hope of the World;* E. D. Walker, *Reincarnation, A Study of Forgotten Truth.*

2. IS THERE A MASTER RACE?

The Nazi betrayers of Germany declared that the Germans are a "master race," to whom other nations should be subservient. Indeed, the German word *herrenvolk*, used freely during the late war, connotes a people which has serfs, upon whose toil the *herrenvolk* live in luxury.

This stupid and insolent claim originated in some conceited brain several generations ago. It was not, at first, taken seriously by the German people. But it had such appeal to human vanity that it was fanned into popular favor by several philosophers. At least one of these, the most often quoted (Nietzsche), was of unsound mind. Hitler, himself mentally ill, used the doctrine of German superiority over all other peoples as a bulwark for his incredibly insane, inhuman ideas which threw the whole world into horrible, bloody warfare. The recent military defeat of the axis powers has laid low for the time being, it is hoped forever, the untenable notion of German superiority among the nations. Belief in a "master race" is an evidence of ignorance of the long history of man on earth. The procession through the ages of Egypt, Babylon, Greece, the various nations of Europe, and many others, refutes the doctrine of the final superiority in any one nation. However, when power came into the hands of these ignorant and mentally oblique proponents of the "master race" theory, they entered into this unhappy war much as a goat butts its head against a solid wall. Ignorance is blind.

Human experience has shown that in all peoples, even in those whom we call semi-civilized or barbarian, lie powers of body, mind, and spirit, which may be developed to match our most "civilized" attainments. Cultivation of these gifts, under the further influence of environment and heredity, will lift men of every land and clime into greater power. It may take longer with some than with others, because of their stage of development, but the possibility of growth is there. As a mass, in innate qualities, there is little difference among races.

There are highly endowed individuals in every land, whose heads are above the crowd—the Platos, Galileos, the Tennysons, who see and do things beyond their fellows. These are the great men of history upon whose thoughts and labors our civilization has been built. They are the artists, writers, scientists, and thinkers who have shaped the lives of the multitudes. They are the Newtons in their respective fields. They are really the final answer to the "master race" question, for every nation has produced some of these mighty minds. They may arise in any society, anywhere. No one nation has built the world of men as it is. Instead, it is the product of people of many lands. Nature has not recognized a "master race" with geographical or racial limitations.

The believer in the "master race" thinks too often of bodily prowess. He is likely to look upon physical strength merely as a means to subjugate his weaker brother. That has been the mistake of Prussianism. He forgets that the members of a "master race" must, above all things, be evenly balanced, and that the developed body is only one mark of superior man. He should also remember that it is a commonplace of knowledge that many people who are on the way to civilization, but yet in the lower stages, have great physical vigor. Witness the Indians of America, the hill tribes of Asia, or the Negroes of Africa. Bodily vigor depends on wise methods of living, notably simplicity in diet and occupation. Among Europeans the self-styled "master race" has no preeminence of physical vigor. Such a claim is idle boasting.

Similarly, no one nation leads in the possibility of intellectual achievement. Nevertheless, it is here that the proponents of the "master race" fallacy have made their greatest claims. They would have us believe that the major conquests by the mind have come from one or a few nations. Even a casual study shows that the world's intellectual history, in every field of endeavor, has been written, painted, sculptured, sung, and played by many peoples. Mental gifts, and those of the emotions, have descended upon poor and rich, just and unjust, from China to America, with no reference to geography.

In the case of science, for example—from the leaning Tower of Pisa to the atom-smashing cyclotron in Berkeley—at least fourteen nations have been concerned with the building of modern science, and nearly all nations are entering the arena.

In the number of notable scientific discoverers, England, France, and Germany shared about equally; but there were key men in the smaller and less known countries without whom the others would have been helpless.

Radio, the wonder gift of science, has come to its present perfection by the labors of men in at least fifteen different countries. Some of the most important radio discoveries and inventions came from the smaller, less esteemed lands. The radio results won in any one country, if assembled, would not give us the radio as at present understood and used. In the number of men who have contributed greatly to radio, Germany is a very poor third.

Likewise, spiritual outreachings are not peculiar to one country. Instead, in every land men have sought the gifts of the spirit. Even the savage has pondered upon the meaning of life. The whence, why, where questions persist in the thinking of every person, great or small. Men have arisen in every land, who have tried to formulate the way to happiness, for the benefit of themselves and their fellow men. And millions of soul-hungry men have followed them. The religions of Egypt, China, India, and Persia, are examples. In the Christian world, this eager spirit has resulted in numerous sects to correct the evident departures from the true gospel of Jesus Christ.

The "master race" claims are sheer poppycock, used by characterless men to further their own interests. There has never been a monopoly of mastery in human achievement by any one nation. To claim so is simply to allow the lawless nationalism to run wild.

Nevertheless, it must be admitted that there is the possibility of a true "master race" or group, excelling all others in human powers. Its membership will include all who seek truth, and, having discovered it, set about at any sacrifice to accept and practise it. They have acquired mastery over themselves.

The Master of that group will be Jesus, the Christ. Conformity to his plan of salvation for men will be their law, for thereby they will win the desired health and strength of body, mind and spirit. Thus they will move towards perfection.

The objective of this group will be not only to help themselves, but also to bless all mankind, and to lift all men to their own stature. That is the difference between the false "master race," and the true redeeming leadership of the world. The first is selfish; the other unselfish. The first is limited to one nation; the other covers the world, believing that "of one blood hath God made all men." The first is of the devil; the other of God.

The "master race" doctrine of the late war was an ugly delusion, conceived by the powers of evil, whose prince is Satan, the devil.

3. ARE COMMUNISM AND ITS RELATED "ISMS" PREPARATORY TO THE UNITED ORDER?

The United Order is the popular name of an economic system revealed to the Prophet Joseph Smith. It is sometimes called the Order of Enoch, since it was practiced by that patriarch and his people. It is also spoken of, and more correctly, as the Law of Consecration because of its vitalizing, directing principle. (D. & C. 42:32) Its structure and operation, as far as given, are described in the Doctrine and Covenants notably in sections 42, 51, and 104.[1]

The United Order rests upon the doctrine that spiritual and temporal activities are based upon the same or similar eternal laws. The laws that prevail in a spiritual sphere must measurably govern temporal existence. A Zion on earth can be built only by the application of the laws of the celestial kingdom. (D. & C. 105:5)

Therefore, since the gospel holds out to all men the promise of eternal life and the possibility of the same degree of exaltation, if certain laws are obeyed, it seems reasonable that there must also be laws which, if obeyed, will enable all men to attain the same degree of temporal salvation. Equality in the life to come is promised the faithful; equality in life on earth is also promised if the way of the Lord is followed. This must be so. "For if ye are not equal in earthly things ye can not be equal in obtaining heavenly things." (D. & C. 78:6; also 104: 15-17)

A full understanding of the United Order requires careful study of the revelations on the subject. In briefest outline it is formed and operated as follows: It is organized under Church authority by the voluntary action of a group of men holding the Holy Priesthood, for themselves and their families. All officers are drawn from the membership of the order. All members, upon entrance into the order, pool

-----

[1]Joseph Smith always referred to the plan as the law of Consecration and Stewardship, whereas the Utah experiments established under the direction of Brigham Young were known as the United Order. For a discussion of differences between the two in principle and practice *see Priesthood and Church Welfare*, pp. 126-131. In the present instance, "United Order" is used as the popular term for the original plan of Consecration and Stewardship.

their resources, that is, place them, as a consecration, in the common treasury of the order (D. & C. 42:32, 33). Each man is then given, from the treasury, his "portion" or "inheritance," that is, the means or capital with which to make a living for himself and his family—a farm and implements for the farmer, a shop and tools for the mechanic, etc. (D. & C. 51:3) As the youth within the order grow into maturity they are likewise given their "inheritances" from the common treasury. His "inheritance" is deeded to each member; it is his very own; it is private property. This "inheritance" he is free to use as he chooses. His free agency is carefully guarded. (D. & C. 51:4; 104:73-75) He is under one obligation only: to be loyal to the order and to be wise and industrious in the use of the "portion" given him. Especially, the idler has no place in the order. (D. & C. 75:29)

Should the use of a man's "inheritance" yield a surplus above the needs of himself, his family, and his business, such surplus is placed in the common treasury, for the benefit of the order, to provide inheritances for the young, to care for the unfortunate, and for all ventures and institutions for the public benefit, as may be approved by the membership of the order.

Should a man, because of insufficient natural endowment, or caught by uncontrollable circumstances, fail to make his inheritance yield enough to meet his needs, he would receive assistance from the common treasury. The fortunate would thus assist the unfortunate. None would be allowed to suffer.

The principles operating in such a "United Order" are almost self-evident. The order rests upon the acceptance of the gospel, faith in God, Jesus Christ, and the prophet of the restoration, and the moral and spiritual life required by the gospel. It is formed for the benefit of each individual member. The members do not exist for the welfare of the order but the order for their benefit. The equal rights of men to seek prosperity are recognized. The right of free agency is strictly respected. Every man is given an equal chance in life as he is given his "inheritance." The unequal powers of man are acknowledged; but no man is allowed to suffer because of lack of capacity or natural inhibitions. Relative equality in possessing the material joys of life is preserved by returning the surplus to the common treasury.

Love of man for man is ever present. In structure the system is not involved, and in practice relatively simple. But it requires, on the part of every member, a recognition of the brotherhood of man, and a rigid will for the common good.

Clearly, the results of the United Order would be most beneficial and glorious. Not only would the poor and weak be assisted, but that earthly equality would be brought about which is a necessary preparation for the celestial world. (D. & C. 78:6, 7) All would have the opportunity of improving their talents; they would seek one another's interest and do all things with an eye single to the glory of God. (D. & C. 82:18, 19)

The United Order, under somewhat differing organizations, has actually been tested by the Church, during short periods, in Ohio, Missouri, and Utah. Its power to benefit humanity has been demonstrated. But it was also found that few men were prepared to render full service in such a venture. Men must cast off their selfishness to be worthy members; they must revise many traditions handed down through generations of time; and they must build in their hearts an unwavering love for their fellow men. All this requires self-discipline over many years. Then, too, persecution from the outside made it difficult to live under the United Order.

These and other conditions led to the suspension of the order, as a mode of life. While it is in abeyance, the law of tithing and wise and earnest cooperation in all affairs of life partially take its place. Yet the United Order remains the ideal under which Latter-Saints hope some time to live.

Today it has a practical value as an ideal by which any proposed economic system may be tested for the degree of its worthiness. The nearer any scheme for economic betterment conforms to the principles of the United Order, the more likely it will be to assist mankind in their efforts to attain material happiness.

It may be observed that the principles appearing in the United Order are those which are applied more or less completely in a democracy. They are certainly in opposition to any form of regimentation or dictatorship, since the order provides personal freedom of action and common consent in all affairs. (D. & C. 104: 21, 71) The student of history will further observe that the periods of greatest human prosperity have been those in which these principles have been most nearly approximated.

An emphatic "No!" is the answer to the question at the head of this chapter. Untruth is never a preparation for truth. Modern communism, facism, nazism, socialism, and other related systems, are all the same in essential theory. They oppose religion, except as they themselves claim to be revelations, and they reject Christian morality. They prohibit free speech and action; eliminate private ownership and initiative; hold without exception the state above the individual; regiment the people; allow the strong to dominate the weak; they take government out of the hands of the governed, and place it in the hands of a self-appointed, selfish, self-styled, super-group, and they culminate in dictatorships. The free agent has no place in their systems. Their claim that they believe in human equality, as shown by their tyrannical behavior, is false. Force and terrorism are their weapons. All that makes for human security and happiness is destroyed.

One need only read the published philosophies of these "isms," and observe them in action, to confirm the above statements. From Plato to Marx and Nietzsche, the same story is told, one of high-sounding objective, but in practice one of subjection of the common man to a self-appointed guardian, masquerading in the stolen robes of human equality —wolves in sheep's clothing.

In stern opposition to these political "isms" is the plan provided by the Lord. As one studies the United Order, the more evident becomes its power for human welfare, for developing human lives, and for providing the prosperity needed on the path of progress. It makes possible the things for which the human soul most hungers. It stands secure and firm above the imperfect inventions of men. It is a mighty and marvelous evidence of the divine inspiration of the Prophet Joseph Smith.

Not communism and its brood, but faithful living within the Church of Christ, reestablished in these latter days, is the preparation for the coming of the United Order. There is no other adequate and acceptable preparation. And let it be remembered that the coming will be authorized through the revelation of the Lord to the President of the Church and not from any other source.

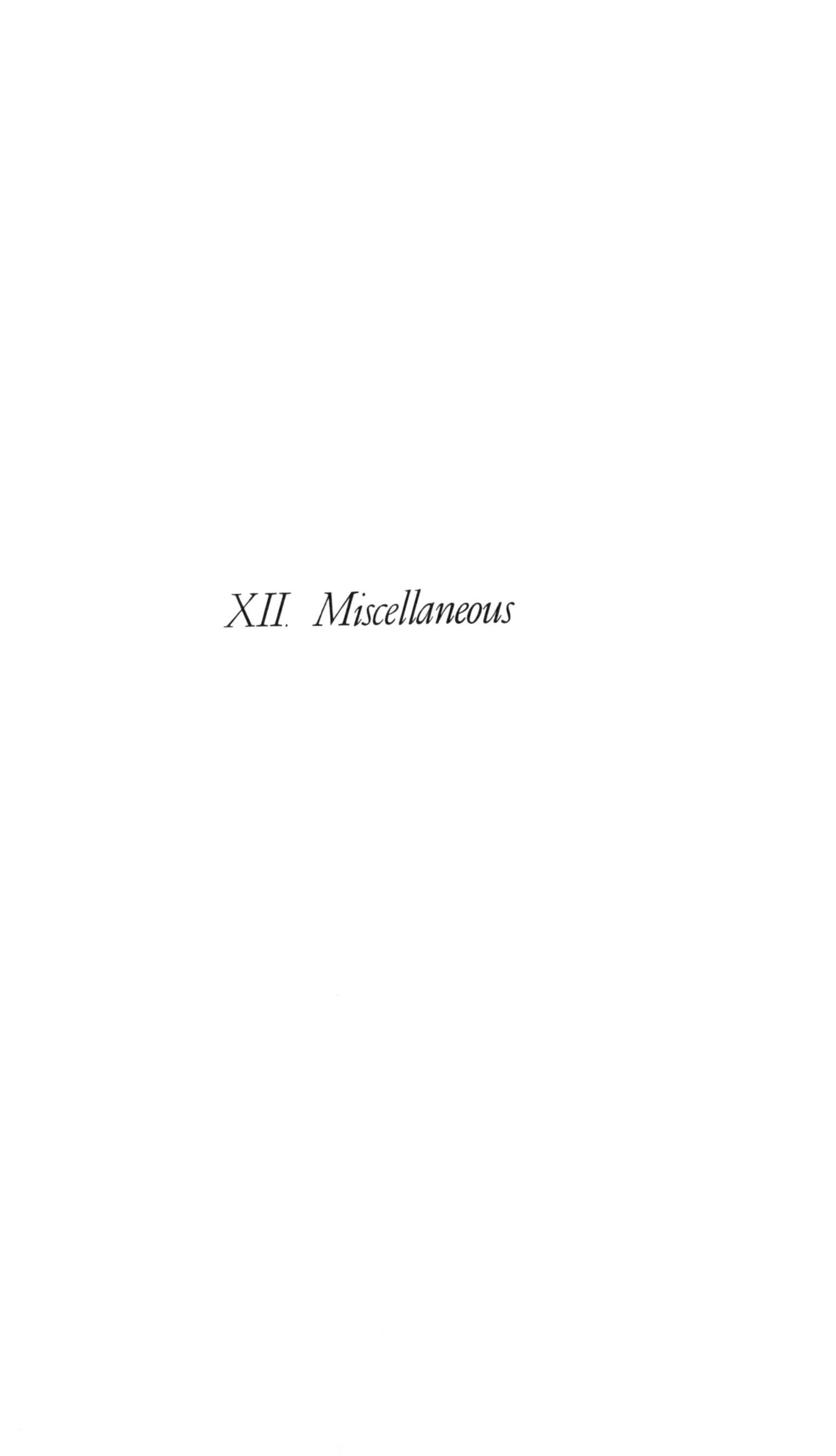

XII. Miscellaneous

1. WHEREIN LAY THE GREATNESS OF BRIGHAM YOUNG?

Brigham Young is recognized the world over as a man who rendered high service to his generation. Generally he is looked upon as a mighty leader of men, and the world's foremost colonizer. More careful students of his life and labors hold him also to be a master in religious philosophy. (See *Discourses of Brigham Young.*) All admit, whether friend or foe, that he belongs among the world's greatest men.

Since Brigham Young, to the age of thirty-three, was a modest carpenter, painter, and glazier in the humble villages of Port Byron and Mendon, New York, men have wondered how he was able to perform the Herculean labors of his life, and to rise to world eminence. The usual explanation has been that he was highly gifted, and that his life's accomplishments were due to the exercise of this natural endowment.

However, this explanation of Brigham Young is not sufficient. Gifted he was, there can be no doubt about that. But, the world is full of gifted men. Hosts of people, performing the average duties of life, have rich talents. The gifts of God are widely and profusely distributed. That is one reason why, when emergencies arise, leaders are found without much searching. Something more than a high natural endowment is necessary to achieve greatness in world or private affairs.

Some say that opportunity is necessary for a person to rise to greatness. True, when the gospel found Brigham Young, he began to show the power within him. Later, when he was called into the Quorum of the Twelve Apostles, responsibility and opportunity shaped his talents to meet the issues of the day. When, in the prime of his manhood, he was made the leader of the Church, he met the then overpowering problems of the Church in the masterful manner that has made him one of the earth's great ones. But, another man, of equal ability and under similar circumstances, might have failed where Brigham Young succeeded. There was something more than natural endowment and opportunity that lifted the colonizer of the West into huge accomplishment, winning world-wide acclaim.

Two basic qualities made Brigham Young capable of his tremendous world service. All other qualities utilized by him were derivatives of these two.

The first of these was his love of truth. Truth, the impelling passion of his life, was placed above all else. From his youth to the end of his days, he sought truth to guide him. When the Book of Mormon first came to him, with its attendant restoration, in its purity, of the gospel of Jesus Christ, he did not accept the offering at once. Through two long years he studied the book and examined the foundations of the newly organized Church. At last, convinced of the truth of the claims of Joseph Smith, he entered the waters of baptism. When he did so, he sacrificed much of a temporal nature. He became a humble member of a small, already hated group, with no prospects of earthly advancement. He could not then foresee that within three years he would be called to a position of leadership in the Church. But, all that did not count, for he had found the truth!

Throughout his life he spoke of truth with an exuberance of love that thrilled his hearers, and thrills the readers today.

"Our doctrine and practice is, and I have made it mine through life—to receive truth no matter where it comes from." (*Discourses of Brigham Young*, p. 11, 1943 edition)

"The Gospel is a fountain of truth, and truth is what we are after." (*Ibid.*, p. 9)

" 'Where is your code, your particular creed?' says one. It fills eternity; it is all truth in heaven, on earth or in hell. This is 'Mormonism.' It embraces every true science; all true philosophy." (*Ibid.*, p. 2)

"There is no truth but what belongs to the Gospel. It is life, eternal life; it is bliss; it is the fulness of all things in the gods and in the eternities of the gods." (*Ibid.*, p 3.)

"Be willing to receive the truth, let it come from whom it may; no difference, not a particle. Just as soon receive the Gospel from Joseph Smith as from Peter, who lived in the days of Jesus. Receive it from one man as soon as another." (*Ibid.*, p. 11)

In eloquent words he placed God as the source of all truth: "God is the source, the fountain of all intelligence, no matter who possesses it. . . . All have derived what intelligence, light, power, and existence they have from God. . . ." (*Ibid.*, p. 18)

"He is our Heavenly Father; he is also our God, and the Maker and upholder of all things in heaven and on earth. He sends forth his counsels and extends his providences to all living. He is the Supreme Controller of the universe. At his rebuke the sea is dried up, and the rivers become a wilderness. He measures the waters in the hollow of his hand, and meteth out heaven with a span, and comprehendeth the dust of the earth in a measure, and weigheth the mountains in scales, and the hills in a balance; the nations to him are as a drop in a bucket, and he taketh up the isles as a very little thing; the hairs of our heads are numbered by him, and not a sparrow falleth to the ground without our Father; and he knoweth every thought and intent of the hearts of all living, for he is everywhere present by the power of his Spirit—his minister, the Holy Ghost. He is the Father of all, is above all, through all, and in all, he knoweth all things pertaining to this earth, and he knows all things pertaining to millions of earths like this." (*Ibid.*, p. 19)

This surrender to truth with the existence of God as the supreme truth, is the first key to Brigham Young's achievements. There is really no other approach to lasting eminence in attainment or leadership. Fame based upon untruth is transient and worthless. This is confirmed by human history. Only those whose feet have rested upon truth, and whose weapon in every affair has been drawn from truth, are secure in the halls of fame.

The second quality that explains the remarkably successful career of Brigham Young was his strict and complete obedience to truth. He held, and correctly, that truth unused has no value in human life.

Truth once found was eagerly obeyed, that is, used. Obedience to truth, whether discovered by man, or received by revelation from God, became the pattern, practice, and concern of Brigham Young's life. His every act and decision squared with truth. He did not therefore choose the easiest path to personal welfare; he followed the way of truth though sometimes thorny.

He understood that many a man knows truth, but does

not obey it. Many know that the restored gospel is true but fail to join the Church. Thousands violate the demands of truth, to satisfy their appetites or improper impulses.

Brigham Young is reputed to have had a strong will. That was needed in the conquest of the desert. Many have failed to understand that in the exercise of his will power he was not autocratic, but firmly determined that truth should be obeyed, so that success could be won in the fierce battle with the wilderness, and with the appetites of men.

The whole world would prosper exceedingly if every man in his life had a will for truth. It is the flabby adherence to truth, or righteousness, the expression of truth, that lies at the bottom of all human disasters.

"Truth is obeyed when it is lived." (*Journal of Discourses,* vol. 7, p. 55)

"A mere theory amounts to but little, while practice and obedience have to do with stern realities." (*Ibid.,* vol. 9, p. 330)

"Some of you may ask, 'Is there a single ordinance to be dispensed with? Is there one of the commandments that God has enjoined upon the people, that he will excuse them from obeying?' Not one, no matter how trifling or small in our own estimation. No matter if we esteem them non-essential, or least or last of all the commandments of the house of God, we are under obligation to observe them." (*Discourses of Brigham Young,* p. 222)

Since the restored gospel contains truth, its welfare necessarily was foremost in all that he did. So complete was his obedience to external truth that all earthly desires had to take second place. Thus:

"I am not bound to wife or child, to house or farm, or anything else on the face of the earth, but the Gospel of the Son of God. I have enlisted all in this cause, and it is in my heart, and here is my treasure." (*Journal of Discourses,* vol. 14, p. 19)

His life was laborious, especially after the burden of leadership fell upon him. Change, travel, service to others crowded his life. But, it was done cheerfully in the cause of truth. He must obey the truth that he had found.

"As I have frequently thought and said, when duty requires I am happy in going from home, and I am happy in returning, for it is my greatest joy and comfort to do what the Lord requires of me, and what I know to be my duty, no matter what it is, if the Lord requires it of me. This course gives joy and peace. When this principle becomes the acting principle of all the Saints, we shall find that Zion is here; we shall be in the midst of it; we shall enjoy it." (*Ibid.*, vol. 3, p. 191)

These two governing principles of his life—loving truth, as God's gift, above all else; and obeying truth at any cost —explain the success that attended Brigham Young. He cannot well be understood unless it is comprehended that these two principles gave power, to every motive and action of his life. That which he did, temporally and spiritually, was hammered out on the anvil of obeyed truth.

Not all are called to high positions of leadership, but everyone can attain honorable distinction in his calling, whatever it may be, if his life is governed by these two principles. That is the important lesson from the notable life of Brigham Young.

2. WHAT DID THE PIONEERS CONTRIBUTE TO THE WELFARE OF OTHERS?

In their westward march from New York State to the Salt Lake Valley, and by ocean to California, the Latter-day Saints established farms, founded cities, and built notable public buildings. Civilization followed in their trail. The states of New York, Ohio, Illinois, Missouri, Iowa, Nebraska, Wyoming, Idaho, Utah, Nevada, Arizona, and California have all profited directly from the pioneers. When at last they found partial peace in the valleys of the Great Basin of North America, they set up practices for their own survival which have become of worldwide benefit. Their pioneer toil became a blessing to all the peoples of the earth.

In all their journeyings the living power of the restored gospel was manifested. Despite a persecution unequalled in modern history, the Saints remained faithful to the new-found truth. They might be driven brutally from place to place into the heartless desert, their cities destroyed, their women ravished, their temples violated, their homes laid waste—but their certain knowledge of the truth of the gospel restored by the Prophet Joseph Smith remained unchanged. Indeed under persecution this knowledge flamed higher, and became an increasing witness of the reality of the new message from heaven to earth. Thoughtful people everywhere, seeing this, knew that in their religion lay the power of truth, which may yet restore peace on earth. This will always be the main contribution of the Latter-day Saints.

In the conquest of the arid and semi-arid area of America, the Latter-day Saints made the United States one land. The two seaboards, Atlantic and Pacific, were at the time of the pioneers separated by a vast area supposed to be unsuitable for successful human settlement. There was no continuity of home and industrial life between the two seaboards. They were separated by deserts and mountains that promised to remain hunting grounds for the trapper and pleasure seeker. Then came the Latter-day Saints and showed how the desert could be tamed. The lessons of the pioneers were quickly taken up; the West was invaded by settlers, by slow but steady degrees, until today "from sea to sea" homes touch homes, and America is one continuous land of prosperous people. It was a glorious gift of the pioneers to their country which they believed to have been founded under divine inspiration.

The experiences of the pioneers served also the needs of the people beyond the seas. One-half of the earth's land surface receives a precipitation of less than twenty inches of water annually. We live on a dry earth. This is true on every continent. America is no exception. Fully two-fifths of the United States lie under an annual rainfall of less than twenty inches.

A precipitation under twenty inches, annually, is insufficient, unless conserved by special methods of tillage, to support crops in any degree comparable with crop yields of the humid region. Since water is so important a factor in plant growth, it has followed that the more humid regions of earth have been sought out as places for human settlement, not because of the greater attractiveness from the point of view of climate or soil fertility, but because of the greater ease in securing large crop yields. The civilized world was waiting, when the pioneers undertook their work in the American west, for modern methods by which the equally attractive other dry lands of the earth might be made to serve human needs better than in the past.

This was the first problem of the pioneers. Naturally they turned first of all to the ancient art of irrigation—the artificial application of water to lands for the purpose of producing large and steady crop yields whenever the rainfall is insufficient to meet the full water requirements of crops. A system of irrigation was set up through the pioneer years, on which rest nearly all later irrigation developments throughout the world. Ancient, time-honored laws, like the one that water in a flowing stream must not be diverted from its main channel, had to be abrogated; substitute laws, like that of the beneficial use of water, fitting the needs of the day needed formulation; proper supervision of the delivery and use of water on lands were to be devised; questions of ownership of water, whether a separate commodity or adhering to the land required answer; and methods of human social organization under the canal demanded attention.

Courageously and intelligently, the pioneers tackled these problems, and in the end gave to the world a set of irrigation principles and practices, used in one form or another by every section under a low rainfall, which means every continent of earth.

Irrigation, however, did not solve the whole agricultural problem. There is not enough water flowing in streams and rivers, anywhere in the arid and semi-arid regions to irrigate more than perhaps one-tenth of the lands in need of the artificial application of water. What about the remaining nine-tenths of this fertile but dry area? With irrigation well under way, many pioneers turned to this problem. It was found that under certain methods of tillage fair crops could be obtained when the annual rainfall was twelve inches or even less, depending on various conditions. This system became known as dry farming. Like irrigation, dry farming is of great antiquity, but primitive methods have limited its practice, and made it hazardous. The work of the Latter-day Saints, in this field has been heralded far and wide, and been the means of bringing under profitable production millions of acres of land in every continent.

The pioneers belonged to the civilization that Anglo-Saxon peoples had won for themselves through centuries of struggle. The gains in that struggle they must maintain. The stark, forbidding desert must be subdued, but not at the price of civilized life and living. Somehow, they must hold on to their social, economic, and spiritual possessions on the conquered desert as well as they had in humid regions. That was the challenge to the pioneers—to build communities of modern, civilized people under the ditch, comparable or superior to those of the rainfall regions from which they came. That accomplishment was a great contribution to the world's welfare, a great lesson to the workers on the half of the earth's surface lying under a low rainfall.

How that was done will yet be the theme of many a book and lecture. Hundreds of peaceful villages, with schools, churches, and the public park; remains of factories and other industries; a people who stand foremost among all people, anywhere under the sun, in educational standing—all these are silent witnesses of the success of the pioneers in learning how, though in the desert, to live a full life.

As their work is studied, the eternal principles of their success stand out boldly. Only by co-operation can the tasks beyond the strength of a single man be accomplished. Industry is demanded by every successful enterprise. Education enables work to be done properly. Faith in God brings to weak, mortal man power to do, and happiness to enjoy, that make all effort worthwhile. These were the cornerstones on which they built faith, education, industry, and co-operation.

The pioneers came to the Great Basin of North America in search of a land of peace. Out of their necessary toil for self-support, came great contributions to general human welfare: America was made one continuous land; the one-half of the earth lying under a low rainfall was taught how the desert can be conquered; all mankind were shown the cornerstones of success in every endeavor; and the path to divine joy on earth and beyond was laid bare.

Thank God for the pioneers!

3. WHY DID THE CHURCH PRACTICE PLURAL MARRIAGE IN EARLIER DAYS?

Plural marriage was practiced by between two and four percent of the Church membership from 1843 to 1890 (according to the Utah Commission appointed by Congress).* In the latter year the Supreme Court of the United States affirmed the constitutionality of the congressional laws against the practice. Obedience to constitutional law is a fundamental tenet of the Church. (D. & C. 98:5, 6) Therefore, after Wilford Woodruff had sought guidance from the Lord, the Church suspended the practice. However, it had been declared, long before, that the Church would cease the practice if constitutional laws against it were enacted. For example, "Would it be right for the Latter-day Saints to marry a plurality of wives in any of the states or territories, or nations, where such practices are prohibited by the laws of man? We answer 'No, it would not be right'; for we are commanded to be subject to the powers that be . . . unless their laws are unrighteous." (Orson Pratt, *The Seer,* p. 111, June, 1853) Today any Church member who enters into plural marriage or who teaches its propriety in these days is promptly excommunicated.

Plural marriage has been a subject of wide and frequent comment. Members of the Church unfamiliar with its history, and many non-members, have set up fallacious reasons for the origin of this system of marriage among the Latter-day Saints.

The most common of these conjectures is that the Church, through plural marriage, sought to provide husbands for its large surplus of female members. The implied assump-

---

*Before 1890 there are no records showing the number of polygamists in the Church. In 1890 it was found by careful survey that there were in the Church 2,451 men with more than one wife. At that time the Church membership was approximately 172,754 individuals. The men living in polygamy in 1890 were therefore 1.4 percent of the total Church population. (Proceedings before the Committee on Privileges and Elections of the United States Senate in the Matter of the Protests Against the Right of Reed Smoot, a Senator from the State of Utah, to hold his seat, Vol. 1, pp. 38, 320-324). The Utah Commission, though distinctly unfriendly to the Church in its presentation and using only population estimates, practically confirms the above percentage for 1880. (Report for 1887, pp. 11, 12.) Probably, the reliable records for 1890 represent the general conditions in the years that polygamy was practiced.

tion in this theory, that there have been more female than male members in the Church, is not supported by existing evidence. On the contrary, there seem always to have been more males than females in the Church. Families—father, mother, and children—have most commonly joined the Church. Of course, many single women have become converts, but also many single men.

The United States census records from 1850 to 1940, and all available Church records, uniformly show a preponderance of males in Utah, and in the Church. Indeed, the excess in Utah has usually been larger than for the whole United States, as would be expected in a pioneer state. The births within the Church obey the usual population law—a slight excess of males. Orson Pratt, writing in 1853 from direct knowledge of Utah conditions, when the excess of females was supposedly the highest, declares against the opinion that females outnumbered the males in Utah. (*The Seer*, p. 110) The theory that plural marriage was a consequence of a surplus of female Church members fails from lack of evidence.

Another theory holds that plural marriage resulted from licentiousness of the Church leaders. This is refuted by the evidence at hand. The founders and early leaders of the Church were reared under the strictly monogamic system of New England. Plural marriage seemed to them an unholy and repellent practice. Joseph Smith has told that he hesitated to enter the system until he was warned of his destruction if he did not obey. (Jenson, *Historical Record* 5:222) Brigham Young said that he felt, when the doctrine was revealed to him, that he would rather die than take plural wives. (*Life Story of Brigham Young*, Gates and Widtsoe, p. 242) Others of the early Church leaders to whom the principle was first taught have related their feeling of resistance to the practice. Undoubtedly the women felt much the same about the practice. However, numerous plural wives have testified to the high moral tone of their relationship with their husbands. Not only was every wife equal in property rights, but also treated with equal deference, and all children were educated and recognized equally. Mormon plural marriage bore no resemblance to the lewd life of the man to whom woman is but a subject for his lusts. Women were not forced into plural marriage. They entered it voluntarily, with open eyes. The men and women, with very few exceptions, who lived in plural marriage, were clean and high-minded. Their descendants, tens of thousands of whom are living, worthy citizens of the land, are proud of their heritage. The story of the Latter-day Saints, fully available, when read by honest men and women, decries the theory that plural marriage was a product of licentiousness or sensuality.

There is a friendlier, but equally untenable view relative to the origin of plural marriage. It is contended that on the frontier, where the Church spent its earlier years, men were often unlettered, rough in talk and walk, unattractive to refined women. Female converts to the Church, coming into the pioneer wilderness, dreaded the possible life-long association with such men and the rearing of their children under the example and influence of an uncouth father. They would much prefer to share a finer type of man with another woman. To permit this, it is suggested that plural marriage was instituted. The ready answer is that the great majority of men who joined the Church were superior, spiritually inclined seekers after truth and all the better things of life. Only such men would be led to investigate the restored gospel and to face the sacrifices that membership in the Church would require. Under such conditions, since, as has been stated, there was no surplus of women in Mormon pioneer communities, there was no need of mating with the rough element, which admittedly existed outside of the Church.

Another conjecture is that the people were few in number and that the Church, desiring greater numbers, permitted the practice so that a phenomenal increase in population could be attained. This is not defensible, since there was no surplus of women.

The simple truth, and the only acceptable explanation, is that the principle of plural marriage came as a revelation from the Lord to the Prophet Joseph Smith for the Church. It was one of many principles so communicated to the Prophet. It was not man-made. It was early submitted to several of his associates, and later, when safety permitted, to the Church as a whole.

The members of the Church had personal testimonies of the divine calling of the Prophet Joseph Smith. They had individually accepted the gospel as restored through the Prophet. When he announced a doctrine as revelation coming from above, the people, being already convinced of the reality of Joseph's prophetic calling and power, accepted the new doctrine and attempted to put it into practice. Members of the Church who were permitted to take plural wives, did so because they believed that they were obeying a commandment of God. That faith gave them strength to meet the many problems arising from plurality, and to resist the encroachments of enemies upon their sacred right of freedom of religious belief and practice.

We do not understand why the Lord commanded the practice of plural marriage. Some have suggested that it was a means of trying and refining the people through the persecution that followed. Certainly, one must have had faith in the divine origin of the Church to enter it. Another suggested explanation is based upon the doctrine of pre-existence. In the spirit world are countless numbers of spirits waiting for their descent into mortality, to secure earth bodies as a means of further progress. These unborn spirits desired the best possible parentage. Those assuming plural marriage almost invariably were the finest types in the community. Only men who were most worthy in their lives were permitted to take plural wives; and usually only women of great faith and pure lives were willing to become members of a plural household. (It should be remembered that permission to enter the system was granted only by the President of the Church, and after careful examination of the candidate.) However, this is but another attempted explanation by man of a divine action.

It may be mentioned that eugenic studies have shown the children of polygamous parents to be above the average, physically and mentally. And the percentage of happy plural households was higher than that of monogamous families.

The principle of plural marriage came by revelation from the Lord. That is the reason why the Church practiced it. It ceased when the Lord so directed through the then living Prophet. The Church lives, moves, and has its being in revelation.

4. WHERE WAS THE GARDEN OF EDEN?

Adam and Eve, the progenitors of the human race, were placed by God in the "Garden of Eden."

> And the Lord God planted a garden eastward in Eden; and there he put the man whom he had formed. And out of the ground made the Lord God to grow every tree that is pleasant to the sight, and good for food; the tree of life also in the midst of the garden, and the tree of knowledge of good and evil. (Genesis 2:8-9)

This very brief statement would lead the reader to believe that Eden may have been the name of a large area of land, perhaps a country or continent, in which a garden of limited area was set aside and "planted" for the use of Adam and Eve.

For many generations Bible students have searched for the location of this home of our first parents. The geography of every continent has been studied minutely in the hope that the location of Eden and its garden might be found. Articles, pamphlets, and books have been written on the subject, but without acceptable conclusions.

The clues that might lead to a discovery are few. The account says that the garden was "eastward" in Eden. What is east or west in such a story depends on the place of the author at the time of writing, since no fixed point is mentioned. It is a fair assumption that the word "eastward" has quite another meaning, so far unknown, than the usual one of direction.

Another clue, which at first promised more, is the statement that

> . . . a river went out of Eden to water the garden; and from thence it was parted, and became into four heads. The name of the first is Pison . . . which compasseth the whole land of Havilah . . .; the name of the second river is Gihon . . . that compasseth the whole land of Ethiopia. And the name of the third river is Hiddekel . . . which goeth toward the east Assyria. And the fourth river is Euphrates. (Genesis 2:10-14)

Despite the apparently specific descriptions given, this clue has not led to the location of the Garden of Eden. Careful scholars have not been able to identify any of the four rivers with certainty. None of the rivers mentioned fits into the lands now known. Since the historically well-known names of Euphrates, Assyria, and Ethiopia do not fit into the use of them in the Garden of Eden story, it is more than probable that they are ancient names variously applied in later times. Clearly, these rivers and countries belong to early ages of the world's history, and do not apply to present-day terminology.

The river which watered the Garden of Eden "went out of Eden," probably out of the country of Eden, not necessarily out of the Garden of Eden. The following statement, that it was parted into "four heads," may refer to a condition at the headwaters area, not within the garden.

In dismay at the failure to locate the garden of Adam and Eve from the description given in Genesis, many students have attempted to spiritualize the whole story. The garden was not, they say, a place on earth, but a heavenly abode, in which the drama of "the fall" was enacted. Others insist that everything in the Bible account of the Garden should be given a symbolic meaning. That is, the events recorded did not really happen anywhere; they were invented as symbols of truth.

In short, the world's scholarship admits that it cannot answer the question, where was the Garden of Eden.

In 1831, the Prophet Joseph Smith received a revelation designating the place called Independence, Jackson County, Missouri, as the center place of the kingdom of God on the western hemisphere. A city called Zion or the New Jerusalem would there be built. There also, the foremost temple to the Lord should be erected. From the temple in Zion the law of the Lord would issue, as the word of the Lord would come from Jerusalem. (D. & C. 57:1-3; Isaiah 2:3; Micah 4:2; *History of the Church,* 1:188)

Later, the Prophet designated "Spring Hill," a hill of eminence about fifty or sixty miles north and somewhat to the east of Independence, as Adam-ondi-Ahman, " . . . the place where Adam shall come to visit his people, or the Ancient of Days shall sit, as spoken of by Daniel the prophet." (D. & C. 116) In a revelation to the Prophet, an early event in the history of mankind, occurring near Adam-ondi-Ahman, was told:

> Three years previous to the death of Adam, he called Seth, Enos, Cainan, Mahalaleel, Jared, Enoch, and Methuselah, who were all high

priests, with the residue of his posterity who were righteous, into the valley of Adam-ondi-Ahman, and there bestowed upon them his last blessing. (D. & C. 107:5)

Since Adam called together seven generations of his descendants at Adam-ondi-Ahman, it can well be believed that there was his old homestead. If so, the Garden of Eden was probably not far distant, for it was the entrance at the east of the Garden which was closed against them at the time of the "fall." (Genesis 3:24) In fact, it has been commonly understood among the Latter-day Saints, from the teachings of the Prophet, that the temple was to be built in or near the location of the Garden of Eden.

That the Prophet actually taught that the Garden of Eden was in or near Independence, Missouri, is amply testified to by many who knew and heard him. Heber C. Kimball, close associate and friend of the Prophet, said on one occasion:

> The spot chosen for the Garden of Eden was Jackson Country, in the state of Missouri, where Independence now stands; it was occupied in the morn of creation by Adam and his associates, who came with him for the express purpose of peopling this earth. (*Journal of Discourses,* 10:235)

Brigham Young, also a close associate of the Prophet, testified similarly:

> In the beginning, after this earth was prepared for man, the Lord commenced his work upon what is now called the American continent, where the Garden of Eden was made. In the days of Noah, in the days of the floating of the ark, he took the people to another part of the earth. (*Discourses,* p. 102)

In conversation with Orson Hyde, on March 15, 1857, President Young said:

> You have been both to Jerusalem and Zion, and seen both. I have not seen either, for I have never been in Jackson County. Now it is a pleasant thing to think of and to know where the Garden of Eden was. Did you ever think of it? I do not think many do, for in Jackson County was the Garden of Eden. Joseph has declared this, and I am as much bound to believe that as to believe that Joseph was a prophet of God. (*Journal History,* March 15, 1857)

That is the position of the Latter-day Saints today, with respect to the much-discussed location of the Garden of Eden.

Adam, after his expulsion from the Garden of Eden, lived in the vicinity of the great Missouri and Mississippi rivers. As his descendants multiplied, they would naturally settle along the fertile and climatically acceptable river valleys. When the flood came in the days of Noah, the Mississippi drainage must have increased to a tremendous volume, quite in harmony with the Biblical account. Noah's ark would be floated on the mighty, rushing waters, towards the Gulf of Mexico. With favorable winds, it would cross the Atlantic to the Eastern continents. There the human race, in its second start on earth, began to multiply and fill the earth.

The location of the Garden of Eden in America, and at Independence, Missouri, clears up many a problem which the Bible account of Eden and its garden has left in the minds of students.

5. WHO ARE THE CHILDREN OF ABRAHAM?

Abraham, the son of Terah, lived in the city of the Chaldees.[1] The family of Abraham had turned from righteousness and had become idolators.[2] Abraham therefore, himself a follower of God's truth, preached righteousness to them but without avail. For his insistence upon the worship of the only true and Living God, he was persecuted and his life sought. So intense was the hatred of the idolators that it was only by the intervention of the Lord that he was saved from being offered up as a sacrifice to the idols of the people.[3]

Abraham was a chosen spirit, destined to be a great leader of the work of the Lord. He was commanded to move into another land to be shown him, where he might be free to worship the Lord of earth and the heavens. The Lord at that time gave Abraham a blessing which has sounded through the centuries and to which all Christians cling: "And I will make of thee a great nation, and I will bless thee, and make thy name great; and thou shalt be a blessing:

"And I will bless them that bless thee, and curse him that curseth thee: and in thee shall all families of the earth be blessed."[4]

In obedience to God's command, Abraham, with believing members of his family, moved into the promised land known to us as Palestine.

In this new and strange land, Abraham became a mighty prince.[5] He received the higher priesthood from Melchizedek himself, to whom he also paid "tithes."[6]

After he was well settled, the promise that the Lord had made to him was reiterated, especially on an occasion when the Lord communed with him.

"And the Lord said, Shall I hide from Abraham that thing which I do;

"Seeing that Abraham shall surely become a great and

---

[1]Genesis 11:31.
[2]Pearl of Great Price: Abraham 1:5-7.
[3]*Ibid.* 1:5-15.
[4]Genesis 12:2-3.
[5]See Pearl of Great Price: Abraham 1:1-4.
[6]Doctrine and Covenants 84:14-16; 27:10; 85:3.

mighty nation, and all the nations of the earth shall be blessed in him?

"For I knew him, that he will command his children and his household after him, and they shall keep the way of the Lord, to do justice and judgment; that the Lord may bring upon Abraham that which he hath spoken of him."[7]

The promise that in him all nations should be blessed, brought Abraham's work beyond that of flesh and blood relationships. It made of him a universal figure in the Lord's plan of salvation for all who were sent upon the earth. It would seem that the acceptance of the knowledge of the gospel, and the possession of the priesthood which Abraham bore would make all mankind heirs to the blessings promised Abraham.[8]

Modern revelation has confirmed this view and has cleared up the true meaning of the phrase, "in thee and thy seed." In the Book of Abraham, translated from Egyptian papyrus by Joseph Smith, the following statement is made: "My name is Jehovah, and I know the end from the beginning; therefore my hand shall be over thee.

"And I will make of thee a great nation, and I will bless thee above measure, and make thy name great among all nations, and thou shalt be a blessing unto thy seed after thee, that in their hands they shall bear this ministry and Priesthood unto all nations;

"And I will bless them through thy name; for as many as receive this Gospel shall be called after thy name, and shall be accounted thy seed, and shall rise up and bless thee, as their father:"[9]

There can be no misunderstanding of this statement. All who accept the gospel become by adoption members of the family of Abraham.

Moreover, there is in the opinion of many, in this process of adoption, a subtle change in the body as well as in the spirit which makes a person a true heir of the promises to Abraham. This was the view also of the Prophet Joseph Smith, in a discourse on the two comforters. "The effect of the Holy Ghost upon a Gentile is to purge out the old blood,

---

[7]Genesis 18:17-19.
[8]See the first chapters in the Pearl of Great Price: Abraham.
[9]Abraham 2:8-10.

and make him actually of the seed of Abraham."[10] This is reflected in the patriarchal blessings of the Church which generally assign nearly all persons to one or the other of the tribes of Jacob, direct descendants of Abraham.

This understanding of the promise to Abraham places a heavy responsibility upon all who accept the gospel. As children of Abraham, they are under obligation to do the works of Abraham. The waters of baptism carry with them the promise on the part of the candidate that he will conform his life to the gospel of Jesus Christ, which of course was the gospel given, accepted, and practised by Father Abraham.

The oft-asked question, "Who are the children of Abraham?" is well answered in light of the revealed gospel.

All who accept God's plan for his children on earth and who live it are the children of Abraham. Those who reject the gospel, whether children in the flesh, or others, forfeit the promises made to Abraham and are not children of Abraham.

---

[10]Joseph Fielding Smith, *Teachings of the Prophet Joseph Smith*, p. 150.

6. ARE THERE GUARDIAN ANGELS?

There are hosts of personages in the unseen world.

Among these, many are used by the Lord as messengers to accomplish his purposes. This doctrine is substantiated by numerous statements in the standard Church works and in sermons by Church leaders.[11]

There are at least three classes of angels: spirits who have not yet attained to the earth estate, and do not possess celestialized earthly bodies; personages who have lived on earth, but have not yet been resurrected; and those who have gone through the earth experience and have been resurrected. Occasionally, also, holy men, yet living, are spoken of in the scriptures, as angels.

It is generally believed that angels who come on earth for any purpose whatsoever are beings who have lived on it. This is confirmed by the Prophet Joseph Smith, who said, "There are no angels who minister to this earth but those who do belong or have belonged to it." (D. & C. 130:5)

President Joseph F. Smith said:

> Therefore, when messengers are sent to minister to the inhabitants of this earth, they are not strangers, but from the ranks of our kindred, friends, and fellow-beings, and fellow-servants. The ancient prophets who died were those who came to visit their fellow creatures upon the earth. They came to Abraham, to Isaac, and to Jacob; it was such beings—holy beings if you please—who waited upon the Savior and administered to him on the Mount. The angel that visited John, when an exile, . . . was one who had been here, who had toiled and suffered in common with the people of God; for you remember that John . . . was about to fall down and worship him, but was peremptorily forbidden to do so. "See thou do it not: for I am thy fellowservant, and of thy brethren the prophets. . . ." (Rev. 22:9) (*Gospel Doctrine*, pp. 435, 436)

President Joseph F. Smith suggested that it is possible that our departed loved ones may be sent to help us who yet live on earth.

> Our fathers and mothers, brothers, sisters and friends who have passed away from this earth, having been faithful, and worthy to enjoy these rights and privileges, may have a mission given them to visit their friends and relatives upon the earth again, bringing from

---

[11]See *Discourses of Brigham Young*, pp. 41-42.

the divine presence messages of love, of warning, of reproof or instruction, to those whom they had learned to love in the flesh. (*Gospel Doctrine,* p. 436)

The purposes of angelic visitors are many. An angel was set to guard the way of the tree of life (Gen. 3:24); to remonstrate with Balaam (Num. 22:22-27); to announce the birth of Samson (Judges 13), of John the Baptist (Luke 1:11-20), and of Jesus (Matt. 1:20-21); to warn Joseph to escape with Jesus into Egypt (Matt. 2:13); to teach Peter the universality of the gospel (Acts 10:3). Angels were means of revelation in ancient days. They guided Nephi and other Book of Mormon characters. In our day Moroni visited Joseph Smith; and he had other angelic visitors, who instructed him in the gospel and in his work.

It would appear also from numerous statements that angels have often been sent out to execute judgments upon the wicked. David sang, "Let them be as chaff before the wind: and let the angel of the Lord chase them. Let their way be dark and slippery: and let the angel of the Lord persecute them." (Psalms 35:5, 6) Angels were sent to destroy Sodom (Gen. 19:1-25); and to smite the Assyrians (II Kings 19:35). The Savior himself said, "The Son of man shall send forth his angels, and they shall gather out of his kingdom all things that offend, and them which do iniquity." (Matt. 13:41)

However, the main service of angels on earth is clearly to be helpers to humankind. They are watchmen, protecting and ministering to us in hours of need. John Taylor says, "The angels are our watchmen, for Satan said to Jesus: 'He shall give his angels charge concerning thee: and in their hands they shall bear thee up, lest at any time thou dash thy foot against a stone.' (Matt. 4:6) It would seem from a careful perusal of the scriptures, that the angels, while God has Saints upon the earth, stay in this lower world to ward off evil." (*The Gospel Kingdom,* p. 31) The scriptures are replete with evidence, that these heavenly visitors are ministering angels for the righteous. Thus an angel brought courage to Hagar (Gen. 16:7); food to Elijah (I Kings 19:5-8); protected Daniel against the lions (Dan. 6:22); and secured the release of Peter from prison. (Acts 12:17)

Undoubtedly angels often guard us from accidents and

harm, from temptation and sin. They may properly be spoken of as guardian angels. Many people have borne and may bear testimony to the guidance and protection that they have received from sources beyond their natural vision. Without the help that we receive from the constant presence of the Holy Spirit, and from possible holy angels, the difficulties of life would be greatly multiplied.

The common belief, however, that to every person born into the world is assigned a guardian angel to be with that person constantly, is not supported by available evidence. It is a very comforting thought, but at present without proof of its correctness. An angel may be a guardian angel though he come only as assigned to give us special help. In fact, the constant presence of the Holy Ghost would seem to make such a constant, angelic companionship unnecessary.

So, until further knowledge is obtained, we may say that angels may be sent to guard us according to our need; but we cannot say with certainty that there is a special guardian angel, to be with every person constantly.

7. WHERE ARE THE LOST TRIBES OF ISRAEL?

In the field of theological-historical speculation, few themes have been more assiduously theorized about than the location of the lost tribes of Israel. The voluminous literature concerning the subject "proves" that the tribes may be in any land under the sun, according to the theory accepted. In the restored Church, several books on the subject, presenting different views, have been written by thoughtful, honest men. Fortunately, so far as human happiness here or hereafter is concerned, it matters not a whit where they are located. Unfortunately, some brethren have entangled the subject with the theology of the gospel to their own discomfiture.

Throughout its long history as one nation, the Hebrews had been in almost continuous warfare with neighboring peoples, and indeed the people of the valley of the Euphrates on the east, and of Egypt on the south and west, mighty nations, had paid their warlike respects to the children of Abraham. Wars and warfare form a large part of the history of united Israel. Only under David and Solomon was the kingdom made into an empire strong enough to dictate terms to weaker neighbors and engender wholesome respect among larger powers.

After the death of Solomon, the divided kingdoms, divided also in strength, were subject to similar warfare. Invasion followed invasion; the larger powers to the east, viewing Palestine as a strategically important corridor to Egypt, descended, with powerful armies, upon the now petty kingdoms. The southern kingdom of Judah and the northern kingdom of Israel became little more than vassals to Babylonian powers.

Following the practice of the times, the victors carried large numbers of the vanquished people into captivity, to serve as slaves, craftsmen, builders, or even statesmen, according to their gifts and talents. There were many such captivities from among the people of Israel.

The captivity connected with the lost tribes is mentioned in 2 Kings 17:6: "In the ninth year of Hoshea the king of

Assyria took Samaria, and carried Israel away into Assyria, and settled them in Halah and in Habor, by the river of Gozan, and in the cities of the Medes." A similar statement is made in I Chronicles 5:26. That is all we hear of them. From that time they are literally lost to history, except for a passage in the Apocrypha, II Esdras, 13:40-47:

> Those are the ten tribes, which were carried away prisoners out of their own land, in the time of Osea the King, whom Salmanasar the King of Assyria led away captive, and he carried them over the waters, and so they came into another land. But they took this counsel among themselves, that they would leave the multitude of the heathen, and go forth into a further country, where never mankind dwelt, that they might there keep statutes, which they never kept in their own land. And they entered into Euphrates by the narrow passages of the river. For the Most High then showed signs for them, and held still the flood, till they were passed over. For through that country there was a great way to go, namely of a year and a half: and the same region is called Arsareth. Then they dwelt there until the latter time; and now when they shall begin to come, the Highest shall stay the springs of the stream again, that they may go through.

Many fantastic theories have been set up concerning the location of the lost tribes. One declares, for example, that in the northern countries are vast subterranean caverns in which the lost tribes live and prosper, awaiting the day of their return. Another, by diagram and argument, suggests that a secondary small planet is attached at the north pole, to the earth by a narrow neck, and that the lost tribes live there. (Dalton, *The Key to This Earth*) Others, even more unacceptable, are in circulation.

The view most commonly held by members of the Church is that a body of Israelites are actually living in some unknown place on earth, probably in the north. In support of this opinion are the common knowledge that the earth is not yet fully explored; and also numerous scriptural references to a gathering of Israel from the north countries. Jeremiah speaks of the house of Israel coming "out of the north country." (Jeremiah 3:18; 23:8; 31:8-11; Hosea 1:11) In the Book of Mormon, also, there are references to Israel coming out of the north in the latter days. Ether prophesies of those "who were scattered and gathered in from the four quarters of the earth, and from the north countries." In modern revelation the north countries are mentioned in connection with the restoration of the ten tribes. "They who are in the north countries shall come in remembrance before the Lord; and their prophets shall hear his voice, and shall no longer stay themselves; and they shall smite the rocks, and the ice shall flow down at their presence." (D. & C. 133:26) Moreover, in the Kirtland Temple, Moses appeared to Joseph Smith and Oliver Cowdery and "committed unto us the keys of . . . the leading of the ten tribes from the land of the north." (D. & C. 110:11)

Another view held by many is that the lost tribes are in the northern part of the earth, thus fulfilling that scriptural requirement, but not necessarily in one body. In support are quoted the many references in scripture to the gathering of Israel from the four corners of the earth and the isles of the sea. Further than that, while north countries are mentioned, nowhere is it specifically stated that the lost tribes are in one body apart from other peoples. It is contended that the wandering Israelitish tribes actually settled in northern Europe and Asia, and throughout the centuries mingled with the people there, until the blood of Israel runs strong among the northern peoples. Thus is explained the relatively ready acceptance of the gospel by the British, Scandinavian, and German peoples. Those who hold this view feel that prophecy has been literally fulfilled by the gathering of Latter-day Saints from Northern Europe to the Church in Western America. The notable British-Israel movement is built upon such a dispersion of the lost tribes. (Stephen Malan, *The Ten Tribes*)

A third view attempts to reconcile the two preceding ones. We are reminded that historically and prophetically it is well known that Israel has been scattered among the nations. By removal from the Holy Land through successive captivities, and voluntary migrations, often due to persecution, and by intermarriage with other races, the blood of Israel is now found in almost every land and among every people. The ancient writers spoke of "the twelve tribes which are scattered abroad." It is suggested that on the northward march of the lost tribes, many fell from the company, remained at various points of the journey, there became mixed with the people living there, until today, along the line of exodus, the blood of Israel may be found. It is further suggested that a part of the ten tribes may be somewhere in seclusion, but also that their blood may be among the nations through which they passed on their long migration, thousands of miles if they reached the arctic regions. (George Reynolds, *Are We of Israel?* Allen H. Godbey, *The Lost Tribes, a Myth*)

The Church of Jesus Christ of Latter-day Saints believes in the restoration of the ten tribes; and that it is a part of the mission of the Church to gather scattered Israel into the fold of truth. It knows that throughout the ages, under the wise economy of the Lord, the blood of Israel, most susceptible to gospel truth, has been mingled with all nations. The scattering of Israel is a frequent theme of writers of the Bible. So firm is this belief that the Latter-day Saints, for over a hundred years, at great sacrifices of money, energy, and life itself, have gone out over the earth to preach the restored gospel, and bring all men into the house of Israel.

The question concerning the location of the lost tribes, of itself unimportant, is interesting in showing how such matters are allowed to occupy men's time and tempers, in a day that calls for helpful action among those who are within our reach. Time will reveal the whereabouts of the lost tribes. It is our concern to help fulfil the plan of God, by eager daily service.

INDEX

John A. Widtsoe, 1935

9 780884 940739 51095>

ISBN 0-88494-073-X
SKU 1475154
$10.95